Complete Guide to
Estate Accounting and Taxes

Second Edition

Complete Guide to Estate Accounting and Taxes

Second Edition

J. G. Denhardt, Jr., C.P.A.

Prentice-Hall, Inc.   Englewood Cliffs, N.J.

Prentice-Hall International, Inc.,*London*
Prentice-Hall of Australia, Pty. Ltd., *Sydney*
Prentice-Hall of Canada, Ltd., *Toronto*
Prentice-Hall of India Private Ltd., *New Delhi*
Prentice-Hall of Japan, Inc., *Tokyo*

Library of Congress Cataloging in Publication Data

Denhardt, J   G
    Complete guide to estate accounting and taxes.

    1. Executors and administrators--United States.
2. Executors and administrators--Accounting. 3. Decedents' estates--Taxation--United States. I. Title.
KF6585.D4 1976   343'.73'053   76-4977
ISBN 0-13-160259-4

This publication is designed to provide accurate and
authoritative information in regard to the subject matter
covered. It is sold with the understanding that the publisher
is not engaged in rendering legal, accounting, or other
professional service. If legal advice or other expert assistance is required, the services of a competent professional
person should be sought.

> *. . . From a Declaration of Principles jointly
> adopted by a Committee of the American Bar As-
> sociation and a Committee of Publishers and As-
> sociations*

Printed in the United States of America

A Word from the Author About the Second Edition

The laws affecting the taxation of estates do not seem to be changed by Congress nearly as often as those relating to income taxation; in fact, there had not been any very basic changes in estate taxation for more than twenty years. In late 1970, however, Congress passed the Estate and Gift Tax Adjustment Act of 1970 (P.L. 91-614), which had sweeping effects on the basic rules under which tax men had been operating for so long.

This second edition of Complete Guide to Estate Accounting and Taxes incorporates the new law's provisions, which in most cases apply to the estates of decedents dying after December 31, 1970, but it also retains enough explanation of the former provisions so that it should serve as a complete guide during the present change-over period.

In addition, the sections of the book dealing with income taxation, particularly the section on fiduciary income taxation, have been brought up to date by taking into consideration the laws and rulings which have come into being since the publication of the first edition. Also, the chapter on fiduciary income taxation has been expanded somewhat, in recognition of the fact that this is one of the most difficult areas of taxation confronting anyone concerned with the tax returns for an estate.

The revised edition retains its character as a complete guide for the individual who has the responsiblity of handling an estate that has already been created, rather than being a book on the planning of an estate before death. Much has been written about estate planning, but as soon as an estate is created, the opportunity for using many of the estate planning technics is gone. The person handling the estate will need to know how to cope with the day-to-day problems, not usually of his own making, which arise as he proceeds with the discharge of his duties, so this book gives a chronological picture of everything he is likely to encounter during the entire administration of an estate, from creation to distribution and final settlement.

The person selected to administer an estate is often a friend or relative of the deceased, who has had no previous experience in this difficult field, and he will probably call on his accountant and his lawyer almost daily for assistance in administrative problems and procedures, in addition to the accounting and tax questions. This book is written, therefore, from the viewpoint of the practicing accountant who may be called on by the administrator, and it covers not only the actual accounting and tax phases of estate administration but also the other phases with which the practitioner should be familiar in order to be of most service to his client. It should also be of value to the attorney who is relatively inexperienced in estate work. Most professional men do not have the opportunity to do estate work often enough to keep in mind a complete picture of the step-by-step procedures in estate administration—and there must also be a "first time" in estate work for the accountant or lawyer—so their task should be made much easier by a study of the guidelines given here.

Although estate planning, as such, is no longer possible after death, there are many important "post-mortem estate planning" opportunities for saving taxes and for helping to make for a smooth administration. Therefore, an effort has been made throughout the book to emphasize these opportunities and to point out alternative procedures the professional man should know about and to help him to "look ahead" and be in a position to measure present action against future effects. There are many pitfalls in estate work that can be avoided by this kind of knowledge.

It must be remembered that estate administration and taxation is governed to a great extent by 50 different sets of state laws, to say nothing of the thousands of different provisions which could be found in a person's will, so no book for general distribution could possibly give specific answers to all estate accounting, tax, and administration questions. It is hoped, however, that enough mention has been made of the various possible problems so that the practitioner may be aware of them and may refer to the specific laws and provisions under which he is operating for the answers he needs.

I would again like to thank the following publishers for granting permission to make extensive use of their published materials: Prentice-Hall, Inc., Research Institute of America, *The Journal of Accountancy*, and The Lawyers Co-Operative Publishing Company, publishers of *American Jurisprudence*.

J.G. Denhardt, Jr.

About the Author

Member of the American Institute of CPA's and the Kentucky Society of CPA's, J.G. Denhardt, Jr. has held positions as staff accountant with Arthur Andersen & Co. of Chicago, chief auditor with the Kentucky Unemployment Compensation Commission, accountant on the staff of Albert B. Maloney & Co. of Nashville, Tennessee, and auditor for Lampkin Hotel Company.

Since 1959 he has served as executor of the C. W. Lampkin Estate and has been an individual practitioner in Bowling Green, Kentucky. He has also taught accounting and taxation at Western Kentucky University on a part-time basis since 1946.

Mr. Denhardt has served as discussion leader a number of times for professional development seminars in the estate field.

He is presently a member of the Kentucky State Board of Accountancy.

He was graduated with a B. S. Degree from Western Kentucky University in 1935 and received his B.S. in Accounting from Bowling Green College of Commerce in 1936. He resides in Bowling Green, Kentucky.

Contents

5 The Executor's Duties and Responsibilities (Cont'd.)

6 Reports to the Court 93

7 Distribution of Assets and Final Settlement 103

8 Estate Accounting Simplified 113

8 Estate Accounting Simplified (Cont'd.)

9 Estate and Inheritance Tax Returns 129

10 Estate Tax Deductions—General 139

11 Estate Tax Deductions—The Marital Deduction 150

11 Estate Tax Deductions—The Marital Deduction (Cont'd.)

12 Estate Tax Credits and Computation of the Tax 159

13 Income in Respect of a Decedent 168

Complete Guide to
Estate Accounting and Taxes

Second Edition

1

The Preliminaries to Administration

The instant a person dies, an estate is created. It may be large or small, taxable or nontaxable, well-planned or unplanned, but in every case it must be handled in some way by somebody.

The person selected to do this job will find that he has a great amount of responsibility and that his procedures are subject to a very technical body of legal requirements. He must become familiar with tax requirements, he must maintain adequate accounting records which will enable him to make the reports required by the various laws, and he must protect himself from any possible charges of mismanagement of the estate's funds and property. There are probably few other endeavors which require as much specialized knowledge and skill in so many different fields as the proper administration of an estate to the best possible advantage of all parties concerned.

Therefore, in addition to the details of estate accounting and taxes, a number of chapters in this book deal in a general and non-technical way with the overall procedures of estate administration.

Creation of an Estate

An estate is a creation of law. The laws of all of the states provide that upon a person's death his property shall be held intact for a period of time, that it shall be "administered" by some individual or corporation, and that creditors shall be paid out of the property before the property is turned over to the decedent's heirs.

Theoretically, administration is always necessary, because state laws generally provide that the title to personal property shall not pass directly to the heirs or legatees

17

but to the person selected to administer the estate. In a few cases, however, formal administration may be dispensed with. These might include very small estates, estates of infants, estates for which a settlement is agreed upon by all interested parties, and, in a community property state, estates in which the property of one spouse goes directly to his survivor. Generally, however, an estate which must be administered comes into being by the operation of state law immediately upon a person's death; and this is especially true where there are creditors, because any creditor has the right to compel administration and therefore to subject the decedent's property to the payment of his debt.

What Is an Estate?

An estate, then, consists of the property owned by a person at the time of his death, property which has been placed by the operation of state law into the hands of some person who is charged with the responsibility and duty of administering this property in such a way that the decedent's creditors may be paid, that taxes and other necessary expenses may be paid, and that any remaining property may finally be turned over to the proper heirs or other beneficiaries in accordance with the decedent's wishes; or, if the decedent left no will, in accordance with the requirements of the state's laws of distribution and descent.

The protection of creditors is the principal reason that a person's property is required to become an estate for a period of time before passing to his heirs. If some heir or distributee not subject to legal control or safeguards should immediately come into possession of a decedent's property, there would be nothing to prevent that person from removing the property from the reach of the creditors, or from squandering it or even giving it away, before the creditors had a chance to present their claims or take other action to collect their debts. Also, the establishing of an estate has proved over a long period of years to be the most systematic and orderly way of winding up a deceased person's affairs. This method appears to have existed from the earliest period of common law, and now the various states have enacted statutes governing in more or less detail the creation and administration of estates.

It should be mentioned that the term "estate" might mean different things in different contexts. For example, the "administrable estate" seldom includes real property but the "taxable estate" usually does; life insurance policies payable to named beneficiaries may be a part of the estate subject to taxation but not of the administrable estate, and other things.

The Estate as a Business and Tax Entity

An estate is an entirely new, distinct entity, not to be confused with the decedent himself, the estate administrator, the beneficiaries, or any other entity. It exists as an entity from the moment it is created by state law until it is settled in accordance with all legal requirements and is dissolved by state law.

It is a business entity to the extent that it may, through its administrator, operate a business, manage property, bring legal action or be sued by others, make contracts, buy and sell property, or take any other action necessary for the preservation of the property of which it consists—all of which is subject, of course, to the limitations and restrictions of applicable state law and to the wishes of the decedent, if he expressed them in a valid will.

It is always a separate tax entity. It exists as a tax entity, also, from the moment it is created until it is dissolved, and it is required to file income tax returns for each year of its existence. A special tax form, known as a *Fiduciary Income Tax Return*, is used by estates. The estate reports on this form all of the income it received during the taxable year, claims deductions from income to which it may be entitled, and pays income tax on the net taxable income, at the same rates which individuals pay, using the schedule for married taxpayers filing separate returns.

The Personal Representative

Since an estate consists of property—property which for a time may not legally belong to any heir—and since property is incapable of controlling and managing itself, it is obvious that there is a need for someone to be placed in charge of the property, someone who has the legal authority to handle it in such a way as to accomplish the objectives mentioned above—satisfaction of the creditors and proper distribution of the property.

This person is known as the personal representative of the decedent. The duties may be handled by an individual or by a corporation, such as a trust company. The personal representative takes the place of the decedent to the extent that he acquires legal title to the decedent's personal property—and in some cases to real estate as well—so that he may be in a position to make legal sales of such property when necessary, and to carry on the other functions of administration of the estate. His power and authority in connection with the possession and management of the property are usually very great. In many cases the personal representative would seem to have almost as much freedom in the handling of the assets as the decedent himself would have had. But his responsibility is also very great, and he is accountable to the court and to the decedent's heirs and beneficiaries for his proper handling of these assets within the limitations placed upon him by state law and by the terms and directions contained in his decedent's will.

The laws of the various states differ greatly in defining the duties, responsibilities, and authority of the personal representative—and there are literally thousands of different provisions and limitations which might be contained in a person's will—so each representative will have to determine for himself exactly what he may or may not do in his particular case. But, there are also many points of similarity applicable in most cases. Throughout this book an effort has been made not only to discuss the more generally applicable rules but to point out the instances in which the personal representative must examine and abide by the particular ones which grant and limit his authority.

Executor or Administrator?

The personal representative of a decedent is known as either an executor or as an administrator. The terms executrix or administratrix are used if the representative is a woman.

An executor is the person named by a testator (a person who has written a will) to carry out the directions and requests in his will, and to dispose of his property according to the provisions of this will after the testator's death. The testator has the right not only to say how his property shall be disposed of but to name any person he may desire to serve as his personal representative. If the person so named is willing to accept this office and if he is able to meet the qualifications required by state law, he will be known as an executor.

Exhibit 1

A Simple Will

I, Fred Watkins, of Springfield, Washington County, Georgia, do make, declare, and publish this to be my last will and testament, hereby revoking all other wills heretofore made by me.

Item One: I bequeath the sum of $1,000.00 to my sister, Jane Watkins, if she survive me. If she does not survive me, I direct that nothing pass under this item of my will.

Item Two: I devise my home at 406 Adams Street to my wife Mary in fee simple if she survive me. This property is subject to a mortgage held by the National Bank which I direct my executrix to pay, it being my desire that my wife shall receive our home free and clear of this mortgage. If my wife does not survive me, nothing shall pass under this item of my will.

Item Three: I bequeath to my wife, Mary, if she survive me, all my household goods, automobiles, and my personal effects including clothing, jewelry and articles of personal use or diversion but not including money, securities or the like. If she does not survive me, then I direct that nothing pass under this item of my will.

Item Four: I direct that all the rest of my estate real and personal be divided into two equal portions one of which I bequeath to my wife and the other to my children. However, if my wife does not survive me her half shall pass to the children also. If any of my children fail to survive me but die leaving issue living at my death, then I direct that such issue receive its parent's share per stirpes. If any of my children die without issue living at my death then the share of such child shall pass to my surviving children and issue of deceased children per stirpes. If I die without being survived by any of my children or their issue, then the children's half shall pass to my wife, Mary, if she survive me. If neither my wife, Mary, nor any of my children or their issue survive me, then I bequeath the rest of my estate to the Community Hospital, a charitable corporation.

Exhibit 1 (cont.)

Item Five: I request my executrix to engage Ronald Colt as attorney to probate this will and to advise her in matters of a legal nature during the administration of my estate.

Item Six: I appoint my wife executrix of this will to serve without bond.

IN WITNESS WHEREOF, I have signed this will consisting of two pages on the _____ day of _____, 19__. Each of the preceding pages I have signed in the margin for identification.

WITNESSES: _____

_____

_____

If the decedent died intestate (without leaving a valid will), or if he left a will but failed to name a personal representative, or if he named someone who is unwilling or unqualified to serve as executor, the court having jurisdiction over the administration of the estate will appoint someone to serve in this capacity, and this person will be known as the administrator of the estate. The term "administrator with will annexed" may be used if there is a will, but the court has to make the appointment of the personal representative.

The differences between the two titles, executor and administrator, are largely technical, therefore, depending upon the way in which the personal representative receives his nomination to the office. But the duties and responsibilities are practically the same for either, so throughout this book the term "executor" will be used to designate either an executor or an administrator, unless otherwise specified.

The Fiduciary Relationship

Although the title to the decedent's personal property vests in his executor, the executor acquires only the legal title necessary for the administration of the estate, but he does not acquire equitable title to the assets. That is, they do not become his, but are his only for a temporary period and for a specific purpose. Equitable ownership will eventually pass to others.

The executor, therefore, occupies a fiduciary or trust position. Executors are trustees and funds in their hands are trust funds, and executors may be held to the responsibilities and duties of trustees.

While an executor stands in the place of, and is regarded as, the representative of the deceased person for the purpose of settling his business affairs and distributing his estate, in reality he serves in a dual capacity. He also occupies the position of trustee for the persons beneficially interested in the estate—the creditors and the heirs of the decedent and those named in the will as legatees or devisees, or those entitled to the property under the law of distribution.

The executor is really more the representative of the creditors of the decedent than of the heirs. Creditors have the first claim against the estate, and it is the principal duty of the executor to protect their interests. It might even be said that the representative of a decedent holds the estate as a trust fund for the payment of the debts. The executor is a trustee for the heirs of the decedent in the limited sense that he is their trustee for the purpose of making a distribution after payment of debts and expenses.

An executor, then, is a trustee, but he usually has even greater power than an ordinary trustee in that he has the power of disposal of property, not usually granted to the ordinary trustee.

In any case, the executor occupies a fiduciary position and is responsible to others. He is under a duty to exercise the utmost good faith in all his transactions regarding the estate, and he also has the duty of determining exactly what he may or may not do in fulfilling his obligations as this particular kind of trustee.

Life of the Estate

The executor's fiduciary relationship exists from the moment he receives his appointment and authority from the court until the estate is settled and he receives his discharge.

How long a period of time might this be? It will vary greatly in different cases. The time for distributing the assets and settling an estate is controlled both by the terms of the local statutes and the terms of the decedent's will. It is, however, the duty as well as the right of the executor to distribute the estate after the debts have been paid, but he will take the risk of personal liability for the payment of debts if he makes distribution before awaiting the period allowed by law for the presentation of these debts.

Taxes on the estate and income taxes on its earnings are also in the nature of debts which must be settled before it is safe for the executor to release the assets to the heirs, and the examination of the tax returns by the Internal Revenue Service and settlement of these taxes will very often necessitate a much longer life for an estate than would otherwise be necessary. Many other factors, discussed later, will also enter into the decision as to what is the proper time for closing an estate.

It is natural for a person to want to complete his job as executor as quickly as possible, and the beneficiaries are also usually in a hurry for him to do so in order that they can get possession of the property, but this is a case where the executor should "make haste slowly" and be very sure that he does not turn the property over to the heirs until all debts have been paid out of it. Again, failure to observe this precaution can make the executor personally liable for any unpaid debts.

Most states prescribe a minimum length of time for settlement of an estate—generally about six months. Many small estates may easily be settled soon after this period expires. If there are few debts, no taxes due, and no other complicating factors, settlement should be made promptly and the executor discharged. More often, however, the executor will find it difficult to complete the job within the maximum time permitted (which is usually about two years), and he may even have to petition the court for an extension of time. It is not at all unusual for the life of some estates to continue for three years, five years, or even much longer.

Probating the Will

A personal representative cannot actively assume his rights to the property of a decedent until officially qualified by the court having jurisdiction over the administration of estates. In some states the county courts, common pleas courts, or superior courts have this jurisdiction. In other states special courts, variously designated as surrogate, orphans', or probate courts, have been established, but all are generally referred to as "probate courts" when they are granted estate jurisdiction, and are the courts in which the will is "probated," or proved.

Generally, the estate will be subject to the jurisdiction of the court of the county of which the decedent was a resident. (If he also owned property in some state other than the one in which he lived, ancillary administration may also be necessary in that state.)

If the decedent left a will, the person named therein as executor should take the responsibility for presenting the will to the proper court for probate. This should be done promptly, but out of respect for the decedent it is not usually done until a day or two after his burial. The estate's attorney will prepare a petition to the court, asking that the will be admitted to probate, a date is set for a hearing and all interested parties are notified (*see* Exhibit 2). At the hearing, which is usually little more than a formality, the witnesses to the will must testify as to the authenticity of the signatures. If the witnesses are dead or cannot appear, persons familiar with the signatures of the testator and of the witnesses may testify as to the authenticity of the signatures. If the court is satisfied that the will is valid, it is admitted to probate.

If an executor is named in the will, and if he is competent and willing to serve, he will be granted "letters testamentary" (*see* Exhibit 3) by the court and may proceed with the administration of the estate, in the capacity of executor.

Exhibit 2

Petition for Probate of Will
and Appointment of Executor or Administrator

IN THE MATTER OF THE ESTATE OF   PROBATE OF WILL AND APPOINTMENT OF EXECUTOR

LETTERS OF ADMINISTRATION AND AP-
<u>   </u> POINTMENT OF ADMINISTRATOR
Deceased

TO THE JUDGE OF THE_____COUNTY COURT:

Your petitioner states that _____died testate on the_____day of_____, 19__, a resident of _____County,_____,

leaving an estate consisting of

PERSONAL PROPERTY OF THE ESTIMATED VALUE OF.............$_____

REAL PROPERTY OF THE ESTIMATED VALUE OF ....$_____

Exhibit 2 (cont.)

The following is a list of the name, age and residence of the spouse and each of the heirs-at-law of the decedent:

_____

_____

_____

_____

Your petitioner offers for probate a paper purporting to be the Last Will and Testament of decedent and asks that he be appointed as executor.

Your petitioner states that there is not to his knowledge any paper purporting to be decedent's will and requests that letters of administration be granted and that your applicant be appointed administrator of the estate of said decedent.

Your petitioner is not indebted to the decedent's estate except as follows:_____

_____

Your petitioner offers as sureties on his bond_____ residing at _____ and _____ residing at _____ and suggests the following three persons as appraisers to wit:_____

_____.

Your petitioner designates_____ as attorney.

_____

PETITIONER

_____

POST OFFICE ADDRESS

_____

ATTORNEY FOR PETITIONER

Subscribed and sworn to before me by_____ this_____ day of _____, 19__.

_____

OFFICER ADMINISTERING OATH

IN THE MATTER OF THE WILL OF: WAIVER OF NOTICE

_____
Deceased

Exhibit 2 (cont.)

We, the undersigned, surviving spouse and next of kin of_____
_____, deceased, hereby waive notice of the presentation of said decedent's will for probate and application for appointment of executor or administrator.

Dated this_____ day of _____19____.

_____

_____

Exhibit 3

Letters Testamentary

WASHINGTON COUNTY COURT

ORDER

A paper purporting to be the Last Will and Testament of Carl Davis having been offered in Court for probate, said paper being dated January 17, 1974, application for the probation of same having been duly made and waiver of notice properly signed, testimony of Mary Welch and George Foster, the attesting witnesses to said paper, having been heard and it appearing from their testimony that Carl Davis signed said paper in the presence of both of the attesting witnesses, and that each of the attesting witnesses signed said paper in the presence of Carl Davis and in the presence of each other, and it further appearing from the testimony that Carl Davis acknowledged said paper to be his Last Will and Testament and requested the attesting witnesses to execute same in his presence; and it further appearing that Carl Davis was of sound mind and disposing memory at the time, that he is now deceased, having died on August 9, 1976, while a citizen and resident of Washington County, and the Court being advised, it is ordered and adjudged that the paper dated January 17, 1974, hereinabove referred to, be probated and recorded as the Last Will and Testament of Carl Davis, deceased.

It appearing that George Foster was named as executor of the will of Carl Davis, deceased, it is therefore ordered that George Foster be and he is hereby appointed as executor of said estate and his bond as such is fixed at $175,000.00.

Whereupon came George Foster and executed bond in the sum of $175,000.00, together with Fidelity & Deposit Company of Maryland as surety thereof, which said bond is hereby approved.

Whereupon came George Foster and took the oath as the law directs and entered upon the discharge of his duties as the executor of the estate of Carl Davis, deceased.

This August 12, 1976.

_____

JUDGE, Washington County Court

If the decedent died intestate (without leaving a will) or if he left a will but failed to name an executor, or if the named executor is unwilling or incompetent to serve, the procedure is very similar to that outlined above, except that the court will name the personal representative. The surviving spouse or next of kin will usually make the petition to the court, notice will be given to interested parties, a hearing will be held, and, if the applicant for the position of administrator can qualify for the office, he will be granted "letters of administration" and may proceed with the duties of administration. (*see* Exhibit 4.)

Exhibit 4

Letters of Administration

No. 1044   WASHINGTON COUNTY COURT

Commonwealth of Kentucky $\Big\}$ Order

County of Washington

On the application filed by George Foster on the 22nd day of September, 1976, as required by law, administration of the estate of Carl Davis, late of this County, is granted George Foster, whereupon George Foster executed and filed herein bond in the sum of $85,000,000, amount fixed, with Mary Davis as surety, which is approved by the Court, and was thereupon duly sworn as required by law and qualified as administrator herein on this the 24th day of September, 1976.

_____

Judge, Washington County Court

Qualifications of Personal Representative

Who may serve as an executor? The appointment of the executor is left solely to the testator. The court cannot appoint an executor but will, so far as possible, carry out the intention of the testator by seeing that the trust is committed to the person named by him. The nominated executor is almost invariably given an opportunity to accept or decline the executorship.

The testator may name different ancillary executors in the several states in which his property lies; he may name conditional executors to serve in case of a vacancy; he may name more than one person to serve as coexecutors; he may name a successor executor.

The rule of common law is that any person may be appointed an executor who is capable of making a will himself, that is, practically anyone except a person of unsound mind. The courts have generally agreed that "whom the testator will trust so will the law." Most states, however, now have statutes expressly disqualifying certain persons. In some states infants are disqualified; in some, habitual drunkards, convicts, aliens, and the like; in some, nonresidents of the state in which the will is probated.

In almost every state corporations can qualify as executors, provided their charters permit this. This, of course, enables most trust companies and banks to qualify.

Who may serve as an administrator? Generally, the qualifications are the same as for an executor, but when an administrator must be appointed the court may have to choose from a number of qualified applicants.

The right to letters of administration is usually regulated by statute, and more or less elaborate provisions are made by such laws determining the priority of the various relatives of different degrees. This priority is usually based on nearness of relationship and extent of interest. Most often, a surviving spouse or the next of kin will receive the appointment, but after these, creditors of the decedent may be preferred.

Anyone may petition the court for the appointment, and in most states if none of the persons in preferred classes apply for administration within a given time after death of the intestate, letters may be granted to any suitable or competent person interested in the estate. However, the courts will almost always give every consideration to the wishes of the surviving spouse or next of kin in appointing an administrator.

In some states there is the office of "public administrator," and this official may be appointed when no members of the classes of eligible persons apply for letters of administration within the given time.

Corporations may also qualify and receive appointment as administrator as well as executor.

Exhibit 5

Petition to Admit Foreign Will to Probate

IN THE COUNTY COURT OF
FRANKLIN COUNTY, ILLINOIS

IN THE MATTER OF THE ESTATE
of
THOMAS LANCASTER, DECEASED

No. 59

Your petitioner, Frances Lancaster, a resident of the City of Greenville, County of Adams, State of Kentucky, respectfully states:

1. That Thomas Lancaster, a resident of the County of Adams, and State of Kentucky, died on the 18th of December 1976, at Greenville, Kentucky, leaving a last will and testament duly signed and attested, which said will was duly admitted to probate in the Adams County Court as will more fully appear from duly authenticated copies of the said will and the probate thereof, which petitioner now presents to the Court for the purpose of having said will admitted to probate pursuant to law.

2. At the time of his death, decedent owned an undivided interest in the Park Apartments, in the city of Johnstown, Illinois, together with the real estate whereon same is situated and the furniture and fixtures therein, of a value of approximately $14,500.00.

3. The names and post office addresses of the testator's only heirs, legatees, and devisees are as follows:

Frances Lancaster, heir, devisee, and legatee	Greenville, Ky.
John C. Lancaster, heir and legatee	Sparta, Ga.
Lucy R. Redd, legatee	Greenville, Ky.
William A. Booker, legatee	Greenville, Ky.

4. Testator, in and by said last will and testament, nominated as Executor William Young, a nonresident of the State of Illinois, who by reason of said nonresidence is not qualified to serve as such executor in the State of Illinois.

Exhibit 5 (cont.)

WHEREFORE, petitioner prays that the said last will and testament of Thomas Lancaster, deceased, be admitted to probate and letters with will annexed be issued to William Whalen, Public Administrator of Franklin County, Illinois.

_____

STATE OF KENTUCKY ⎱
COUNTY OF ADAMS   ⎰ SS.

Frances Lancaster, being first duly sworn, says that she has read the foregoing petition by her subscribed, knows the contents thereof, and that the matters and things set forth therein are true.

Subscribed and sworn to before me this_____day of_____

_____19__.

_____

Notary Public

Exhibit 6

Letters of Ancillary Administration

The State of Ohio, Grant County, SS.   PROBATE COURT

BE IT KNOWN, That by the Probate Court of said County, administration of all and singular the moneys, goods, chattels, rights, credits, and estate of which were of Frank Marder, deceased, late of Franklin County, Indiana, located in Ohio has been granted unto David Green, whose duty it shall be to:

1. Make and return to the Court on oath, within the time required by law, a true inventory of all moneys, goods, chattels, rights and credits of the deceased, which are by law to be administered, which come to his possession or knowledge, and an inventory of the real estate of the deceased;

2. Administer according to law all the moneys, goods, chattels, rights and credits of the deceased, the proceeds of any action for wrongful death, or of any settlement, with or without suit, of a wrongful death claim, and the proceeds of all his real estate, sold, which came to the possession of the Ancillary Administrator or to the possession of any person for him;

3. Render upon oath, a just and true account of his administration at the time or times when required by the Court or the law. Failing to do so for thirty days after he has been notified by the Probate Judge of the expiration of the time, he may forthwith be removed by the Court and he shall receive no allowance for services, unless the Court enters upon its journal that such delay was necessary and reasonable;

4. Pay any balance remaining in his hand, upon the settlement of his accounts, to such person as the Court or the law directs;

5. Deliver the Letters of Ancillary Administration into Court in case a Will of the deceased be thereafter duly proved and allowed;

6. Faithfully and honestly discharge the duties devolving upon him as such Ancillary Administrator.

WITNESS my signature and the seal of said Court, this

_____day of_____19__.

_____

(SEAL)   Judge and Exofficio Clerk

By _____

Deputy Clerk

Bonding the Personal Representative

Upon receiving his appointment, the executor or administrator is generally required to take an oath of office. He is also required to give a bond for the faithful handling of the funds and assets coming into his hands and the faithful performance of the duties of his office, unless the decedent specified in his will that no bond shall be required.

State laws usually prescribe the form and conditions of the bond. Sometimes the signature of a personal surety on the bond will be approved by the court; sometimes it will be necessary to purchase a bond from a bonding company, the premium being an expense of the estate rather than of the executor personally.

Exhibit 7

Executor's Bond

WASHINGTON COUNTY COURT

Whereas George Foster has been appointed Executor of the estate of Carl Davis, deceased, we the undersigned, George Foster, and John Hanson and Howard Stone, his sureties, do hereby covenant to and with the Commonwealth of Kentucky, in the penal sum of $85,000.00, that the said George Foster will faithfully discharge all the duties of his trust.

Witness our hands, this the _____ day of _____ 19__.

_____
Principal

_____
Surety

_____
Surety

As for the amount of the bond, this is fixed by the court and is usually based on the estimated value of the personal property in the estate. It may be fixed at that amount, twice that amount, or some other amount, depending on the state law. It will not often have to be large enough to cover the estimated value of the real estate also, since the executor seldom gets possession of the real property and therefore has little chance to commit fraud in connection with it. But, in states where he does acquire title to it, or in cases where the will directs that he shall have control over it, the amount of the bond may be made large enough to cover the real estate too.

Letters Testamentary

These, then, are the preliminaries to the administration of an estate—someone makes a petition to the proper probate court for probate of the will and for appointment of the executor; if the executor can qualify he takes the oath of office and gives a bond, and the court issues letters testamentary to him (or letters of administration if an administrator), which is his authority to take possession of the estate's assets and to proceed with the many urgent duties discussed in Chapter 2.

2

Tasks Requiring Prompt Attention

The *executor* will find that he is a very busy person during the first few weeks of his administration. As he becomes familiar with his duties and his responsibilities he may be somewhat awed by the weight of these responsibilities, and he will find that his immediate duties consist of a number of different tasks, each of which seems to need to be done first.

It is true that there are several duties which require prompt attention, especially if the estate is large or if it includes businesses or property which must be carried on and managed, but all of these can be worked out one at a time. This chapter points out the various tasks which are usually necessary for the executor to do to get the administration of the estate under way. It should serve as a check list to prevent his overlooking something during this time when there is so much on his mind.

Prior to Issuance of Letters

There is always some lapse of time between the decedent's death and the issuance of letters to the personal representative, but during this time it is the executor's duty to do everything necessary to preserve the estate. His authority during this period is limited, however, to those acts which are strictly necessary and indispensable—preserving the property, assisting the surviving spouse or next of kin in the proper burial of the deceased, providing for the support of the family until the will can be probated, and others.

A person does not always know that he has been nominated as executor until possibly several days after the testator's death, when the will is found. This can create a situation in which no one assumes the responsibilities for doing the things which may be urgent during this period. It is desirable, therefore, for the testator to inform his executor of the nomination beforehand so that this person can take charge immediately upon the testator's death. Otherwise, it is up to the surviving spouse or some other close relative to assume this interim responsibility.

Probably the most urgent step is an immediate examination of the decedent's papers, memoranda, and records to try to find a will and any directions he might have left regarding his funeral arrangements, and so forth; and to learn who is the executor, if that is not already known. Any life insurance policies found at this time should be turned over to the beneficiaries so that they can file their claims with the company.

Custody of the corpse and the right of burial do not belong to the executor but to the surviving spouse or next of kin, but the executor should certainly cooperate with the survivors in making the funeral arrangements. The duty to erect a suitable tombstone or monument does, however, usually rest with the executor, but he should be guided by the wishes of the surviving spouse or next of kin in this matter.

Other steps which may be necessary during this interim period include notifying the decedent's banks and brokerage firms, if any, of the death; putting into safe custody any jewelry, cash, securities, or other valuable property which should not be left lying about; and, possibly, selling any highly perishable property.

The issuance of letters legalizes all proper acts prior to their issue.

When the executor receives the letters testamentary, he should ask the clerk of the court to give him a number of attested copies of this order. He will need a copy to give to each bank where the decedent had an account, one for each stock transfer, one for the bonding company, and for others. Securing a sufficient number of attested copies at once will save time later. Provision should also be made for obtaining a number of attested copies of the *will*, as these will be needed for the same purposes.

Opening a Bank Account

The next step, which should be taken immediately upon receipt of the letters testamentary, is for the executor to make arrangements for the opening of a bank account in the name of the estate. This is urgent because there will be certain expenses which must be taken care of at once, such as the court costs for probating the will, copies of the letters, and others.

The executor may select any bank he wishes for this account, but he will usually use the one his decedent favored. He should take a copy of the letters testamentary to the bank and find out the bank's balance in the decedent's account. He should then request that this balance be transferred to a new account in the name of the estate, sign a signature card for this account as executor, and secure a new checkbook for use with this new account.

The bank's balance will be the one which the estate will start out with as a checkbook balance, because the bank will not pay any of the decedent's outstanding checks which are presented to it after his death. The bank will either notify the executor as these checks are presented or will return them to the payees; the executor will then write checks on the estate's account to cover them, charging such payments to the account "Debts of the Decedent."

It is seldom necessary for the estate to have more than one bank account. If the decedent had other bank accounts the executor should file a copy of his letters with each bank, determine the bank's balance, and have it transferred to the bank in which he opened the estate's account. However, any accounts, including savings accounts, which are left where the decedent had them should be transferred to a new account in the name of the estate with the executor authorized to draw on them.

Taking Possession of the Property

The executor should proceed to take actual physical possession of all items of personal property which the decedent owned at the time of his death, except certain items which may be specifically exempt by law from the general category of assets available for the payment of debts. Examples of these exemptions might be wearing apparel, household furniture, bibles, schoolbooks, and certain provisions and supplies.

Cash should, of course, be deposited in the estate's bank account; a bank deposit box should be rented for the safekeeping of securities, deeds, insurance policies, and other important papers; records of accounts receivable, mortgages, and other documents should be put in a safe place; furniture, cars, and all other personal property should be kept under lock and key. The executor has a definite responsibility for the safekeeping of all such assets, but he will often decide that he can safely permit the surviving spouse or some other close relative to retain custody of certain things, such as jewelry, household furnishings, and automobiles, rather than disturb their living arrangements by demanding immediate actual possession of the property.

A word of advice might be well at this point. The executor should be courteous and co-operative with the decedent's beneficiaries at all times during the administration. He must never forget that the property is really theirs, not his. He must not be overly impressed with his powers and authority but should accede to the wishes of the heirs, if legally possible. His kindness and consideration to these heirs at the time of the decedent's death, and during the trying days for them after the death, will pay great dividends to the executor in the form of better relations and smoother administration during the months ahead.

The executor, of course, is very often one of the heirs himself, who will have somewhat more freedom than the outsider who might have been appointed—but he, too, should be most considerate of any other beneficiaries.

Subject to the above comments, the executor must exercise due diligence in discovering the assets, and all proper legal steps must be taken to obtain possession of them. If the decedent kept a set of books, such records will assist in determining just what assets there are.

The rule seems to be that if assets are lost through the executor's neglect, he will be held personally liable for such loss.

Personal Property vs. Real Property

The authority of the executor to impound the decedent's personal property is based on the fact that legal title to such property actually passes to him at the time of death.

This is not usually true of the decedent's real estate, however, as mentioned earlier. In most states the title to real property vests immediately in the heirs or devisees, the executor has no power or control over it, and it is not a part of the administrable estate.

But this general rule regarding the real estate has several exceptions. First, in a few states the executor does acquire title to the real estate. Next, in many jurisdictions statutes expressly make the realty assets of the estate to the extent necessary for the payment of debts and expenses of administration and authorize the executor, after he has exhausted the personal estate, to apply to the court for permission to sell as much of the real estate as will be sufficient to take care of the rest of the debts. Finally, in many cases the testator directs in his will that his real estate be a part of the administrable estate and subject to the control of the executor.

A person writing a will should consider the advisability of giving his executor title to and control over the real estate, if his state's laws do not already provide for this, as it always makes the administrative processes simpler and more definite. Also, since real property is generally a part of the taxable estate the executor is equally concerned with its discovery, location, and valuation; and since he has a certain amount of responsibility in connection with it he might as well have some authority also. Furthermore, some states give the executor the authority to manage the real estate and collect rents on it during the period of administration.

The distinction between real property and personal property is discussed thoroughly in Chapter 4, but it should be mentioned here that mortgages on real estate and real estate sold under contracts are considered personal property, and that any real estate sold during administration becomes personal property.

The Administrative Team

The administration of an estate is seldom a one-man job. So much specialized knowledge is required in several different fields that the executor usually needs professional help. Unless the executor is himself an expert in the areas of business, law, estate and income taxation, and accounting, he should retain whatever professional assistance he may need. This is expected and permitted. A team effort is usually required, and the ideal administrative team consists of the *executor, his attorney*, and *his accountant*.

There is rarely ever an estate which can be administered without the aid of a lawyer—unless the executor himself is so qualified. The very least that the lawyer might need to do would be to file the petition for probate of the will. A number of probate courts require that an attorney must do this. In the larger estates, an attorney will be needed for many different duties, such as the preparing of deeds, opinions of title, contracts, and so forth; defending any litigation brought against the estate; filing such actions as may be necessary in the protection of the estate; bringing any actions necessary to foreclose on deliquent notes, accounts, and claims or debts due the estate; handling any legal matters arising in connection with businesses the decedent owned; defending or prosecuting any tax action necessary; and, in general, consulting with the executor on any matters requiring legal advice.

It seems that in the large estates there is always much more for an attorney to do throughout the administration than anyone anticipates at the beginning. Therefore, the importance of retaining a competent attorney cannot be overemphasized.

The third member of the team, a competent tax accountant, is also a very necessary person in the administration of an estate of any size. He will be needed for setting up adequate bookkeeping records; seeing that entries are made to these records in accordance with good estate accounting practices; preparing financial reports required by the court; preparing the decedent's final income tax return; preparing the executor's fiduciary income tax returns; preparing the estate and inheritance tax returns; working with the attorney in any tax litigation which may arise; and, in general, advising the executor in any matters of business, accounting, or tax planning for the benefit of the estate.

The executor of a small estate might be able to handle most of these matters himself, but the services of a competent accountant are most indispensable in larger estates.

Just what does all of this leave for the executor to do? He certainly will not be idle, even though he is permitted to retain a lawyer and an accountant and to employ any necessary clerical help, property managers, agents, and others. The executor is the executive, the director of the administrative team. All final decisions and responsibilities are his, and he is the one responsible for getting things done.

The office of executor is far more than just an honorary office. At the same time, an executor is not expected to devote his full time to the performance of these duties. Many business and professional men serve as executor without first discontinuing their businesses or practices. Nor do trust companies devote full time to any one estate. The office is more in the nature of a part time job, and if more time is required the executor is expected to engage the necessary help. If he chooses to devote more time than normal to the business of the estate and does more of the actual work than is customary, the executor may petition the court for an additional fee for these management services.

Engaging an Attorney and Accountant

The engaging of professional services will be near the top of the list of things to be done in getting an administration under way. The services of an attorney are usually necessary in order to probate the will in the first place, so the executor should immediately make arrangements to retain a competent person.

It has been held that a provision in a will selecting an attorney is not necessarily binding on the executor and may be disregarded by him, but unless there are unusual circumstances the executor will certainly want to abide by his decedent's choice in the matter.

The attorney may be engaged just to probate the will; he may be engaged on a fee or retainer basis for the performance of whatever services the executor specifically calls on him for; he may be engaged for a flat fee to take care of all legal matters during the administration of the estate. The flat fee basis is generally the most desirable arrangement for the executor of a large estate, because he will know, then, what the total final cost will be for these services. When the arrangement is agreed upon, the executor should suggest that a written contract be drawn up setting forth the details of this arrangement. No reputable attorney will object to discussing his fees and services in advance or to having a written contract to cover them.

Exhibit 8

Contract With Executor's Attorney

THIS CONTRACT made and entered into this the＿＿＿＿＿＿day of＿＿＿＿＿＿, 19＿＿, by and between Anthony Ross, Executor of the estate of Guy Wallace, deceased, party of the first part, and Donald Jackson, attorney-at-law, party of the second part.

WITNESSETH: That for and in consideration of the terms and conditions hereinafter set out the party of the first part has this day employed the party of the second part as the attorney for the Guy Wallace Estate to represent the estate and the executor in all legal matters pertaining to the administration and settlement of said estate.

In addition to rendering such general legal services as may be required, it is understood that the services of the second party under this contract shall include the defense of any litigation brought in Court and the filing of such actions as may be necessary in the protection of the interest of the estate; that he shall be available for consultation and conferences with the executor, with the Certified Public Accountant who will be employed by the executor, and with such others as may be employed by the executor in the administration of the estate in the determination of any problems which may arise; that he shall prepare all deeds, opinions of title or title bond contracts which may be required in connection with the sale of real estate and such necessary instruments as may be required in the consummation of the sale of personal property; that he shall bring such actions as may be necessary to foreclose on delinquent notes, accounts, claims or debts due the estate; consult with the Certified Public Accountant in the preparation of the final settlement and in all legal matters which pertain to the accounting, and in general to do each and every act and deed of an attorney in the proper administration and settlement of an estate.

It is agreed that there is excepted from the duties of the second party the duty of preparing and filing income tax returns, inheritance tax returns and estate tax returns. Since the executor will employ a Certified Public Accountant to handle such matters, the second party shall not be required to do so as part of the duties of his employment.

The consideration for the employment of Donald Jackson as attorney for the estate of Guy Wallace is the sum of Ten Thousand Dollars ($10,000), of which Two Thousand Dollars ($2,000) shall be paid by the

Exhibit 8 (cont.)

executor to Donald Jackson during the year 1975; Four Thousand Dollars ($4,000) during the year 1976; and the balance of Four Thousand Dollars ($4,000) to be paid on the final settlement of the estate.

The party of the first part does, in addition to the above, hereby agree to reimburse the party of the second part for all expenses, such as telephone calls, travel expenses and other expenses which may be required of the second party in carrying out his duties set forth in this contract.

IN TESTIMONY WHEREOF, witness the signatures of the parties hereto this the day and date first above written.

_____

Executor, Estate of Guy Wallace

_____

Attorney

The executor may also engage his accountant on a specific job basis or for a flat fee. Again, the flat fee is generally more satisfactory to the executor; again, a written contract should cover the details of whatever arrangements are agreed upon.

An executor who is himself a lawyer may not properly claim an extra fee for the legal work he does for the estate. He may, however, engage another attorney or he may engage a law firm of which he is a member, if it has been agreed between him and his partners that he is not to share in the fee received by the firm. (This is the general rule, but certain jurisdictions do permit a fee in both capacities.) The same principles would apparently hold true for an executor who is an accountant.

The contract of employment of an attorney or accountant is essentially one made by the executor in his individual, and not his representative, capacity. The estate itself is not generally bound by such a contract. The executor is responsible for the payment of the fees, but he will be entitled to an allowance for them, provided the amount is considered by the court to be reasonable.

Opening the Lockbox

If the decedent had a lockbox in some bank, the executor should visit the bank and make an inspection of the contents of this box as soon as he can conveniently do so.

The lockbox is likely to contain all of the decedent's most important papers. Many of them will be of help to the executor in discovering the estate assets. Deeds, titles, mortgages, insurance policies, contracts, and other such papers will give the executor clues as to the existence of certain assets.

Other assets, themselves, may be found in the lockbox. These might include stocks, bonds, notes, jewelry, and other articles of value.

The executor will have to take a copy of his letters testamentary to the bank in order to obtain the bank's permission to open the lockbox. Also, most states having inheritance tax laws require that the bank seal the box upon the death of the renter of the box, and not even permit a qualified executor to open it for the first time unless he is accompanied by a representative of the state tax department. This, of course, is so that the state may have a list of any assets found in the lockbox and be able to trace these items into the inheritance tax return filed later. The executor, therefore, will have to make an appointment with a state tax department representative to accompany him to the bank the first time he wishes to open the lockbox.

It is advisable, at this time, for the executor to make a detailed listing of every item found in the lockbox. (The tax department representative will do so, and a carbon copy of his list will usually serve for the executor.) Care should be taken to furnish complete information about each item. *For example,* the description of securities should include the exact name of the issuer, kind and par value, quantity or amount, date of acquisition, name of co-owner, if any, and whether or not there is a survivorship provision.

For the sake of completeness, the listing should include everything found in the box, even though some of it appears to belong to others than the decedent. The time spent in making an accurate, complete listing will save unnecessary trips to the bank in the future.

The executor will seldom need to remove anything from the lockbox at this time. He will usually prefer to continue to rent the box and leave the valuables in it for safekeeping.

As mentioned earlier, it might be necessary for someone to enter the lockbox before the personal representative receives his appointment—possibly even before the decedent's funeral. This is true when it is believed that the will and directions regarding the funeral are in the box. In this case, the executor (if he knows of his appointment) or some close relative of the deceased will have to petition the probate court for an order to the bank permitting access to the lockbox. He will also have to be accompanied by a state tax department representative at this time.

Keeping a Going Business Going

One of the most troublesome immediate problems for the executor is likely to be the proper handling of a trade or business in which the decedent had been engaged.

From a legal standpoint, it is no part of the duty of an executor to carry on a business conducted by the decedent; it is, on the contrary, a breach of trust for him to do so except for the purpose of disposing of the stock in trade or of disposing of the business as a going concern.

From a practical standpoint, however, the executor is frequently expressly authorized and directed to operate such a business. This authority may be granted by statute, by an order of court, by the decedent's will, or, in some cases, by the consent of the beneficiaries. Without such authority, the executor may be held personally liable for any losses resulting from the business operation, even though he acts in the utmost good faith and believes that he is proceeding for the best interests of the estate.

The executor's first concern, then, is to determine just what authority he does have regarding the decedent's trade or business, so that he can shape his thinking and planing toward either an early liquidation of the business or toward a profitable continuing operation.

But in either case, he will immediately have an urgent responsibility—keeping the business going. Most businesses are likely to flounder when suddenly deprived of the owner's leadership. The executor must step in at once and furnish the necessary management and guidance to keep the operations running as smoothly and successfully as possible until more permanent arrangements can be made.

Even though the executor may not have the authority to carry on the business, he does have the power to continue it for a reasonable time and sell the stock in the ordinary course of trade. He should also keep in mind that a going business will usually command a higher sale price than the piecemeal sale of its stock in trade and other assets. Therefore, it can be said that he actually has a duty to keep a going business going, at least for a short period of time.

If the business is supposed to be continued indefinitely, circumstances in each case will have to determine whether the executor himself will permanently assume the management or engage additional help to fill the vacancy. An executor has no obligation to take over these extra duties; but if the business is very small or is one to which the decedent had not had to devote very much time, the executor might prefer to manage it himself rather than incur the expense of additional salaries for management.

The foregoing discussion applies only to a decedent's proprietorship business. Theoretically, it would not apply to any corporation in which the decedent was interested, even though he owned all of the corporate stock, because a corporation is supposed to have continuity of existence and autonomy of operation even upon the death of any of its stockholders.

Practically, however, if the decedent was the principal stockholder and an active officer of a close corporation, the executor will be equally concerned with the immediate and continued successful operation and management of this business as with a proprietorship. His responsibility to take whatever action is necessary to accomplish these objectives is based on his obligation to try to prevent any devaluation of the decedent's stock in the corporation. His authority derives from the fact that the title to this stock, which is personal property, vested in him at the decedent's death.

What are the executor's duties in respect to a partnership of which the decedent was a member? This will depend on the terms of the partnership agreement and any instructions contained in the decedent's will.

The partnership agreement should definitely state whether the business is to be dissolved or continued; and if it is to be continued, whether the decedent's representative shall come into the partnership in place of the decedent or leave the management to the other partners. Where the agreement provides simply that the deceased partner's capital shall remain in the business, his executor cannot exercise the control of a partner in the conduct of the business but is bound to leave the capital in it, leaving its management to the surviving partners.

Directions in the will regarding a partnership will also govern the executor, provided they are not in conflict with the partnership agreement. In the absence of definite directions in either the partnership agreement or the will, state law will determine the handling or disposition of the partnership business.

The determination of exactly what to do with a decedent's partnership business can be very tricky and complicated, so the executor should have his attorney make a thorough investigation of the circumstances in each case and advise him of his exact duties.

Opening an Office

In a few cases the executor will have to arrange for office facilities for the administration of the estate. In most cases, however, the duties do not warrant the expense of a separate office; the executor simply uses his own office or even his residence as his base of operations. Many times, the decedent's office is available, especially if it is located in a business which is being continued.

The executor may choose whatever location is most convenient for him. If there is a real need for a separate office, the executor should rent one. He will be guided in this decision by the size of office force needed, whether or not the location needs to be convenient to outsiders, the nature of the business to be handled, the probable duration of the administration, and so forth; but only a very large or complex estate would be likely to require an office of this kind.

If an office must be rented, the executor might also have to buy furnishings for it. But the renting and furnishing of an office are not usually acts within the scope of an executor's authority, and, if they are considered necessary, he would be wise to petition the probate court for such authority beforehand.

(If the estate's beneficiaries are friendly toward the executor and inclined to go along with his decisions and judgment, the executor may often simply secure their consent for certain borderline acts rather than follow the more formal procedure of petitioning the court for authority.)

When the executor uses his own office or residence for the estate's business, he is often granted a reasonable rent allowance for this, payable out of the estate's funds.

Temporary Books and Records

The executor, fortunately, does not have to be concerned with setting up a permanent, complete bookkeeping system during the first few weeks of his administration. This is one thing which can be postponed and, in fact, must be postponed until the correct opening entries are available. These entries will not be available until after the appraisal of the estate is completed.

In the meantime, however, the executor must be certain to keep a complete record of all transactions which occur. These entries will be transferred to the formal books of account later, as of the date the transactions occurred.

The temporary records can be very simple, even for a large estate. A listing of cash receipts and disbursements will suffice, but care should be taken to include a complete explanation with each item. Better still, even this simple listing might be dispensed with. The record of cash disbursements can consist of only the checkbook stubs (with complete explanations), and cash receipts can be written up in a duplicate money receipt book with the original copy of the receipt being given to the person paying the money and the carbon copies serving as the temporary receipt book.

Such records, if kept accurately and reconciled with the bank's balance, will serve admirably, even for several months; and this will eliminate much of the worry and bother of bookkeeping during the executor's first, busy weeks.

When the formal books are opened, the bookkeeper can make the necessary journal entries from these temporary records.

There are rarely any transactions during this early period other than cash receipts and cash disbursements. If there are any, proper memoranda can be made for later entry in the permanent journals. (One executor even kept a day by day diary of everything that happened concerning the estate—dates, times, and details of every transaction, conference, visit, decision, agreement, order, and other events that occurred—not a bad idea, but probably more trouble than most executors would care to undertake.)

Advertising for Creditors

One of the principal duties of the executor is to see that the decedent's creditors are paid. The executor should therefore promptly try to determine just who these creditors are and the nature and amounts of their claims.

The executor is permitted to advertise for creditors and should do so for his own protection. In some states he is required to do this. Notices are inserted in one or more newspapers published in the county, requesting persons who have claims to present them to the executor along with supporting affidavits and vouchers within the time specificed by law, usually six months (*see* Exhibit 9).

Exhibit 9

Notice To Creditors To Present Claims

EXECUTOR'S NOTICE

Notice is hereby given to all persons having claims against the estate of Carl Davis, deceased, to file the same with the undersigned at the address given below and to prove the claims as required by the statutes.

_____

Executor of the Will of Carl Davis

_____

Address

The executor's failure to publish such a notice promptly may extend the time for presentation of the claims, when the statutes allow a certain period for presentation of claims after publication of the notice. Prompt determination of the debts due by the decedent will also help the executor in planning to have funds available at the time when they must be paid.

Some probate courts make a practice of publishing a notice to creditors each time an executor or administrator is appointed; if the court does not do this, the executor should.

Preliminary Estate Tax Notice

The estate tax preliminary notice, which formerly had to be filed with the Treasury Department, is no longer required for estates of decedents dying after December 31, 1970.

The executor's attorney or accountant can inform him as to whether there is any requirement in their state for filing any such preliminary notice with the state inheritance tax division.

Selection and Appointment of Appraisers

The statutes of the various states usually provide for an appraisal of a decedent's estate by a specified number of disinterested persons. Either two or three appraisers are generally required, and they are appointed by the probate court. Their appointment is frequently included in the letters testamentary or letters of administration given the personal representative.

Exhibit 10

Order Appointing Appraisers

At a regular session of Washington County Court held at the Court House in Springfield, Iowa, on the 14th day of August, 1976, present, Hon. Lewis Ballard, Judge, presiding.

It is ordered and directed that Ralph Gary, James Boyle, and George Drake be and they are hereby appointed Appraisers of the Estate of Carl Davis.

_____

JUDGE, Washington County Court

Although the appraisers' appointment is made by the court, the courts will almost invariably appoint anyone named for this duty by the testator in his will. In the absence of such testamentary directions, the executor has the right to suggest the names of suitable persons to the court; the court will most often base its appointments on these suggestions.

In suggesting appraisers, the executor should try to select men or women who will be willing to undertake these duties and who have the time to perform them without undue delay. Close friends of the decedent or of the executor are frequently thought of first, but the position of the appraiser is not just an honorary position and even the closest friends should not be favored over other persons who are better qualified to make the appraisal.

A good appraisal of the estate's assets is an extremely important step in a good administration, because the values established at this time will be used as the basis for the estate's accounting, as the basis for its taxes, as the basis for computing certain fees, and possibly as the basis of certain assets in the hands of beneficiaries years after the estate is terminated.

The executor, then, should try to secure appraisers who will be co-operative with him, and who are qualified to establish proper values for the particular kinds of assets which make up the estate. Good appraisers might be found among the following: the decedent's surviving business partner; a real estate man familiar with the decedent's property or with property values in general; a banker or broker; the decedent's accountant or attorney; and others having specialized knowledge of values in specialized fields.

If the estate includes property in other states, a team of appraisers will be appointed to work with the ancillary administrator in each such state.

The appraisers may be paid a fee for the performance of their duties. The amount is usually nominal and is usually governed by state law. It will vary from a few dollars to possibly several hundred dollars each, depending on the time spent in making the appraisal. It is not uncommon, however, for an appraiser who was a good friend of the deceased to refuse to accept any fee for his services.

The Appraisers' Duties

It is the appraisers' duty to agree on a fair market value, as of the date of death, for each item of personal and real property which the decedent owned. It is not their duty to discover what property is to be appraised—that must be done by the executor.

It may be several months before the appraisers can begin their work. The executor should wait until he has satisfied himself that he has a substantially accurate listing of everything to be included in the inventory before calling on the appraisers.

The appraisers will then meet and proceed to place values on each item on the executor's list. This may be a small job requiring only a brief time or it may require a number of days. The appraisers should never just arbitrarily guess at a valuation; they should make a physical inspection of each item or piece of property, if they are not already familiar with it, and use whatever means are available to arrive at a reasonable estimate of its value at the date of death. This may necessitate travel to other locations, correspondence with experts, and other means, but the great importance of what they are doing justifies the effort.

The executor should work closely with his appraisers. He should guide them in their duties and use every means to make their job as easy as possible—such as having the various assets readily available for inspection, furnishing any necessary transportation, furnishing clerical help, if needed, and the like. He should remember that the appraisers are most often giving of their time and effort out of respect for the decedent rather than for whatever small fee they might receive.

The Inventory and Appraisal

Upon completion of the appraisal, the executor will be in a position to file an inventory of the estate with the court. Most states require the filing of an inventory, within a prescribed time. The object of the inventory is to show creditors and other interested persons of what the estate consists.

The executor should secure from the court clerk the form usually furnished for the inventory (*see* Exhibit 11). On this form the executor will list every item of which the estate consists, showing the value for each as determined by the appraisers. This listing will usually be in great detail, but any large group of relatively low value items—such as household furnishing—might be grouped and appraised as a unit rather than piece by piece.

Exhibit 11

Inventory and Appraisement

INVENTORY AND APPRAISEMENT

We, the undersigned, Appraisers, appointed by the Washington County Court to appraise the personal property of Guy Wallace, deceased, after being first duly sworn, proceeded on the_____day of _____, 19____ to discharge said duty, and did appraise the property not exempt from distribution exhibited to us by Anthony Ross, the personal representative, described and valued as follows, viz:

(Detailed listing of property)

Total Amount of Appraisement $_____

Given under our hands, this_____ day of _____, 19____.

_____

_____ APPRAISERS

_____

Exhibit 11 (cont.)

I, Anthony Ross, as the personal representative of the late Guy Wallace, deceased, of Washington County, do certify that the foregoing_____ pages of the Inventory and Appraisement of the personal estate of said decedent is a true and full Inventory of said estate, which came to my hand as Executor, this _____day of _____, 19____.

_____

Executor

Real estate may or may not be a part of the estate subject to administration, but in either case it is advisable that such property be included in the inventory and appraisal. The valuation of the real property will be needed in fulfilling the requirements of state inheritance tax laws and the Federal estate tax law. Moreover, in some states the inventory, filed with the county recorder, serves as evidence of the passing of title.

Accruals of income up to the date of death should not be overlooked when inventorying and appraising the estate. Rents receivable, interest receivable, salaries receivable, and any other accruals must be computed and included in the inventory.

No liabilities are shown in the inventory—only the gross assets are included. Assets pledged to secure a loan, or real estate subject to a mortgage, are listed without deduction for the amount of the liability.

Upon completion of the inventory form, the appraisers will sign it, acknowledging that they appraised the property exhibited to them by the executor. The executor also signs it, acknowledging that the listing is a true and full inventory of the property which came into his hands as executor.

In some jurisdictions, if property not included in the first inventory later comes into the possession or knowledge of the executor, he must make an additional or supplementary inventory after the discovery.

Valuation of Property

Chapters 3 and 4 contain a detailed discussion of the problems and methods of valuation of various kinds of property which may be found in an estate. In general, however, all property is supposed to be valued at its fair market value as of the date of the decedent's death.

It seems that most appraisers are inclined to assign the lowest possible values to the property, in the belief that they are doing the decedent and his estate and heirs a favor by reducing the valuation on which the death taxes will be computed. This, of course, may be a fallacy, because the valuations assigned at this time may become the bases on which gain or loss is computed when the property is sold in the future; a low basis might result in a gain taxable at a much higher rate than the death tax rates would have been.

But overvaluation can be equally harmful tax wise and otherwise, so, unless the executor has a reliable crystal ball, he should try to lead the appraisers into agreeing on the fairest possible market values for each item of property.

The Optional Valuation Date

The property valuations assigned, as discussed above, may or may not be the same as those on which the estate tax will be based.

The executor has an option when preparing the Federal estate tax return. He may use the values assigned as of the date of death or he may use values as of the "optional valuation date," which is six months after the date of death (one year for estates of decedents dying before January 1, 1971). He does not have the privilege of using one date's valuation for some assets and the other date's for others. The entire estate must be valued as of either the date of death or six months later; except that any property sold, distributed, or otherwise disposed of during the six months is valued as of the date of disposition when the later date is used for estate tax purposes.

This option can be a valuable tax saving device. It should be considered during periods of falling values, or when the estate has suffered a shrinkage in its aggregate value, or when the first appraisal was very much out of line. But the executor might consider electing the higher of the two valuations if comparative tax rates indicate that a beneficiary would be better off in the long run by having a higher basis in the property. The following chapters, however, are based on the assumption that the values at the date of death will be used, unless otherwise specified.

3

The Estate Inventory— Assets

It was pointed out in Chapter 2 that the estate inventory should not include any liabilities, only the estate's assets. There is often some question, however, as to just what assets should be included, and there is almost always a question as to just what is the proper valuation for each asset so included.

This chapter deals with the question of what assets must be included, and Chapter 4 deals with the valuation of these assets.

The answers to these questions sometimes seem to depend on a mixture of various laws, not all of which are always in agreement with each other. Local property laws, state inheritance tax laws, and the Federal estate tax law all have something to say about what property should be included in an estate inventory and how it should be valued. The most universal of these laws is the Federal estate tax law, and in a vast majority of cases if the provisions of this law are followed there will not be any great conflict with other laws.

The Federal estate tax code, supplemented by a set of regulations and numerous rulings and decisions, is much more complete and thorough than any of the other governing laws. Also, it frequently provides that local law may control some of the issues. Therefore, the executor and his appraisers will usually be well advised to make every effort to follow the Federal provisions and directions in preparing the estate inventory and placing valuations on the various items.

This is true even though the estate may be too small to be subject to the Federal estate tax.

Inventory Should Include All Assets

As mentioned earlier, the administrable estate is not always the same as the taxable estate. The assets passing through the probate estate are generally only those in which the decedent had an interest at the time of his death; the taxable estate can include additional assets, such as certain lifetime transfers, life insurance, or other funds.

Since this is the case, it is recommended that the inventorying and appraising of the estate should include *all* assets, both administrable and taxable, as all will be needed in preparing the Federal estate tax return. Those not subject to administration can simply be deleted from the listing in preparing the inventory to be filed with the court.

The information contained in these chapters on inventory is, therefore, based on the all-inclusive Federal law, with any important exceptions and options being noted.

Importance of the Inventory

It would be very difficult to overemphasize the importance of the estate inventory. The inventory is certainly the most important of the many documents with which the executor must be concerned.

Its importance lies in the fact that the inventory is the basis for everything accounting wise and tax wise that takes place during the course of the estate's administration. It is, first, the basis for the opening entry in the estate books, and many of the figures recorded from the inventory will last not only during the estate's life but into future years as well.

Secondly, these values will usually be the basis of distributions to the various heirs when the estate is settled and will continue to be the tax basis of the property in the hands of the heirs from that time on.

Thirdly, the inventory is the basis for listing the assets on the estate and inheritance tax returns, and the inventory values are those on which the taxes will be computed. If the inventory is listed and valued completely and carefully, and in accordance with the tax laws, there is much less chance of the tax returns being questioned and changed by the revenue agents examining them. Time and effort spent on the inventory will be amply repaid by a saving of time and worry when the tax returns are being examined later. A revenue agent will be much more inclined to accept the inventory valuations if it appears to him that the inventory was conscientiously prepared by a team of qualified, informed appraisers.

Finally, the inventory filed with the court establishes the executor's accountability for the estate assets. It is an enumeration of the property with which the executor is charged and is the basis for his reports to the court showing what disposition he has made of this property. Also, reliable inventory valuations will be of great help to the executor in determining sales prices for any of the property which he must sell; they wll eliminate—at least as far as the executor is concerned—arguments among the various beneficiaries as to the relative values of unsold property being distributed among them.

It is at the time of inventory preparation that the executor's accountant will first prove to be a very valuable person to have around. His knowledge of the estate tax laws will be indispensible; he is the one who will keep the appraisers on the right track in establishing valuations which are in accord with these tax requirements; his ability to foresee the future effects of actions taken at this time will go a long way toward accomplishing some of the desirable objectives mentioned above. It is certainly worthwhile for the accountant to spend as much time with the appraisers as may be necessary to assure their doing the best possible job. The accountant will not be wasting time by doing this, because he, too, will be well repaid in great savings of time later.

Property Owned by the Decedent

For administration purposes, property is generally considered as being owned by the decedent only to the extent that he had a *beneficial* interest in the property. If the decedent had only a *legal* title to the property, *for example* as a trustee, no part of the property is considered a part of his estate. On the other hand, if the decedent had a beneficial interest in the property, the value of the property is included in his gross estate even though title (or possession) is held by another person, such as a trustee or pledgee.

The decedent must not only have had a beneficial interest in the property but also must have had an interest which survives his death in the sense that it can be transmitted to others by his will or through intestacy laws. This eliminates such interests as life estates which terminate with the decedent's death, property expected to be owned in the future, certain contingent interests, and so forth.

But for estate tax purposes, property transferred to others by the decedent during his lifetime may have to be included in the inventory. Certain powers over property, such as powers of appointment, may also have to be inventoried. This is explained more fully later in this chapter.

Real estate situated outside of the United States (defined as the fifty states and the District of Columbia) is excluded from the gross estate, unless the decedent died after July 1, 1964, in which case it is included, but personal property, regardless of its location, is included.

Property subject to homestead or other exemptions under local law must be included in the gross estate for tax purposes and should, therefore, be inventoried. Notes or other claims held by the decedent should be included even though they are cancelled by his will. Accrued interest and rents are includible even though they are not collected until after the death, and so also are declared dividends payable to stockholders of record when the record date occurs on or before the date of the stockholder's death.

Various statutory provisions which exempt bonds, notes, bills, certificates of indebtedness of the Federal government or its agencies and the interest thereon from taxation are not applicable to the estate tax, so such assets should also be inventoried.

The above mentioned types of property interests, as well as others which might have to be included in inventory, are discussed more fully in the following sections.

The problem of determining actual ownership of property can be very tricky at times, but this determination must be made for every asset in question before an accurate inventory can be completed. As a general rule, local property law is controlling on the issue of ownership for estate tax purposes as well as for inventory purposes. If there is a local decision settling the issue it will ordinarily be given effect. The executor's attorney, therefore, should make a study of each question that arises regarding ownership, and the executor should be guided by his attorney's opinion in deciding whether to include or exclude any questionable asset.

The decision to exclude any such asset should be supported by a written memorandum or letter from the attorney, setting forth the details and reasons for the decision. This letter will be valuable later on when the estate tax returns are being examined, because it is very easy to forget such details after several years, and a letter filed at the time might quickly answer a revenue agent's question and save having to re-study the decision to exclude an item of property.

Dower and Curtesy Interests

There is no reduction in gross estate due to any dower or curtesy interest of the surviving spouse. The entire value of the property must be included in the gross estate of the decedent.

In those states which have created by statute interests in place of dower and curtesy the same rule applies; the entire value of the property must be included in gross estate.

State law, therefore, is relevant only in determining the quality and quantity of the marital interests, but Federal law determines the question of taxability. Where under local law the spouse of a decedent has certain privileges as to the estate, such as the right of the widow under Pennsylvania, Illinois, and Ohio law to retain a certain part of the deceased husband's real or personal property, the amount retainable cannot be excluded from the husband's gross estate. The same is true of the husband's right to a "marital portion" under the laws of Louisiana, support payments allowed under local law for the surviving spouse, homestead rights, and personal property set aside for the widow under the New York law.

Transfers and Gifts

Strange as it may seem, there is sometimes property in which the decedent had neither a beneficial nor a legal interest which might still have to be considered a part of his gross estate. This would generally be certain property which the decedent had given away during his lifetime or property which he had otherwise transferred for less than a full and adequate consideration.

The reason for such a requirement is, of course, to prevent a person from defeating the application of the estate tax by ridding himself of the title to all or a part of his property before his death, leaving little or nothing subject to tax in his estate. State laws relating to trusts and other property rights make it easy for a person to dispose of certain property but at the same time retain control or beneficial ownership for life. Also, if it is obvious to a person that he does not have long to live he could dispose of any remaining property by outright gift, thereby removing such property from the gross taxable estate.

To combat these possibilities, the estate tax law provides for inclusion of almost every type of lifetime transfer in which the decedent did not dispose of every consequential right. There are five general types of lifetime transfers the value of which might have to be added to the decedent's gross remaining estate for tax purposes.

1. *Transfers in contemplation of death.* Any transfer made by a person within three years prior to his death is deemed to have been made in contemplation of death, and presumably for the purpose of avoiding estate taxes, even if the decedent disposed of his entire interest in the property. Such property must be included in the gross estate unless the executor can satisfy the Treasury Department that the transfer was *not* motivated by the expectation of death, but rather by motives associated with life. The burden of proving this is placed upon the executor. The executor will have to determine the facts as best he can and should support them with affidavits from various people who were acquainted with the decedent and familiar with the circumstances surrounding the particular transfers in question (*see* Exhibit 12).

Exhibit 12

Affidavit—Contemplation of Death

AFFIDAVIT

The affiant, Gordon Keith, states that he was a friend and close business associate of Guy Wallace for eighteen years prior to his death; that he worked with Mr. Wallace in the operation of their business for eighteen years prior to his death; that Guy Wallace was active in business transactions and in daily and regular activities of life on up to the day of his death; that he had an optimistic and forward outlook on life, and at no time anticipated sudden death; that he was in good health, took good care of himself physically, watched his diet and in other ways protected his health, that he at no time made any gifts or conveyances in contemplation of death.

The affiant further states that Guy Wallace took good care of himself, had frequent physical examinations, felt confident that he would live at least as long as his father who died at the age of eighty-six, was optimistic about the future and made plans for future business transactions and was never apprehensive of the attack from which he died, which was very sudden and wholly and duly unexpected both to him and to all associated with him. He had been in the office and worked on the date prior to his death.

The affiant states that the gifts and conveyances which Guy Wallace made to his wife during the last three or four years of his life were no more numerous or extensive than during any other period of their

Exhibit 12 (cont.)

married life, and that Mr. Wallace at no time tried to get his affairs ready or in shape for death, but rather kept his estate going forward in a progressive way looking for future profits.

_____

Gordon Keith

An important consideration in these cases is the decedent's physical condition at the time of the transfer. If he was well, active, and looking forward to continued life, it is probable that he did not act in contemplation of death. If the decedent was advanced in years, was suffering from some ailment likely to result in his death, and was conscious that he had the ailment, it is probable that the transfer was made in contemplation of death.

Transfers generally held *not* to have been made in contemplation of death are those made for the financial assistance of members of the family, or even friends; transfers made to help children get established in business; transfers made for the purpose of reducing income taxes and property taxes, and the like.

No transfer made prior to the three years immediately preceding the decedent's death will be considered a transfer in contemplation of death.

2. *Transfers taking effect at the decedent's death.* A transfer made by the decedent of an interest in property which takes effect at the decedent's death is includible in the gross estate if the decedent retained a reversionary interest in the property, which interest exceeds five percent of the value of the property at the time of death; and if possession or enjoyment of the transferred property can be obtained only by beneficiaries who must survive the decedent. The decedent's reversionary interest is to be valued by the usual methods, using mortality tables and actuarial principles.

3. *Transfers with possession and enjoyment retained.* If the decedent made a transfer, either outright or in trust, under which he retained possession or enjoyment of the property or of the income from it for his life or for any period which cannot be ascertained without reference to his death, the property must be included in his estate. If the rights were retained for a specified period only, they are not includible unless the decedent died within that period.

The date on which the transfer was made has a bearing on its includibility, and the other rules governing the taxability of this type of transfer are rather technical. If such a transfer is encountered, the code and regulations should be studied in the light of the specific case.

4. *Transfers whereby the decedent retained the right to designate who shall possess or enjoy.* Retaining such a right in the transfer of property will make the value of the property taxable in the decedent's estate, even though he did not retain the kind of interest described in (3) above. The requirements as to the period for which he retains such a right are the same as mentioned for the preceding type of transfer.

5. *Revocable transfers.* Transfers are also includible if the decedent retained the right to alter, amend, revoke, or terminate the transfer. Such transfers are taxable whether

the decedent had this power at the time of his death or whether he relinquished it in contemplation of death (and within three years prior to his death). This, also, is a very technical question, and a thorough study of the governing law should be made when it arises.

The executor should search for all of the above types of lifetime transfers at the time he is listing the estate property. If at all possible, he should make an investigation at this time of any such transfers and try to determine whether they must be included in the gross taxable estate. The executor's accountant and attorney should join in this investigation and determine the correct method of handling the transfer.

If there are transfers which the executor thinks he should not include, he should make a written memorandum of the details and his reasons for excluding the transfer and retain it for later presentation to an examining agent.

All transfers of a value of $1,000 or more made by the decedent within three years prior to his death, and all transfers made at any time of a value of $5,000 or more (except bona fide sales for an adequate and full consideration) must be shown on the estate tax return, whether the executor regards such transfers as subject to the tax or not. If the executor believes that such a transfer is not subject to the tax, a statement of the pertinent facts should be made and its value not added in to the total taxable estate. Transfers included in the gross estate should be valued as of the date of the decedent's death (or the alternate valuation date).

If any of the various types of transfers was for a consideration in money or in money's worth, then the transfer is taxed only on the excess of the fair market value *at the valuation date* over the consideration received by the decedent. If the transferee has made additions or improvements to the property, the enhanced value of the property at the valuation date due to these additions and improvements should not be included.

Transfers of property which the executor believes are non-taxable should not be included in the estate inventory. Inclusion in the inventory is recommended for those transfers which appear to be taxable; they may also be recorded in the books as a part of the estate assets, then finally written off as a distribution to the transferee. However, since local laws generally do not require their inclusion as a part of the administrable estate, it is usually better to omit them from the books and simply make a notation of their existence and value for use in preparation of the estate tax return.

The gift tax consequences of transfers made for less than a full and adequate consideration is discussed in Chapter 12.

Life Estates

The foregoing section refers to transfers made *by* the decedent prior to his death. But what about limited interests in property which had been transferred *to* the decedent?

If the decedent had an interest in property which terminated with his death, this interest is not to be included in his gross estate. Such an interest is generally known as a "life estate" in the property, with the property usually being held in trust; and since the life estate ended with the life tenant's death, he had no right in the property which he could transmit to others.

If the decedent's interest is measured by a fixed term of years or by the life of another person, the interest for the balance of the term or the unexpired life of the other person is an interest which can be transmitted at the decedent's death. The value of the interest so transmitted is included in the gross estate.

If there is undistributed income in the trust at the life tenant's death, this income is included in his gross estate.

Trusts generally are established for the benefit of two classes of persons—the life tenant mentioned above and the "remainderman," to whom possession or enjoyment of the property will pass upon the death of the life tenant. This raises the question of whether a remainderman, who dies before obtaining possession or enjoyment of the property, might have any taxable interest in the property.

In general, the value of this future interest must be included in the estate unless it was extinguished by the remainderman's death and therefore cannot pass to his heirs, legatees, and devisees.

There are generally two types of remainders. One is a "vested" remainder, which cannot be defeated by any contingency or condition contained in the instrument of transfer. The other is a "contingent" remainder, which gives the remainderman the future right to enjoyment or possession of the property only if a certain event occurs or a certain condition is fulfilled. In either case, the taxability of the property interest depends on whether or not the decedent had an interest which survived his death and which he could transmit by will or by intestacy law.

The question of whether the decedent had any interest in property and the nature of the interest is basically determined by the local property law. Local law, therefore, should be studied in trying to decide whether the decedent had merely a life interest in property which need not be included in the estate inventory or a larger interest which might have to be included.

If such interests must be inventoried, their valuation presents a problem. The present value of a life estate, remainder, or reversionary interest must be computed on an actuarial basis; the method of doing this and the tables to be used are given in the estate tax regulations.

The valuation date for such interest is the date of death, whether or not the optional valuation date is used. If the optional date is used, the value at death is adjusted for any difference in value between the two dates which is due to causes other than the mere lapse of time.

Powers of Appointment

Another class of property right which the decedent may have had, and which the executor should search for and determine the status of, is property over which the decedent had a "power of appointment."

A power of appointment is a right to designate, by will or by deed, the persons who are to receive certain property which came from the estate of a prior decedent. Such a power is usually held by someone who had the income from the property for life—a life tenant. However, it is possible, of course, for one person to have the life income and another person to have the right to designate who shall receive the property after death of the life tenant.

The tax effects of a power of appointment depend primarily upon its scope. The holder of the power (donee) may have been given a degree of discretion which in effect makes him the economic owner of the property. If the donee can exercise the power in favor of himself or his estate (and without the joinder of someone else who has a substantial adverse interest), the power is a "general" power of appointment and the estate tax law will treat the donee as the owner of the property.

If the power is sufficiently restricted in scope, the donee will not be regarded as owning the property himself, but as acting on behalf of the donor in whose estate the property has already been taxed.

Taxability upon the *donor's* death raises no particular issue. The property is taxable as a part of his gross estate. It is the *donee's* death that brings up the question whether there is another estate tax due, by including the same property in the donee's estate, or whether upon the donee's death the property may go tax-free to the person he designates as the appointee.

Tax laws do not unqualifiedly follow local property law in the case of powers over property. The estate's accountant, with his knowledge of tax law, must work with the estate's attorney, who will be familiar with local property law, in determining the exact status of any such powers discovered by the executor.

In making this determination, it is necessary, first, to ascertain when the power was created. A power was created when a testator who conferred it by his will died (or when some other instrument conferring it became effective). October 22, 1942 is the crucial date. A power created before that date is taxable in the donee's estate only if he exercised the power by his will, or if he disposed of it during his lifetime in such a way that if it had been a transfer of his own property it would be includible in his gross estate. A power created after October 22, 1942 is taxable whether the holder of the power exercised it or not. If exercised during his life there may be gift tax; if by his will, or not exercised at all, estate tax. In either case, however, the donee's power must have been of sufficient scope to have been a "general" power of appointment.

The donee of a power of appointment does not always have the opportunity beforehand of accepting or refusing the power. If one is granted to him, he may prefer not to have it on account of the potential estate tax liability due to the property being in his estate. In this case, he may disclaim or renounce the power, provided he does so within a reasonable period after having learned of its existence. The donee may also escape estate tax liability by releasing or exercising the power, provided he does not act in contemplation of death and provided he reserves no rights such as would cause a transfer of his own property during his lifetime to be included in his gross estate.

The executor must determine if his decedent *ever* possessed a power of appointment and, if so, must disclose it on the estate tax return. He must also file a certified copy of the instrument granting the power and a certified copy of any instrument by which the power was exercised or released, even though it is his contention that the power was not a general power of appointment and that the property is not otherwise includible in the gross estate.

There is one additional point which it is important to know if the estate tax has been increased by the inclusion of appointable property—the executor of the donee's estate is entitled to recover from the recipient of the appointable property the portion of the estate tax paid by the donee's estate which is allocable to the property. The recipient from whom the executor may claim proportionate reimbursement is the person who received the appointable property, by reason of exercise, nonexercise, or release of the power. Where there are several recipients, the executor may recover from them in the same ratio.

Jointly Owned Property

Joint ownership is a widespread method of property ownership throughout the country, so it is very likely that the executor will find some such property among the decedent's assets and will have to investigate its status and take a stand regarding its taxability and its includibility in the estate inventory.

Following again the principles laid down by the Federal estate tax law, there are only three specific types of property interests which are considered as "joint interests."

The first of these is a *joint tenancy*. This exists where two or more individuals own a single estate in property, either real or personal, under one instrument or act of the parties. The distinguishing feature is that the interest of a deceased tenant passes under right of survivorship to the surviving tenant. It is not descendible and cannot be disposed of by will, but can only pass to the surviving tenant.

The next type is a *tenancy by the entirety*. This is similar to a joint tenancy, but is limited to property acquired by husband and wife jointly after marriage. It is based on the amiable common law fiction that the husband and wife are but one person because of the joining together in the bonds of matrimony. Like property held jointly, the interest of the deceased spouse is not descendible and cannot be disposed of by will. Upon the death of either spouse, the survivor takes the entire estate.

The third type is *joint bank accounts*. This can be either money or securities deposited with any bank in the name of the decedent and any other person or persons, and payable to either or to the survivor.

It will be noted that in each of these types of ownership the element of survivorship is present.

As for the includibility of such property in the gross estate, the rule is that the entire value must be included, *except* such part of the value as the executor can prove to be attributable to an actual investment in money or money's worth furnished by the other joint owner. Thus, if the survivor paid a portion of the purchase price for property held in joint tenancy or by the entireties, that portion of the value on the applicable valuation date may be excluded from the gross estate.

In all cases where the executor seeks to exclude a part of the value of the jointly held property from the gross estate, he has the burden of proving that he should include only the reduced value. The law is not satisfied with the mere showing that consideration was furnished by the other joint owner. It inquires into the source and origin of the consideration. Thus, if a husband and wife buy securities in joint tenancy, each contributing one-half of the purchase price, but the wife contributes only money previously given to her by her husband, the entire value of the securities is included in the estate of the husband, if the husband is the first to die.

Funds in a joint bank account will be included in full in the decedent's estate in the absence of proof positive that part of the funds originally belonged to the survivor. Such proof may be difficult, or even impossible.

The difficulties in proving the contribution made by surviving tenants often make it inadvisable, for estate tax purposes, to hold property as joint tenants or tenants by the entirety. However, a number of advantages derived from joint ownership by husband and wife may outweigh estate tax considerations. *For example*, on the death of one spouse, the survivor immediately acquires sole ownership of the property without the cost and delay of probate proceedings. In addition, the property is ordinarily free from the claims of the deceased's creditors, and others.

Little difficulty is encountered in excluding a portion of the value if the property was acquired by the decedent and the other joint owner or owners by gift, devise, bequest, or inheritance from a third person. In the case of property received as a tenant by the entirety, the value of only one-half is included in the decedent's estate. For property held under a joint tenancy, the value of the deceased's interest as fixed by local law will be included in the estate. If such interest is not specified by local law, then there is included only the fractional part of the total value obtained by dividing the full value by the number of joint tenants.

Complete information to support the executor's decision to exclude any portion of the value of jointly owned property should be retained for use in preparing the estate tax return, on which there is a page or reporting all such property and for giving full details supporting the exclusion of any portion.

There are two other types of multiple ownership of property, neither of which is subject to the above rules. One of these is community property, discussed in a subsequent section, and the other is tenancies in common.

Only the value of the decedent's undivided share of property held under a tenancy in common will be taxed as part of his estate. Property of this kind should not be listed under the "Jointly Owned Property" schedule of the estate tax return, but the value of the interest should be shown under the appropriate schedule for real estate, securities, cash, or whatever the property happens to be.

Life Insurance

The proceeds of life insurance policies on the decedent's life are classified as (1) those receivable by the executor, payable to the estate, or in fact receivable by or for the benefit of the estate; and (2) those payable to all other beneficiaries.

Those in the first category are always includible in the gross estate for estate tax purposes. They must be included even though the premiums may have been paid for by someone other than the decedent, someone who retained complete control over the policy during the insured's lifetime. They are even includible when they are payable to a trustee if the trustee is *required* to apply the proceeds to any of the estate's expenses. They are includible if any other recipient of the proceeds is *required* to use them to pay estate taxes.

Proceeds falling into the second category are subject to special rules. If the decedent had not merely named the beneficiary of a policy on his life, but had retained any incidents of ownership normally attaching to a policy, the proceeds must be included just like any other property. This is true even though the proceeds are paid directly to the beneficiary and never come into the executor's possession.

If the decedent had disposed of *all* rights over the policy, the entire proceeds may be excludable, even though he had paid all of the premiums on the policy.

In determining the application of the term "incidents of ownership," the following rights must be considered, and if it is found that the decedent had retained any one or more of them this will result in inclusion of the insurance proceeds in the gross estate;

(1) The right to change the beneficiaries or their shares.

(2) The right to surrender the policy for cash or to cancel it.

(3) The right to borrow against the policy reserve.

(4) The right to pledge the policy as collateral.

(5) The right to assign the policy or to revoke an assignment.

(6) A reversionary interest with a value of more than 5 per cent of the value of the policy immediately before the decedent's death. A reversionary interest includes the chance of the policy or proceeds returning to the decedent or his estate, and the power in the decedent to dispose of the policy.

Even though the decedent had relinquished all of these rights of ownership during his lifetime, the proceeds may still be includible in his estate under the special rules governing lifetime transfers. *For example*, the transfer may have been in contemplation of death, a revocable transfer, a transfer taking effect at death, and so forth.

Life insurance is frequently used in connection with various types of business transactions. In all such instances the method of treating the insurance for estate tax purposes depends on the terms of the agreement, if any, and the insurance contract.

When insurance on the decedent's life was taken out by a corporation of which the decedent was a stockholder, the proceeds will not be included in the decedent's estate, because the insured under such an arrangement usually has no interest himself in the insurance. The proceeds will be felt, however, in fixing a value for the decedent's stock in the corporation, as they will be included among the corporate assets in determining the stock value.

Life insurance is often used in connection with agreements calling for the purchase and sale of stock in a close corporation following the death of a stockholder. If the agreement is such that it requires the purchase and sale of the stock following the death of the insured, there will be included in the insured's estate either the value of the stock which is to be sold or the proceeds of the sale of the stock.

The taxability of partnership insurance is dependent upon the possession of incidents of ownership and upon whether the insurance arrangement is a true funding plan to provide for continuance of the business by the survivor.

Benefits payable on the decedent's death under retirement and pension funds are not considered life insurance as such. If they are proceeds of a policy of life insurance, whether group or individual, they may qualify.

There is no exclusion for endowment policies, group insurance, or war risk insurance and national service life insurance.

The amount at which a policy should be valued if it is payable to or for the benefit of the estate is the amount receivable. If the proceeds are payable to some other beneficiary and not to or for the benefit of the estate, the value is also the full amount receivable. In case the proceeds of a policy were made payable to the beneficiary in the form of an annuity, the value is the lump sum payable at death if there was such an option, or, if there was no option, the sum used by the insurance company in determining the amount of the annuity.

In filing the estate tax return, each policy must be listed, whether or not it is considered taxable. In addition, the executor must secure from each insurance company a Form 712, "Life Insurance Statement," and file it with the return.

The foregoing discussion of life insurance is perhaps an oversimplification of a very complex subject in estate taxation, and the executor should be warned to investigate fully the nature and status of any insurance on his decedent's life.

This is one area in which Federal estate tax law and local law are sometimes widely divergent, and local law should be studied to determine the includibility of insurance proceeds for probate inventory purposes. Insurance payable to beneficiaries other than the estate is not generally held to be a part of the administrable estate, even though it may be a part of the taxable estate; but again, it is wise to include such an asset in the inventory for the sake of completeness.

One word of caution, however, is that insurance payable to beneficiaries other than the estate is, in many states, not subject to state inheritance taxation, and, if this is the case, the executor must be careful not to include it in the inheritance tax return.

A reminder—if any taxable insurance proceeds are receivable by a beneficiary other than the executor, the executor is entitled to reimbursement of a portion of the estate tax. The portion to be reimbursed by the beneficiary is so much of the tax paid as the proceeds of the policies bear to the sum of the taxable estate and the $60,000 exemption.

Annuities and Pensions

Annuities and payments from various employee's benefit plans are treated separately from life insurance and other kinds of property for estate tax purposes. Benefits provided for in annuity, pension, profit-sharing or stock bonus plans or trusts, may or may not be includible in the gross estate of the decedent, depending upon the nature of the contract and the payment made.

Generally, the value of an annuity or other payment payable to any beneficiary by reason of his surviving the decedent is includible in the decedent's estate. This value is included only if prior to death the decedent was receiving or had the right to receive payments under the annuity contract, either alone or in conjunction with any other person for life, or for a period which did not in fact end with his death. Here are the estate tax rules, covering the various possible situations, whether the annuity was purchased by the decedent on his own or through some employee benefit plan.

1. *Life payments.* Under a life plan, the employer, insurance company, or trustee is obligated to make payments only for the life of the annuitant. At his death, all installments cease even though death occurs before a single payment is received. No person other than the annuitant is entitled to receive any payments, so there is nothing to be included in the estate.

2. *Return of employee's contributions.* Where a retirement plan merely provides that the amount contributed by the employee shall be returned with interest to his named beneficiaries in case of his death before retirement, the sum returned is a part of the decedent's estate.

3. *Refund plan or annuity.* A refund plan or annuity usually provides for payments to the employee or annuitant for life, and a refund if death should occur before the contract cost (or employee's contribution) is recovered. If this refund is in cash, the amount actually paid to the beneficiaries upon the annuitant's death would be includible in the gross estate. If the plan or annuity provides for continuing the installments after the decedent's death, the total amount receivable by the beneficiary, discounted to its present value, would be includible. (Sec. 2039).

4. *Survivorship plan or annuity not connected with employment.* There are two general types of annuity plans. One is the contingent annuity plan whereby the annuitant receives payments for life or for a designated period, and upon his death, payments are made to a named beneficiary for life or for the remainder of the designated period. The other is the joint and survivor annuity plan whereby payments are received by joint annuitants during their lives, and upon the death of one annuitant the payments continue to the survivor. The value of the annuities going to a beneficiary of a contingent plan or to the surviving annuitant of a joint and survivor annuity plan is includible in the

gross estate if the recipient is entitled to the payments by reason of surviving the decedent, *and* the decedent up to the time of death was receiving or was entitled to receive payments under the annuity plan.

5. *Employee's annuity and benefit plans.* If the decedent was an employee entitled to payments under an employee's annuity or benefit plan, the value of the payments going to his beneficiaries after his death is includible in his gross estate if (a) the decedent employee made any contribution to the plan from which the payments are to be made, regardless of whether or not such plan qualified as tax-exempt under the income tax laws, *or* (b) the employer's contributions to an unqualified plan were made as an inducement to employment or as a substitute for additional compensation. If the plan is a qualified pension or profit-sharing plan, financed entirely by the employer, the annuity escapes inclusion in the decedent's estate. If the employee contributed to the cost of the annuity under such a plan, the portion of its value attributable to his contributions is includible. (Sec. 2039 (c)).

6. *Self-Employed Retirement Plans.* When the decedent was an owner-employee who had made payments to a retirement plan (Keogh Plan), most of the rules that apply to plans for employees are brought into play, depending on the nature and provisions of the decedent's plan, and the amount includible for estate tax purposes must be determined. It must be noted, however, that any portion of this total which represents amounts for which the decedent obtained an income tax deduction, as well as all the tax-free income accumulated during the period the plan operated, must be treated as income in respect of a decedent (see Chapter 13). The same principles apply to the new Individual Retirement Accounts.

The valuation of annuities is determined as of the date of death of the primary annuitant. Where the benefits are payable in a lump sum, the value is obvious—the amount payable is the value, though this may be reduced on a proportionate basis because the entire cost of the annuity may not have been borne by the decedent.

Where the benefits are payable in installments, the value of this continuing annuity to the survivor is to be based on the cost of an annuity of such amount at the time of the decedent's death.

Where the payments to the survivor are fixed in duration or amount, they are valued as an annuity for a term certain under tables provided in the estate tax regulations.

The subject of annuities and pensions is another area which is covered in great detail in the estate tax law and regulations, to which the executor should refer if additional information concerning the particular annuity involved is needed.

Debts and Claims Due Decedent

Valid and enforceable debts and claims owned by the decedent are includible in his gross estate. A claim is not includible unless it is enforceable; thus, a debt barred by the statute of limitations should not be included.

Debts or claims supported by notes or mortgages are discussed in Chapter 4, but there are likely to be other claims which would fall into the category of miscellaneous claims, and which should be reported on the "miscellaneous property" schedule of the estate tax return. A number of these are listed and discussed briefly:

1. The decedent's right to a fee or commission as an executor or trustee.

2. A claim for a contingent fee for legal services.

3. A claim for a bonus for services rendered prior to death, provided the employer was under a legal liability to pay the bonus.

4. A claim for salary, bonus, or severance pay payable under a contract.

5. The value of a right of subrogation. This is included in the estate as an offset to the deduction for liability as an endorser.

6. A claim for refund of income taxes, even though it is being contested or is in litigation. This is includible although the refund claim is filed by the executor, not by the decedent before his death.

7. A claim for overpayment of income tax for the decedent's last taxable year ending with his death, through overpayment of his estimated tax or overwithholding by his employer. If a joint return is filed covering the decedent's last taxable year, the estate includes that portion of tax paid by the decedent which exceeds his pro rata share of the tax shown on the joint return. The pro rata share is the proportion of the total tax which his taxable income bears to the total taxable income.

8. A claim for refund of gift taxes paid.

9. Accounts receivable (unless already included as a part of an interest in a business).

10. Debts and claims due at date of death, even though they are cancelled by the decedent's will.

11. Advances to heirs (unless it is evident that there was no intention that the debt was to be paid).

12. Commissions receivable.

13. Benefits payable on the death of a Federal employee from the Civil Service and Disability Fund.

14. Social security and unemployment compensation receivable. But the value of a decedent's interest in uncashed social security checks jointly payable to him and his wife is not includible. Rev. Rul. 75-145).

15. Unpaid legacies.

Receivables which are *not* includible in a decedent's gross estate include death benefits payable under the Social Security act to the widow, children, or parents of the decedent; Congressional death gratuity payments; armed forces death benefit; workman's compensation death benefits; lump-sum benefits under the Railroad Retirement Act payable to a spouse or parent under age 60. (Rev. Rul. 73-316).

It has been held that the proceeds of a wrongful death settlement are not includible in the gross estate; they were not owned by the decedent at his death, since the claim did not arise during his lifetime when he was capable of owning property. (Rev. Rul. 75-126).

All includible debts and claims should be itemized in the inventory, and if any of them bear interest the accrued interest to the date of death should also be shown.

Community Property

If the decedent was a resident of a community property state, his executor will have the additional problem of determining the correct method of including any community property in the gross estate.

Community property exists in the following jurisdictions: Arizona, California, Idaho, Louisiana, Nevada, New Mexico, Texas, and Washington. Each jurisdiction has developed the general idea in its own way and by its own methods, with the result of widely divergent local differences. However, the principles governing the inventory and tax treatment of community property can be fairly well summarized.

The underlying principle of community property is that a husband and wife, by the industry and labor of either or both, have created the community estate and that this estate belongs beneficially to both during the continuance of the marital relation. It is dissolved upon the death of either spouse, by divorce, or separation of property without divorce.

Community property is not regarded as being held by husband and wife as either joint tenants or as tenants by the entirety, so only the value of the interest vested in the decedent by state law is included in the gross estate. It is not necessary to trace the surviving spouse's investment in the property or to prove that the survivor actually made any investment in it.

Ordinarily, one-half of the community property held by husband and wife is included in the deceased spouse's estate. Local law will determine the nature and extent of the decedent's interest, and the Federal estate tax law defers almost entirely to local law in this regard. Local laws regarding community property, however, are usually rather intricate, and the advice of the estate's attorney should be sought whenever this problem is encountered. Property which the attorney believes is community property should be inventoried at only one-half of its appraised value.

On the estate tax return, it should not be listed as jointly owned property but rather on the schedules for the various kinds of assets it might consist of.

The exclusion of the surviving spouse's one-half interest in community property applies not only to property in which the decedent had an interest at the time of his death, but also to property which was the subject of his taxable lifetime transfers (discussed earlier in this chapter) and to life insurance purchased with community funds, and so forth.

Although the limitation on the taxability of community property seems to place such property in an especially favorable position, its effect is balanced for noncommunity property by the "marital deduction," which permits a deduction for property passing to a surviving spouse to the extent of up to one-half the value of the property. (*See* Chapter 11.)

4

The Estate Inventory— Valuation

The discussion of the estate inventory has, up to this point, dealt principally with the various kinds of property interests which the decedent might have had, and with whether or not those interests were subject to inclusion in the estate inventory and were a part of the gross estate for estate tax purposes. The relatively unusual types of property interests were mentioned so that the executor, his accountant, and his lawyer might have a check list to help prevent their overlooking something which should be inventoried.

When the decision is arrived at that a certain property interest must be included, the specific makeup of that interest must then be determined and each part of it valued according to the rules for the particular assets involved. *For example*, a taxable transfer may have consisted of real estate, bonds, and cash. These cannot be listed and valued as a unit, but each of the three assets must be valued separately.

In most instances, however, there is little question as to the includibility of property; but there is frequently a lot of difficulty in arriving at the proper valuation at which the property should be shown.

This chapter discusses the problems and methods of valuation of the various kinds of assets. Again, Federal estate tax law is the basis for the rules and procedures suggested; these will serve as a guide to correct valuation for inventory purposes as well as for estate tax purposes.

It is very unlikely, of course, that any estate would include all of the kinds of property mentioned in these chapters on inventory, but any executor would be well advised to think about each one of them in the light of his particular decedent's estate and to use these chapters as a check list to insure against his overlooking some assets.

Valuation of Property in General

The value of every item of property includible in a decedent's gross estate is its fair market value at the time of the decedent's death. Even though the alternate valuation date (six months from date of death) is later decided on for estate tax purposes, the values at the date of death are used in preparing the estate inventory.

The fair market value is the price at which the property would change hands between a willing buyer and a willing seller, neither being under any compulsion to buy or to sell and both having a reasonable knowledge of relevant facts. The fair market value of a particular item of property is not to be determined by a forced sale price.

The value is generally to be determined by ascertaining the fair market value of each unit of the property. For example, in the case of shares of stock or bonds, such unit is generally one share of stock or one bond. Livestock, farm machinery, harvested and growing crops, and the like, must generally be itemized and the value for each item determined separately.

Property should not be valued at the amounts assessed for local tax purposes. Such assessments are not often very accurate, but they might be of some help to the appraisers in giving them a general idea of the relative values if there have been recent sales of comparable property.

Specific valuation problems are discussed in the following sections in connection with some of the various assets which might be found in the estate.

Real Estate

As pointed out earlier, a decedent's real estate may or may not be a part of the administrable estate but it is a part of the taxable estate. Regardless of how little authority the state law and the decedent's will might give the executor in connection with real estate, the executor has, at the very least, the responsibility of locating the real estate, reporting it on the tax return, and paying the tax on it.

For all practical purposes, therefore, the executor should make very little distinction between real estate and personal property. This applies particularly to the estate inventory, in which every parcel of real property should be included.

All real property owned by the decedent at death and situated in the United States is included, whether the decedent is a citizen or alien, resident or nonresident. Real property situated outside of the United States is excluded, unless death occurred after July 1, 1964 or the real estate was acquired after January 1962. (Personal property is included in the gross estate regardless of its location.)

Real estate is included even though it is subject to homestead and other exemptions under local law. The only exclusion of real estate is the part of a cemetery lot designated for the burial of the decedent or members of his family; the salable value of any other part of the lot is included.

Each parcel of real estate should be listed separately. Each should be described in enough detail so that it could be readily located, and a short description of any improvements should be included.

The valuation of real property is always difficult. This is particularly true of land in rural districts, but even expert appraisers of city real estate frequently vary materially in their valuations. At best, in the absence of bona fide sales, the valuation is a matter of opinion.

It should not be forgotten that correct values in estate tax cases are doubly important inasmuch as the government makes a careful field investigation and also, subject to certain exceptions, because the value finally determined in the estate tax proceeding is the value which must be used as the basis for determining subsequent gain or loss on the sale of the property by the beneficiary, for income tax purposes.

An appraisal by experts is not required where the executor can arrive at a fair market value through personal knowledge or by consulting bankers or other business associates, but in general, where important holdings of real estate are involved, it is advisable to obtain experts of good standing. The appraisals of such experts are usually given serious weight.

One or more of the appointed appraisers may qualify as such an expert. If not, the appraisers may ask for additional help on especially troublesome valuations. Copies of any appraisals should be filed with the estate tax return.

Each valuation must be fixed individually, in accordance with the requirements and circumstances of the particular situation. General market activity, recent sales of comparable property, rentals, local tax assessment values, and so forth are helpful factors in establishing value. The value decided upon should not be an inflated one, but rather a conservative value which will stand the test of an investigation.

If a piece of the decedent's real estate is sold, either by the executor or by a devisee, prior to completing the estate inventory, the sale price usually helps to establish the fair market value for inventory purposes. Likewise, a sale taking place before the time of filing the estate tax return might help establish the correct value to show on that return. But in either case it should be remembered that the fair market value at the date of death is supposed to be used, and a subsequent sale price is not necessarily the same as the correct value at the earlier date.

Mortgages Payable on Real Estate

As a general rule, the estate inventory includes only the decedent's assets, not his liabilities. This is true even though the liability is in the form of a mortgage payable, to which a certain piece of the real estate is subject. The full value of the property should be inventoried without any deduction for the mortgage.

For estate tax purposes, the rule is a little more technical—if the mortgage is enforceable against other property in the estate and not just the mortgaged property, or if the decedent was personally liable for payment of the mortgage, the full value of the property is shown in the schedule for real estate and a deduction taken for the amount of the mortgage in the schedule for the decedent's debts; if only the mortgaged property can be subjected to the payment of the mortgage, then only the net value of the property less the indebtedness should be entered on the real estate schedule.

Conversion of Real Property to Personal Property

When the decedent's will directs the executor to sell certain real estate, this real estate is deemed converted to personal property on the death of the testator. The same is true if the property is sold for any other reason, such as by court order for the payment of debts. Also, real property purchased by an executor at a foreclosure sale under a mortgage belonging to the estate is generally considered, for the purposes of administration, as constituting personal assets of the estate.

These distinctions between real and personal property are rather technical, but they may become important in cases where certain fees, such as the executor's compensation, are based on the amount of the personal estate.

For inventory and estate tax purposes, however, real estate will still be listed as such and mortgages will be listed as personal property.

Contracts for Purchase of Real Estate

If the decedent had entered into a contract to purchase real estate, the property should be listed as real estate and appraised at its full value, without any deduction for the unpaid portion of the purchase price. It would not be proper to show only the decedent's equity in the property.

The amount remaining payable on the purchase price at the date of death may be deducted, for estate tax purposes, as a debt of the decedent.

Stocks and Bonds

The estate inventory must include a listing of each stock and each bond of which the decedent was possessed.

All corporate stocks—whether listed or unlisted, closely held or widely held— must be inventoried and complete information given about each issue. This would include the exact name of the corporation, number of shares, whether common or preferred, par value, the principal exchange on which it is sold or, if not listed on a stock exchange, the state of the company's incorporation and address of its principal business office.

Stock actually sold by the decedent before his death is not included, even if all or a portion of the purchase price remains unpaid. Stock purchased by the decedent before death is fully includible regardless of the amount actually paid before death, and a deduction is allowed for the balance payable.

The description of bonds should include the quantity and denomination, the name of the obligor, kind of bond, date of maturity, interest rate, interest due dates, the exchange on which listed or, if unlisted, the principal business office of the company.

Bonds and other obligations, the income of which is exempt from income tax, must be included for estate tax purposes. This rule applies not only to bonds issued by the United States government but to Farm Loan Bonds and to state and municipal bonds as well. Thus, the value of all Federal, state, and municipal bonds, notes, and bills, is included in the gross estate as well as bonds issued by private corporations.

Certain United States Treasury Bonds are redeemable at par in the payment of estate taxes. If any of these are owned by a decedent at his death and are used to pay estate tax, they must also be included in the inventory of the estate—at the higher of their par or market value. (Any not used in paying the estate tax are simply included at their current market value.) It has even been held that the full value of U.S. Treasury Bonds purchased by a terminally ill decedent with funds he borrowed is includible in his gross estate and the bonds are redeemable at par in payment of the estate taxes; and the borrowed funds are deductible from gross estate as one of his debts.

Valuation of Listed Stocks and Bonds

In the case of stocks and bonds which are listed on a stock exchange, no great difficulty arises in fixing their values. The fair market value per share or bond is the mean between the highest and lowest quoted selling prices on the valuation date. In cases where there were no sales on that date, the fair market value is arrived at by taking the mean for the last day prior to the valuation date on which there was a sale, and a mean for the first day after the valuation date. In addition, there is an apportionment based on the number of days which elapsed between the date of sale and the valuation date.

An exception to the above procedure in valuing listed securities is sometimes proper when the decedent owned a large block of the stock of a single company. The executor may contend that because of the depressed market value which often results from the sale of a large block at one time, a lower sales price per share is obtainable than if only several shares of the same block had to be sold. This is known as the "blockage rule," and a lower valuation may often be sustained by this rule, provided the other factors involved in the specific case will also support the lower valuation.

Valuation of Unlisted Stocks and Bonds

If the security is not listed on any exchange but is traded "over-the-counter" and there have been bona fide sales, the same valuation procedures are followed as with listed securities. If there have been no sales, some factors to be considered in arriving at the fair market value are the bid and asked prices for the stock, the company's net worth, the dividend capacity of the company and its earning power, and the value of securities of a like corporation engaged in a similar business which securities are listed on an exchange.

The above factors are also relevant in valuing stocks for which there is no active market. In the case of bonds having no active market, consideration is also given to the soundness of the security, the interest yield, the date of maturity, and so forth.

The greatest valuation problem arises, of course, in connection with the stock of close corporation. It is obvious that where an estate owns the stock of a close corporation it is usually taxed on a much higher basis than that of an estate owning listed securities. In the later case the value is definitely established by actual quotations, and experience has shown that sales of such stock are usually made at a much lower price than the theoretical fair market value determined for closely held stock by an examination of financial data and the application of the usual methods of valuation.

A number of factors which may be helpful in determining the fair market value of closely held stock are as follows:

1. The nature of the business and the history of the enterprise from its inception.

2. The economic outlook in general and the condition and outlook of the specific industry in particular.

3. The book value of the stock and the financial condition of the business.

4. The earning capacity of the business.

5. The dividend paying capacity of the business.

6. Whether or not the business has goodwill or other intangible value.

7. Sales of the stock and the size of the block of stock to be valued.

8. The market price of stock of corporations engaged in the same or similar lines of business having their stocks actively traded in a free and open market, either on an exchange or over-the-counter.

9. Opinion of expert witnesses.

10. The possible effect of the death of the stockholder if he was the principal stockholder or active in the operation and management of the business.

Complete financial and other data upon which the appraisers base their valuations should be retained to support these values on the estate tax return. The executor is also required to submit balance sheets of close corporations and statements of net earnings and dividends paid by the corporation for each of the five years preceding the valuation date.

Securities considered worthless, obsolete, or of nominal value should be listed, and the address of the company and state and date of incorporation should be given. Copies of correspondence or statements used as the basis for showing no value for the security must be submitted with the estate tax return.

Options to Buy or Sell Stock

If, at his death, the decedent held an unexercised option to buy stock, which survives his death and is transferred to his executor or heir at death, the gross estate includes the value of the option, if any, and not the value of the stock. If the option expires with the decedent's death, there is nothing to be included in the estate on account of the option.

If stock owned by the decedent is subject to an unexercised option by another to purchase, the value of the stock is includible in the gross estate. However, depending on its terms, the option may affect the value at which the stock is includible.

Business Interests

The correct valuation of a decedent's interest in a proprietorship or partnership business is often a troublesome problem for the executor and his appraisers. It is helpful to keep in mind, however, that such an interest should be valued as a unit, rather than as the many different assets which go to make up the business.

In the case of a proprietorship, the executor should attempt to place a net value on the business equal to the amount which a willing buyer would pay to a willing seller in view of the net value of the underlying assets of the business and its demonstrated earning capacity.

This value is arrived at by making a fair appraisal of all the assets making up the unit, and deducting from their total value the amount of the outstanding liabilities. The book values of the assets should not be given too much weight in this appraisal; fair market value is the amount being sought.

In valuing these assets, intangibles such as goodwill, patents, advantageous leases, trademarks, and so forth must not be overlooked, even though they may not be recorded on the books of the business.

The most improtant of these intangibles is usually goodwill, and its presence or absence must always be determined. There may be good reasons for assigning no value to goodwill. *For example*, the earnings record may show no profits in excess of a fair return on the tangible assets; the death of the owner may have destroyed much of the business prospects; increased competition may have reduced the goodwill to a purely nominal figure. In other cases, goodwill is obviously present. The growth, development, and the prospects of a business may be so exceptional as to warrant an appraisal at a much greater value than the net asset value, even taking into account the owner's death.

A bona fide sale of the business, or even an attempt to sell it, may furnish a good indication of what the business in general, and the goodwill in particular, may be worth.

The method of valuing a partnership interest is governed largely by the terms of the partnership agreement, or, in the absence of such an agreement, by the provisions of state law.

The agreement or the law might provide for immediate dissolution of the partnership, liquidation, and a final accounting. If it is permissible to sell the business as a going concern, including the trade name, goodwill, and so forth, then the valuation of the decedent's interest must be arrived at as for a proprietorship—appraisal of the various assets, including goodwill, and deduction of liabilities. If the business cannot be continued for long enough to sell it as a going business, goodwill will likely be destroyed and should not be included among the assets being appraised.

(The valuation thus arrived at in cases of liquidation of a partnership at death of a partner will automatically, of course, include the decedent's share of the profits of the business earned to the date of death as well as his share of the capital at that date. The total is properly included in the gross estate, but the profits are not "income in respect of a decedent;" they must be reported on the decedent's final income tax return since the partnership year ended on the same date as his final taxable year.)

The partnership agreement may provide for the continuation of the business; this often makes valuation of the decedent's interest much less difficult.

Particularly where the partnership consists of many members, it is usually provided that upon a partner's death the partnership shall be continued among the surviving partners, who agree to pay the decedent's estate or beneficiaries for his interest. Such agreements are common where the valuation of the interest would be difficult, or where outsiders would be unwilling to pay full value, or where sole ownership of the business by the surviving partners is desired.

The sale price specified in these "buy and sell" agreements will usually fix the value of the decedent's interest, provided the agreement (1) binds the estate to sell, either by giving the survivors an option or by binding all the parties, and (2) sets a price which is not so grossly inadequate as to make the agreement a "mere gratuitous promise."

Buy and sell agreements are often funded by insurance on the lives of the parties, so that the death of one provides the survivors with cash to purchase his interest.

The continuance of a partnership means that the partnership's taxable year does not end on the date of the partner's death. The decedent's share of profits to that date cannot, therefore, be reported on his final income tax return, but will be reportable on the estate's fiduciary income tax return. In this case, these earnings to date of death are considered "income in respect of a decedent." (*See* Chapter 13.)

The executor, when filing the estate tax return, should submit all evidence bearing on the valuation of a business interest, including the financial statements for the last five years, copies of any buy and sell agreements, opinions of technical experts, and so forth.

Mortgages Receivable

Mortgages owned by the decedent are generally valued at the face amount of the mortgage at the date of death.

The executor may, in some cases, be able to sustain a valuation lower than the face value. Consideration must be given to the value of the property securing the mortgage, applying the same factors as are used in fixing the valuation of the decedent's real estate. Where the mortgage is amply secured, face value is used, but where the security is insufficient the mortgage may be valued on the basis of the fair market value of the property less back taxes, estimated foreclosure expenses, and, where justified, the expense of rehabilitation.

In valuing a mortgage, a distinction must be drawn between the mortgage itself and the underlying personal obligation. A mortgagor personally liable on a mortgage note may be in a financial condition that makes full collection a certainty although the property mortgaged may only partly secure the note. In this case the note is worth face value. More often, however, the debtor is unable to pay out of other assets and the valuation will depend primarily on the underlying property value.

In addition to the value of the property, factors to consider are the rank and maturity date of the mortgage relative to other encumbrances on the same property and the necessity of expensive refinancing when prior mortgages become due. These factors may even warrant a discount of 20 or 30 percent or more of face value.

The inventory listing of the mortgage should include the name of maker, date of the mortgage and date of maturity, face value and unpaid balance, property subject to the mortgage, interest dates and rate of interest, and the appraised valuation at date of death.

The burden of proof is on the executor if he attempts to establish a value lower than face value for a mortgage. In such cases he must file a statement giving a summary of the relevant factors on which he bases his valuation. This will be used by the Treasury Department in the final determination of the value of the mortgage.

Notes Receivable

The value of promissory notes and claims held by the decedent at his death must be included in his gross estate. Notes are includible even though they have not matured and are not due and payable until after the decedent's death. They must be included even though they are cancelled by a provision in the decedent's will.

The valuation of notes is similar to that of mortgages. Fair market value is presumed to be the face value of the note unless the executor can establish that the actual value is lower or that the notes are worthless.

A reduced value might be based on an unfavorable interest rate or maturity date or other cause; the note may be uncollectible, in whole or in part, by reason of the insolvency of the party or parties liable; any property pledged as security may be insufficient to satisfy the obligation. The facts in each case must be considered in arriving at a proper valuation.

As with mortgages, the burden of proof is on the executor whenever he attempts to establish a value lower than face value for notes receivable.

Contracts to Sell Real Estate

Real estate held in the name of the decedent, but subject to a contract to sell (title bond contract) which the decedent had entered into, should be inventoried as a contract receivable rather than as real estate. Such a contract is similar to a mortgage, the principal difference being that the property has not yet been deeded to the purchaser.

The listing of these contracts should include the name of the purchaser, date of the contract, description of the property to be sold, sale price, initial payment, amount of installment payments, interest rate, and the unpaid balance of the principal.

As with mortgages and notes, the proper valuation is the face value of the obligation at date of death, unless the executor can support a lesser value by consideration of the factors mentioned in connection with the valuation of mortgages.

Interest and Dividends Receivable

At the time of inventorying the decedent's securities, the executor should also determine the amount of interest and dividends receivable on these securities up to the date of the decedent's death.

Such accruals (as well as others discussed later) are a part of the gross estate and must be included in the estate inventory and reported on the estate tax return. This is true even though the decedent was a cash basis taxpayer.

The determination of accrued interest is not difficult. A simple computation is made of the amount accrued on each bond, mortgage, or note receivable inventoried and covering, of course, the period from the date of the obligation (or the date to which interest had last been paid) up to the date of the decedent's death. It is proper to list the accrued interest on each obligation immediately following the listing of the obligation itself, and it is well to note the period covered by the computation in each case.

One exception is that interest is not accruable on certain U. S. Savings Bonds. If saving bonds, such as Series G and K bonds, pay interest semiannually, and the decedent dies between interest dates, the accrued interest since the last payment date is not included in the gross estate; at the date of death the holder had the right to redeem the bonds but had no right to the unpaid interest accrued to that date. Series E bonds are noninterest-bearing bonds; their redemption value at the last redemption date preceding the date of death is a part of the gross estate, but there is no accrual of interest from that date to the date of death. However, if a cash basis decedent had not elected to report the increment in value as income, the increment becomes "income in respect of a decedent," explained in Chapter 13, unless the executor elects to report this increment in value on the decedent's final income tax return. Comparative tax rates will govern the exercise of this option. (Rev. Rul. 68-145).

There is really no such thing as accrued dividends, of course, because dividends on stock do not accrue like interest but must be declared by the corporation. In certain cases, however, unpaid dividends must be handled in the nature of accruals in an estate.

The rule is simply that if a dividend has been declared by the corporation whose stock the decedent owned, and if the date of record for the dividend is prior to the decedent's death, the dividend is considered to be a receivable and must be included as such in the estate inventory and the estate tax return. The date of record governs; if it is after the date of death there is no receivable, even though the dividend may have been declared earlier.

Interest and dividends receivable are among the assets included in the group known, for tax purposes, as "Income in Respect of a Decedent." These assets are subject to a special income tax treatment, explained fully in Chapter 13.

Cash in Possession and in Banks

There is little difficulty in the valuation of the decedent's cash, but it is not always easy for the executor to be sure that he has located all of it.

Cash may be in several different forms—the currency and coin in the decedent's pocket at his death, currency and coin in his office safe or in a bank deposit box, cash on deposit in a checking account, cash on deposit in a savings account, the "shares" of a savings and loan association, a certificate of deposit, and so forth.

It is the executor's duty to locate all such cash. Bank books, check books, deposit certificates, and the like found among the decedent's effects may furnish clues to the location of the cash, but the executor must also make inquiry of any other depository where he suspects the decedent may have had an account.

Cash in possession or in a savings account will be listed at its actual amount. Cash in checking accounts should be listed at the amount shown by the bank's books at the date of death, not the balance shown in the decedent's checkbook. Any difference in the two amounts caused by checks written prior to death but not yet cashed by the bank will be ignored. The reason for this is that most banks will stop paying a decedent's checks immediately upon receiving notice of the death. The result is that the bank's entire balance becomes an asset of the estate and the outstanding checks must be presented to the executor later as debts of the decedent.

(If the bank does subsequently honor outstanding checks, charging them to the decedent's account, the balance remaining in the account may be inventoried and there will be no such debts for the executor to pay.)

The proper handling of joint bank accounts—either checking or savings accounts— is discussed in Chapter 3 in connection with jointly owned property.

Interest on savings bank accounts generally does not accrue between interest payment dates, and therefore, is treated the same as interest on certain government bonds. However, a savings account deposit book should be balanced up to the bank's last interest payment date before the executor lists any balance shown therein. But if a savings account is one which is withdrawable at any time and interest is added to the date of withdrawal, the entire amount including interest to date of death must be inventoried.

In instances where the cash consists of foreign currency or foreign bank accounts, the value should be stated in terms of the official rate of exchange unless, by reason of restrictions or convertibility, or by any other reason, it can be shown that a lower value is proper.

Cash in possession should be listed separately from bank accounts. Each bank account should be listed individually, showing the name and address of the bank, the serial number and nature of the account, and the amount.

Household and Personal Effects

All household furnishings and personal effects are a part of the decedent's gross estate, even though they are used exclusively by members of his family, unless any of such property actually belongs to others. The controlling factor is title, not use, but ownership by the decedent may be inferred if he disposed of certain articles by his will or if his funds were used to purchase them.

Generally speaking, where the widow claims such property, she must substantiate her claim by showing one of the following situations:

1. That the items in question were owned by her prior to her marriage.

2. That she purchased the items in question during marriage out of her separate funds.

3. That the items in question represent gifts from a third person to the wife individually during marriage. This includes bequests and legacies.

4. That the items in question were given to her during marriage by the decedent; that such gift was not in contemplation of death; that the transaction was fully executed by the delivery of the property to her; and that the decedent clearly and unmistakably expressed his intention that title should be given her.

The Treasury Department holds that household effects and like personalty used by husband and wife in the marriage relation are presumed to be the property of the husband, and, in the absence of sufficient evidence to rebut this presumption, must be included in his gross estate.

The preferred method of listing and valuing household and personal effects is to make a room by room itemization of them, valuing each item at the price which a willing buyer would pay a willing seller. All articles in a room with individual values of $100 or less may be grouped. A separate value should be given for all other items.

In lieu of the itemized listing, the executor may obtain a written statement containing the aggregate value of the property as appraised by competent appraisers or dealers. Also, if there is included among the household and personal effects articles having an artistic or intrinsic value of more than $3,000, such as jewelry, furs, works of art, books, collections, and the like, the appraisal of an expert under oath is required. The appointed appraisers may be able to make these appraisals or they may find it necessary to call on outside experts.

The above appraisal methods are the ones outlined by the estate tax regulations, but, as a practical matter, a lump sum estimate of the total value of the household and personal effects will often suffice, especially if these assets are relatively unimportant compared with the total estate. When a lump sum appraisal is used, however, it is usually wise to list separately any specific items of unusual value or any which were specifically mentioned as legacies in the decedent's will.

Property subject to homestead or other marital interests is includible in the gross estate.

If the executor desires to sell or distribute any of the household or personal effects in advance of an investigation by an officer of the Internal Revenue Service, notice should be given to the district director.

Interests in Other Estates

One of the most troublesome problems an administrative team can have will arise if it is found that the decedent was a beneficiary of a prior decedent's estate, the prior estate still being in the process of administration.

A situation of this kind is not at all commonplace. As a result, there is not a very large body of law, regulations, or decisions to guide the executor in the proper methods of inventorying, reporting, and accounting for such an interest. But a way must be found to value this asset in accordance with the general principles of estate tax law and to set up the value in such a way that the subsequent accounting for it may be as accurate and simple as possible.

The executor's first thought might be that an interest in a prior estate is in the nature of a receivable, that it should be valued as a lump sum which will eventually be written off by credits for the cash and property he will receive from the other executor during the administration and liquidation of the prior estate.

Following such a course can only lead to trouble. The cash received might include not only distributions of corpus but also of income, and it would be impossible and incorrect to try to anticipate the future income to be included in the lump sum. Distributions of income cash from the prior estate will seldom agree with the amount of income taxable to the present estate. Capital gains and nontaxable income of the prior estate will further complicate the matter. Considering the prior interest as a receivable will often create such accounting difficulties that the account for the asset might even increase rather than decrease over a period of time, making this an impossible situation.

The proper way to value a prior interest may not seem to be the easiest, simplest way, but this is an area in which any attempt at a "short cut" would be very unwise in the long run. The executor must think of his decedent as having owned a proportionate interest in *each* individual asset in the hands of the prior estate at the time of death. The interest in the prior estate is more in the nature of a business interest, therefore, and the underlying assets must be valued individually.

The executor and his appraisers should meet with the executor of the other estate and determine a current fair market value for each asset held by that estate. The values at which they were originally appraised should not be used—those values may be several years old. A new fair market value at the date of the second decedent's death is proper. Each piece of real estate, security, note, bank account, and other assets should be valued separately and the decedent's proportionate interest shown for it.

No anticipated earnings or expenses for the remainder of the administration should be considered. Values will therefore be established exactly as if the decedent himself had actually owned the assets (or his proportionate share of them) at the time of his death. An attempt should be made, however, to estimate the remaining administrative expenses which will have to be paid out of the assets, and the fair market value of the various assets will be reduced proportionately by this deduction.

Local property laws will seldom consider that the decedent had an undivided proportionate interest in the individual assets of the prior estate, but, for practical purposes, this is exactly the way the executor should consider the problem.

When the accounting problems involved in handling income and distributions from the prior estate are discussed in a later chapter, the wisdom of handling the matter in this way will become apparent.

Other Miscellaneous Property

A number of other assets which the decedent might have owned, but about which there are seldom any very difficult problems of valuation or of inclusion in the inventory, are discussed briefly below.

1. *Prepaid Items.* Prepaid fire insurance premiums on rental property have been held to be includible in gross estate. Other prepaid items, such as prepaid rent, prepaid interest, and so forth, would presumably be includible also.

2. *Accrued Income.* Dividends receivable and accrued interest were mentioned earlier as being includible in gross estate. Accrued rents receivable up to the date of death must also be inventoried, and the amount is listed immediately following the listing of the property on which the rent is receivable. The fact that the decedent may have been a cash basis taxpayer does not eliminate the necessity for including all income accrued at the date of his death.

3. *Judgments.* The amount of a judgment receivable must be listed, including the name of the judgment debtor, date of the judgment, name of the court, interest rate on the judgment, if any, and other necessary information.

4. *Shares in Trust Funds.* The fair market value of the decedent's interest in a trust fund at the date of his death must be determined and included in gross estate.

5. *Insurance on the Life of Another.* Life insurance policies owned by the decedent on the life of another person who survives him are valued at their replacement value at the date of death. A Form 938 should be obtained from the insurance company for each such policy and filed with the return.

6. *Royalty Interests.* The valuation of a royalty contract is based on the guaranteed minimum payments required under the contract.

7. *Patents and Copyrights.* There is no definite rule for valuing these intangibles, but the burden is on the executor to prove their value based on the probable earning power, previous earnings, remaining life, and other factors.

8. *Farm Products and Growing Crops.* Farm products, growing crops, farm machinery, and miscellaneous materials are valued at the price at which such items would change hands between a willing buyer and a willing seller—fair market value.

9. *Automobiles.* Fair market value must also be determined for the decedent's automobiles, trucks, or other vehicles, as well as for any other asset of any kind owned by the decedent at the date of his death.

5

The Executor's Duties and Responsibilities

When the executor completes the difficult task of locating, inventorying, and appraising the estate assets, and when he has filed this inventory with the probate court, he may well feel that he has cleared one of the most formidable hurdles in his path to a successful administration of the estate.

By this time the executor will probably have taken care of most of the things which required his prompt attention, so this will be a good time for him to pause and take stock of his position. He should now familiarize himself with his duties and his responsibilities, if he does not already have them well in mind, and start planning a course of action and of policy for the remainder of his term.

The principal duties of an executor include the collection of the estate's assets, the exercise of proper care in the custody of the assets and the management of the estate, preservation of the assets, prosecution and defense of suits in behalf of the estate, payment of the decedent's debts, payment of taxes and the expenses of administration, distribution of the residue to those entitled to it, and the making of such accounts as are required by statute or by the court.

Caring for Estate Funds and Assets

An executor is under a duty to exercise good faith and is required to use ordinary care, prudence, skill, and diligence in the discharge of his trust.

This is especially true in connection with the custody and safe-keeping of the estate's assets. Obviously, cash or securities should not be left where they may be stolen;

perishable goods should be disposed of promptly; certain machinery should be protected from the elements, and so forth. But it is equally important for a receivable to be collected before the statute of limitations expires; for necessary repairs to be made before the property is extensively damaged by the lack of such repairs; for employees and agents to be properly bonded; for a suit against the estate to be defended if any defense is available; for the proper kinds and amounts of insurance to be carried on insurable property, and the like.

The executor's failure to care for the estate's assets with the same care and diligence as a prudent and cautious person would bestow on his own property may result in his being held personally liable for losses to the estate due to his negligence. The executor may, *for example,* be personally liable for damages resulting from fire following a failure to insure the property of the estate in a proper manner.

Furthermore, since the executor's duties include collecting the assets in the first place, he may even be liable for a loss caused by his neglect in seeking out these assets.

An executor is not ordinarily responsible, however, for a loss due to a decline in the market value of stocks or bonds, provided he sells them within a reasonable time. But he does have a duty to use diligence and care to preserve the value of securities, and retaining them beyond a reasonable time may be considered negligence.

It should always be remembered that the executor is holding the assets for only one purpose—to liquidate them to the extent necessary to satisfy the creditors and the beneficiaries. He must do his very best to prevent any kind of loss while the property is in his hands and to pick the most propitious time to convert each asset into cash.

Management of the Estate Assets

To what extent is an executor responsible for managing the estate's assets during the administrative period?

The first point to remember is that the personal representative has a greater responsibility for safeguarding the assets so that they, or the proceeds from their sale, may be available to the beneficiaries than he has for making these assets produce income while they are under his control. His duties as to management refer principally to the acts necessary to preserve the property rather than to things he might do if he owned the property outright and was trying to get the best possible return on it.

On the other hand, the executor would seem to be negligent and derelict in his duty if he failed to exercise reasonable care and diligence in securing some return on the assets, if he can do so safely and within the limitations of his authority. *For example,* it would be foolish to leave an excessive amount of cash on demand deposit when it could be transferred to an interest paying savings account without any loss of security.

In any case, the executor's responsibility is based on the authority conferred on him by state law or by his decedent's will. If the will can be interpreted as directing the executor to exercise his judgment in managing the assets, or if it authorizes him to buy and sell, invest and reinvest, and so forth, the executor should assume this responsibility and try not only to preserve the assets but to make them produce a satisfactory income. It is possible for the executor, in many cases, to have almost as much freedom in the management of the assets as the decedent himself had.

The question of whether the decedent's proprietorship or partnership business should be continued and managed by the executor was discussed in Chapter 2—businesses are sometimes continued by the executor, but more often he does not have this authority.

As for personal property in general, the executor usually has great latitude in its management. He always has the power to sell personalty, which implies that he may also invest the proceeds from such sales. In making these investments he is under the duty of so placing the money that it will be safe and productive, safety being the primary objective. If he fails to make an investment within a reasonable time after the receipt of the money, he may even be chargeable with interest on such funds.

Personal property which is already producing a satisfactory income, such as notes, mortgages, bonds, and the like, should usually be left in their present form—if these investments were the choice of the decedent his executor cannot be criticized for continuing them. But the executor should watch them carefully and liquidate them whenever they stop producing income or appear to be becoming unsafe. Nonproductive personal property such as jewelry, furnishings, autos, and possibly machinery, will be the first which the executor will try to dispose of in order to secure funds for the payment of expenses, taxes, legacies, and other urgent payments.

The executor has the privilege of spending estate funds whenever it is necessary and advisable for the protection of the personal property—*for example,* he should not neglect to insure the personal property when advisable; he should rent a lockbox for the safekeeping of jewelry and other valuables; he should bond employees, agents, and others, if necessary.

The executor has no responsibility for managing the real estate which passes directly to the heirs. But he should certainly be courteous enough to deliver deeds and other papers on the property to these heirs—who may have little knowledge of such matters—and to explain to them any rental payments and dates due, remind them to see that the property is adequately insured, advise them regarding repairs, upkeep, and maintenance. After all, these heirs are likely to be the same people for whom the executor is administering the personal estate, and both will benefit from close cooperation.

The executor may be requested, in these cases, to assume the management of the real estate. This may even be required in a few jurisdictions. If so, the executor should try to keep the property rented advantageously, take care of necessary repairs, carry adequate insurance, and handle various problems that may occur. Income and expenses on the property must be carefully segregated in the accounts. They are not estate funds, and the executor is simply acting as an agent or trustee of the heir in respect to this particular property.

In a few states, the decedent's real property does pass to the executor. In some states the executor may take possession where there is no heir present and competent to take over. Also, it is not uncommon for a testator to direct that real property, as well as personal property, shall be administered by his personal representative. He may even display such confidence in his executor as to permit him to buy and sell real estate, invest and reinvest the funds, and so forth. In these cases the executor's authority will be almost absolute with regard to the real property, the same as with personal property. His responsibility, too, will be great, and he will have the duty of keeping the property rented, collecting rentals (which in this case will be estate funds), preserving its value through necessary repairs, carrying adequate insurance, and other duties. He has no authority to make major improvements or to erect new buildings, unless specifically authorized by the will or where, *for example*, a building paying a good rental is destroyed by fire and where the new building can be paid for in a short time out of the rental.

If the decedent's will does not make it clear whether the title to real property vests in the executor or in the heirs, this question must be answered promptly—usually by petitioning the court for an interpretation. This is important. It fixes the executor's responsibility over the real property; it determines whether the executor or the heir will sign the deed to property which is sold.

Exhibit 13

Court Order Interpreting Will

No. 1366   WASHINGTON CIRCUIT COURT

MARK SHELBY, Executor under
  the will of Constance Hapworth,
  deceased, et al   PLAINTIFFS

vs.   JUDGMENT

ROBERT SHELBY, et al, infants under
  14 years of age   DEFENDANTS

It appearing to the court that Mark Shelby has been duly appointed Executor under the will of Constance Hapworth, deceased, and that he has qualified as said Executor according to the law; and that the said will of Constance Hapworth, deceased, was on November 14, 1975, duly probated in the Washington County Court; and

It further appearing to the court that the defendants, Robert Shelby, James Shelby, and Eleanor Shelby, all infants under 14 years of age, are residents of Washington County, and have been duly summoned and Richard White, an attorney regularly practicing at this bar, has been appointed Guardian ad litem to represent the interests of said defendants, and having filed his answer herein making no defense or objection to the relief prayed for herein; and

Exhibit 13 (cont.)

The court being sufficiently advised, it is hereby adjudged that the will of Constance Hapworth, deceased, when read as a whole, clearly indicates the intention of the testatrix that the real property located at 1516 Thirteenth Street, Springfield, be sold and the proceeds received therefrom be used to pay the specific bequests contained in the will with the balance, if any, to be paid to Mark Shelby as trustee to be used by him for the education and welfare of his children as he sees fit; therefore, none of the defendants herein, all infants under 14 years of age, have any interest in the real property to be protected.

It is further adjudged by the court that the said will of Constance Hapworth, deceased, does not name any donee as having the express power to sell and convey the real property, and that to carry out the intention of the testatrix in the disposition of the real property and the use of the proceeds as directed in the will, Mark Shelby, acting in his official capacity as the duly qualified executor under the said will, has the implied power to sell and convey said real property and execute a valid deed thereto.

It is further adjudged that all of the property of Constance Hapworth, deceased, was disposed of by the testatrix under the terms of her will, and that there is no property that will pass by the laws of descent and distribution; therefore, John Hapworth, as the only heir at law of Constance Hapworth, deceased, would have no interest in the real property.

ENTER this December 28, 1975.

_____

JUDGE, Washington County Court

The executor must remember that even in cases where the real estate does not come under his control he still has the right to take it for the payment of creditors in case the personal estate proves insufficient to pay the debts of the estate and the expenses of administration.

Payment of the Decedent's Debts

The executor is usually required to advertise for creditors, giving them notice of the decedent's death and specifying the period (usually fixed by law) within which these creditors must file their claims against the estate.

The executor is not required to pay any debts or make any distribution of assets until after the expiration of this statutory period, during which he must attempt to determine the decedent's liabilities. If he does make any payments or distributions within this period, he may be held responsible if the remaining assets are not sufficient to meet the remaining liabilities.

The burden of presenting a claim for a debt is on the creditor. His failure to do so within the time prescribed will bar the allowance of the claim.

The executor must make a careful review of all claims presented and should object to any which are doubtful. A doubtful claim may sometimes be settled by a reasonable compromise in good faith. In other cases, litigation may be necessary to establish the amount and validity of a debt.

Typical claims which might be presented to an executor would be claims for services rendered the deceased; claims founded on a contract, bill, or note; mortgages; judgments; claims for purchases made or obligations incurred by the decedent before his death; claims for checks written and delivered by the decedent but not cashed by his bank before his death; and all other debts or demands of a pecuniary nature which could have been enforced against the decedent in his lifetime. Claims for taxes are not generally required to be presented. Claims for funeral expenses and all other debts arising after the decedent's death are not included in the category of debts of the decedent.

The executor has a duty to the creditors to pay their claims as promptly as he can do so, providing there is no question as to the solvency of the estate. There is seldom any time limit within which claims must be paid, however, because it is often necessary for property to be liquidated before it can be known whether funds will be available for the payment of all the debts. Therefore, it is best for the executor to delay these payments until he is very sure that he is safe in paying them.

Funeral and Administration Expenses

Although funeral expenses and the expenses of administration of the estate are not classed as debts of the decedent, they too constitute claims against the estate.

The amount of the funeral expenses allowable is not fixed by law, but is should be reasonable and correspond with the decedent's circumstances and social condition, including his station in life and the value of his estate. The reasonableness of such an allowance is nearly always subject to the review of the court. The term "funeral expenses" includes not only the ordinary costs of burial but may also include a reasonable amount for flowers and expenditures for a burial lot, a vault, monument, and tombstone.

Administration expenses include court costs, the compensation of the personal representative, fees paid the estate's attorney and accountant, and all other costs and charges that are necessarily incurred in the settlement of the estate. The character and amount of the estate and the complications of the particular situation will govern the decision of the court as to the reasonableness or necessity of an expenditure.

Order of Claims

The decedent's debts, funeral and administration expenses, and taxes constitute all of the claims against the estate's property which the executor must consider and provide for before making distributions to the legatees, devisees, and other beneficiaries and heirs.

By the time the list of debts is completed, the executor will probably have finished the inventory of the assets and should be in a good position to make a close estimate of the amount which will be needed for administrative expenses. With this information, the solvency or insolvency of the estate can be determined.

If the assets are obviously enough to cover the payment of the debts and expenses, the order of their payment is immaterial. If the liabilities seem to be in excess of the assets, the statutes defining the order of preference of the various kinds of claims must be consulted, and the executor must be careful to follow the order required in his state.

The order of classification and payment varies in the different jurisdicitons, although in general the statutes require payment to be made in the following order:

1. Funeral expenses.
2. Expenses of administration.
3. Widow's and children's awards.
4. Expenses of decedent's last illness.
5. Claims for wages.
6. Debts and taxes due the government.
7. Judgment creditors.
8. Lien claims.
9. All other debts and demands against the estate.

Claims within any one preference group must be paid pro rata if the assets are not sufficient to pay all of them in full.

Where the estate is solvent, there should be no delay in paying the decedent's debts. Interest bearing debts, especially, should be paid as soon as possible in order to stop the interest expense. Administration expenses may be paid as they are incurred. But the executor has no obligation to sell estate assets at a sacrifice to obtain funds for the quick payment of claims. He is generally allowed a reasonable time to convert property into cash advantageously before the court will insist that the claims be taken care of.

The assets of the estate are used in the following order in the payment of claims:

1. Personal property not bequeathed.
2. Personal property bequeathed generally.
3. Personal property bequeathed specifically.
4. Realty not devised.
5. Realty devised generally.
6. Realty devised specifically.

The personal property of a decedent is primarily liable for his debts. The realty is liable only after exhaustion of the personalty. This is true even though the debt is secured by a mortgage or lien on the realty. Real property which passed directly to an heir at the decedent's death is still subject to a possible claim for unpaid claims against the estate.

Exhibit 14

Court Order Directing Sale of Securities

WASHINGTON COUNTY COURT

ORDER

RE: CARL DAVIS ESTATE

This cause coming before the Court on motion of George Foster, Executor of the estate of Carl Davis, deceased, it appearing to the Court that it is necessary for George Foster, Executor, to reduce a part of the estate to cash for the purpose of paying inheritance and estate taxes and for the purposes incident to the settlement of the estate, it is ordered that George Foster, Executor, be, and he is, hereby authorized and

Exhibit 14 (cont.)

directed to sell for and on behalf of the estate of Carl Davis, deceased, the following stocks belonging to the estate:

    50 shares National Bank and Trust Company stock
    500 shares Pacific Company stock
    100 shares General Motors Company stock
    120 shares Franklin Mills stock
    150 shares American Telephone & Telegraph stock

It is further ordered that the above stock be sold by George Foster, Executor of the Carl Davis estate, at the fair cash market value, and, if necessary, same may be sold through regular brokerage channels or by direct sale.

This January 20, 1976.

_____

JUDGE, Washington County Court

Payment of Legacies

Although the payment of legacies really amounts to a partial distribution of the estate, it is mentioned at this point because legacies are usually taken care of well in advance of the time for final distribution of the estate assets.

A legacy is cash or other personal property left to a person by a testator's will. A specific legacy is one of specified property. A general legacy is one payable out of the general assets. A residuary legacy is one which includes all the property not otherwise distributed.

In the absence of any provisions in the will as to the time of payment, legacies other than residuary legacies are usually payable one year after the date of death of the testator. But the executor may pay them before the expiration of the year, or even before discharging all the debts, if the estate is such that he can safely do so. He should try to pay these legacies quickly out of consideration for the legatees—a year can seem a very long time to a person waiting for a legacy.

The entire legacy need not necessarily be paid at one time. The executor may make advances on the legacy as funds become available. But most states provide that if a legacy is not paid within the year it will start drawing interest from that time.

Legacies are payable from the personal property only, unless there is a definite intent of the testator that real estate shall also be used.

If there are insufficient assets to meet the debts and claims, the legacies will have to be reduced or abated. Certain classes of legacies have priorities over others. *For example,* a specific legacy takes priority over a general legacy, and both are prior to a residuary legacy.

Certain deductions may have to be made from legacies. An example is that a debt due to the decedent by the legatee would be deducted from the legacy. Also, since state inheritance taxes are generally levied on the person receiving property from an estate rather than on the estate itself, such taxes should be withheld from the legacy.

Payment of Estate and Income Taxes

The Internal Revenue Code makes the executor personally liable for the amount of the estate tax to the full extent of the assets which come into his possession, even though a major portion of the estate does not pass through his hands for distribution.

The preparation of the estate tax return and the accumulation of enough cash with which to pay the estate tax usually presents one of the most serious problems for the executor, especially in the larger estates. A later chapter explains in detail the various factors involved in correctly preparing and filing the return and the way in which the tax must be paid. For the present, however, the executor must determine whether or not an estate tax return will be required and, if so, an approximation of the amount of the tax, so that the requirement of accumulating enough cash for the payment of this tax may become a part of his over-all planning.

It should also be determined at this time whether state inheritance tax returns are required by any state in which the decedent owned property. If so, this requirement must also be taken into consideration.

The executor also has the responsibility for filing an income tax return reporting the estate's income and deductions for each year, or portion of a year, during which the estate exists as an entity—from the date of the decedent's death until the time of final distribution and settlement. This "fiduciary" income tax return is discussed in Chapter 14.

Theoretically, a fiduciary income tax return is always required (unless the estate's gross income is less than $600 for the year). This return bridges the gap between the decedent's final income tax return and those later filed by the final recipients of the decedent's property. Many accountants seem to think that a fiduciary return is unnecessary if the estate is small and if all of its income is distributable and taxable to a beneficiary. This practice cannot be condoned, however, if for no other reason than that the law requires the executor to file income tax returns for the estate and makes him personally liable for failure to do so.

The executor is personally liable for the payment of any income taxes due from the estate, so he should be careful not to distribute or otherwise dispose of any of the estate's net income until he has provided for the payment of the taxes on it.

State income tax returns will also be required from the fiduciary in those states having income tax laws.

Decedent's Final Income Tax Return

Another of the executor's duties is to file a final income tax return for his decedent. This return will cover a fractional part of the year in which the decedent died—January

1st to the date of death for a calendar year taxpayer. The due date for filing a decedent's final income tax return is the same as if the decedent had lived the entire year—three and one-half months after the close of the taxpayer's calendar or fiscal year.

The executor must determine all of the decedent's taxable income and deductions for this period and report them on an individual income tax return in the name of the decedent. It should be indicated that the taxpayer is deceased, and the return should be signed by the executor in his capacity as personal representative of the deceased taxpayer.

If the return shows additional tax due, the executor is responsible for the payment of this tax out of the estate assets. The tax will be considered as a debt of the decedent—it was a liability of the decedent at the date of his death, being based on his income prior to death. If the return discloses that a refund of tax is due (because of over withholding or over estimation by the decedent), this refund constitutes a receivable to the estate and must be included as an asset in the estate inventory.

When there is a surviving spouse (who has not remarried by the end of the tax year), it is permissable for a joint return to be filed just as if the decedent had lived throughout the year. Since joint returns usually result in a smaller tax than separate returns, the executor should go into this matter with the survivor and obtain the survivor's consent to a joint return—if joint filing is determined to be the better way. A joint return will include the decedent's income and deductions for the portion of the tax year he was living and the survivor's income and deductions for the entire year. Personal exemptions are allowed as if both parties had lived all year. The surviving spouse will have to sign the joint return, along with the executor who signs for the decedent.

The executor has no responsibility in connection with later income tax returns for the surviving spouse (nor for the year of death, for that matter, except that it is usually advantageous to the estate). He should be thoughtful enough to remind the survivor that he or she may be entitled to the benefits of a joint return for the two years following the spouse's death, if certain requirements are met. If the survivor is inexperienced in business and tax matters, the executor should consider volunteering to take care of the preparation of her income tax returns during his term as executor. This can often be a very great service to a surviving spouse and will seldom be any great burden to the executor, as he will probably be set up to handle such matters easily; and since there is usually a close relationship between the fiduciary tax return and that of the surviving spouse (who is frequently the principal income beneficiary), the executor will have the satisfaction of knowing that the two returns are in agreement with each other.

Another point to remember is that if the decedent died before filing his income tax return for the last full tax year he lived, the executor must prepare and file the return for that year as well as for the year in which death occurred.

At the time of preparing the decedent's final income tax return, the estate's accountant would be well advised to make a careful review of the decedent's tax file for the past several years. Such a review might result in the discovery of errors in the returns for the earlier years which could necessitate the payment of additional taxes; or the opportunity for claiming a refund of an overpayment might be disclosed, and the executor could be considered negligent in overlooking such an opportunity.

The above discussion of the decedent's Federal income tax returns also applies to his state income taxes in those states having income tax laws.

Defense of Suits Against Estate

An estate cannot sue or be sued as such. The only way in which an action can be brought against it is to sue the executor in his representative capacity. This is particularly true in regard to actions arising before the decedent's death, but since an executor who contracts for necessary matters relating to the estate does so on his personal responsibility, actions to recover on such contracts must be against him individually.

The executor has the responsibility of defending any such actions, if there is any defense available. Unless he is himself a lawyer, the executor should always turn such matters over to the estate's attorney for defense of the action or for advice as to a compromise or settlement. The executor could be considered negligent if he should take such matters into his own hands and attempt a settlement without professional advice

When a suit has been begun against the decedent and is still pending at his death, it is the duty of the executor to defend that action also, and for that purpose to be substituted as defendent. He may not call on the legatees and heirs, whose interest he must protect, to assume the burdens of litigation which his office imposes on him.

The executor of a large estate can well expect to have to defend one or more suits during his term.

When the executor has faithfully defended a suit against the estate, he will generally be protected from liability to the beneficiaries even though the outcome is adverse.

It also frequently becomes the duty of the executor to prosecute suits in favor of the estate. He may often have to bring a suit for the collection of assets. It may even be his duty to sue the decedent's widow when she wrongfully disposes of the effects of the decedent. The court may compel an executor to bring suit in a proper case and punish him for contempt if he fails to do so.

Again, all such matters must be discussed with the attorney, whose judgment should be relied upon by the executor for his own protection.

The executor is sometimes charged with the duty of trying to uphold the will where a contest results over its probate, but the laws of the various jurisdictions are not in agreement on this question and the applicable ones should be studied before deciding on a course of action.

Planning Deadlines

The administration of a large estate often seems to resolve itself into a constant struggle to accumulate enough cash to meet the deadlines which require large cash outlays. It is not always easy to build up the estate's cash balance quickly without sacrificing some of the property, but this may not be necessary if the executor has clearly in mind just what cash will be needed and the dates it must be available. And there are a number of things the executor can do, discussed in later chapters, which will help in his quest for cash or in postponing some of the cash payment dates.

It is a good idea, therefore, for the executor to prepare a "timetable" of the deadlines he must plan for, and he should include not only those which will require large cash outlays but also the ones requiring little or no cash.

A typical schedule of deadlines, with brief explanations, is given below. The order in which they are listed will vary somewhat depending on the time of the year the decedent died, the requirements in the various states, and other factors.

1. *Preliminary Steps.* Probation of the will and qualification of the executor and other acts necessary to get the administration started.

2. *Inventory and Appraisal.* Seldom any definite time requirement for filing, but usually completed and filed with court within two to four months after date of death.

3. *Decedent's Final Income Tax Return.* Due to be filed three and one-half months after end of decedent's regular tax year. Cash may or may not be required, depending on amount decedent has prepaid on the tax.

4. *Gift Tax Returns.* Not often required, but examination of decedent's affairs and inventory of his property might disclose gifts in the year of death or unreported gifts in earlier years requiring the filing of gift tax returns. If for prior years, or quarters, file as soon as possible to stop the accrual of interest. Cash requirement is variable. The return is due within one and one-half months after the end of the calendar quarter in which gifts were made, but can be filed even before the end of the quarter for a deceased donor.

5. *Payment of Debts and Funeral Expenses.* Not payable until after the statutory period for filing claims (usually six months). Amount determinable after this period. Pay promptly thereafter if funds are available, within the next month or two if possible. May be paid at any earlier time if the estate is unquestionably solvent.

6. *Payment of Estimated State Inheritance Tax.* Not always necessary, but some states having inheritance tax laws offer a discount on the tax for early payment, *for example,* a discount of five per cent if paid within nine months after death. An estimate of the amount is permissible; filing of the return not required at this time. Usually requires large cash outlay, but advantage should be taken of discount if at all possible. (This is one case where the executor might consider borrowing money for a short time, if he has the power to do so.)

7. *Payment of Legacies.* Usually payable one year after date of death, unless otherwise specified by the will. Amount is fixed and determinable from the will. Try to make earlier payment if other cash requirements do not make this impractical. Consider partial, periodic payments on legacies. (Specific legacies of property other than cash may be given to the legatees promptly if there is no possibility that they will have to be sold in order to take care of claims having priority over them.)

8. *Fiduciary Income Taxes.* Return due three and one-half months after the end of the estate's first fiscal year and each year thereafter, as long as the estate is in existence. Amount of tax based on estate's net income less amounts distributed or distributable to beneficiaries.

9. *Federal Estate Tax Return.* Return is due to be filed nine months after decedent's death. Tax due in full with the return. Cash outlay is likely to be the largest of any required from the executor. Plans for taking care of this expense must be foremost in the executor's mind. (But see Chapter 15 for ways of postponing some or all of this payment).

10. *State Inheritance Tax Return.* Return is due at different dates in different states, usually not earlier than the filing date for the Federal estate tax return. Cash requirement likely to be large unless advance payment of this tax was made (*see* 6 above).

11. *Administration Expenses.* Payable at various times as incurred. Probate fees, filing fees, executor's bond, settlement fees, appraisers' fees, and other expenses not likely to require any large cash outlays. The larger administration expenses are listed under 12 and 13.

12. *Legal and Accounting Fees.* Payable in accordance with the contracts with the attorney and the accountant, either periodically during the administration or in full upon settlement of the estate. Amounts readily determinable and can usually be accumulated after taking care of more pressing cash needs.

13. *Executor's Fee.* Usually payable at end of administration period. Amount is fixed by state law, generally based on size of the estate. This is usually the final cash outlay necessary before the estate can be closed. An executor's fee is frequently sizable enough to delay the settlement of the estate until the cash can be accumulated.

14. *Distribution of Estate Assets.* The remaining assets after payment of all debts, fees, taxes, and expenses are transferred to the proper heirs and beneficiaries. No cash is required unless the assets are in a form not acceptable to the recipients or not easily divisible among a number of different beneficiaries. The necessity for liquidation of all or a part of the assets might delay the final distribution.

Temporary Investments

Cash which is being accumulated over a period of months in anticipation of some cash deadline will often become sizable enough in amount that it would be foolish to leave it in a nonproductive bank account.

In these cases, the executor should determine whether he has the authority, either under the statutes or under the will, to invest these funds temporarily. If he does not, the court may grant him this right.

In selecting temporary investments, safety is the most important consideration. Corporate stocks should never be selected; corporate bonds seldom, if ever. Government bonds and U.S. Treasury notes are considered safe investments, even though they may be subject to small market fluctuations. Bank savings accounts or certificates of deposit are also favored from a safety standpoint—but it would be prudent, if possible, to distribute these deposits among several different banks, investing no more than $40,000 (the insured amount) in any one account.

The other factor to consider in making temporary investments is the availability of the funds at the time they will be needed by the estate. No security should be acquired unless there is certain to be a ready market for it at any time. Also, it would obviously be futile to purchase a one year certificate of deposit with funds which are going to be needed within, say, eleven months.

Adequate Accounting Records

The foregoing discussion of the executor's duties emphasizes his responsibilities, and it obviously follows that he must keep sufficient records of his administration to safeguard himself from any possible charges of neglecting his duties. This, together with the necessity of making reports to the court—explained in Chapter 6—makes it imperative for the executor to see that an adequate accounting system is installed and maintained for the estate.

The accounting system may be very simple or highly complex, depending on the size and nature of the estate. Estate accounting is fully explained in later chapters, but its great importance warrants its mention here as one of the executor's duties and responsibilities.

6

Reports to the Court

The *probate court* is usually given complete jurisdiction over the administration of estates. It has the power to examine into the accounts and vouchers of the executor or administrator, and to consider and determine objections which may be made by interested parties in reference to the estate's administration.

A person accepting the position of executor or administrator subjects all of his actions in connection with the administration to the review of the court, and his knowledge that this is true forces him to be more careful in complying with the governing statutes and the provisions of the decedent's will than he might be if he expected no such review.

The effect of such a system is that it emphasizes to the personal representative that his position is a fiduciary one, and it strengthens the possibility that he will faithfully accomplish the objectives of any administration, namely, satisfaction of the decedent's creditors and proper distribution of the remaining assets.

Necessity for Periodic Reporting

The probate court does not, however, actively supervise the day-to-day activities of any executor. This would be manifestly impossible because there might be many estates in the process of administration within the jurisdiction of the court at any time.

The court's review and control are accomplished, instead, by the statutory requirements making it mandatory for the personal representative to file with the court periodic reports and accountings of his stewardship. One of the first and most important duties of an executor is to keep and render full and accurate accounts concerning the estate in his hands.

These reports, when filed by the executor and passed on by the court, become a matter of public record, which any interested parties may examine and to which they may file objections, if desired. In many jurisdictions such an account is not immediately passed on by the court, but is first referred to an auditor or referee, whose report is subject to confirmation, modification, or rejection by the court. The auditor is generally empowered to take testimony and make findings of fact. Exceptions to his report may be filed by either the executor or any other interested person.

Many courts do not pretend to make a thorough study of an executor's reports, but more or less rely on objections being filed by anyone believing himself to have been injured by improper acts of the executor.

The court also needs a report from the executor so that it can review the disbursements made by the executor, for the purpose of determining whether the executor is entitled to reimbursement for these expenditures. Theoretically, the executor's expenditures are considered as having been made from his own personal funds but, if they are approved, he is reimbursed for them by being permitted to deduct them from the amount of the estate's cash for which he is accountable. The court will permit the executor to be reimbursed for, or credited with, all proper claims against the estate which he has paid and for all actual and necessary expenses incurred in good faith and with exercise of reasonable judgment in the care, management, and settlement of the estate.

When Reports Are Required

Reports of the progress of the administration of the estate are made to the court as often as the executor cares to make them, or upon order of the court, or as required by statute. If the administration is not completely settled at the end of the first year, the executor is frequently required to make an accounting annually.

When the assets have all been collected and reduced to cash as far as possible or desirable, and when all obligations and expenses have been ascertained and settled as far as it is necessary to do so, a final report or accounting is always made. An exception to this requirement may sometimes be permitted if all the interested parties make and file an agreement with the court which makes the accounting unnecessary.

Interim Reports

Any report or accounting made to the court prior to final settlement is known as an interim report.

It is a good practice for the executor to prepare an interim report at the end of each year of the administration, even though he may not be required to do so. It is well to have the approval of the court, or to learn of any objections, periodically as the administration progresses rather than wait until the executor thinks he can make a final settlement.

Reports covering each twelve-month period from the date of the decedent's death are acceptable, but equally acceptable, and usually much easier to prepare, are reports covering periods corresponding to those covered by the fiduciary income tax returns;

that is, the first report will include a period of less than a year (from the date of death to the end of the estate's first fiscal or calendar year) and each succeeding report will cover a full twelve-month period, except that the final report may again be for less than one year. Estate books, like those of most businesses, are closed only at the end of each annual tax or accounting period, at which time any figures needed for reports are easily available either in summary form or in detail. Attempting to gather such information at some odd date in the middle of the accounting year is unnecessarily difficult.

The Final Report

The probate court might accept a final report from the executor covering only the period which has elapsed since the date of his most recent interim report, but a final report must generally cover the entire period of administration—from the date of the decedent's death to the date of final settlement. This may cover several years, but its preparation should pose no particular problem, particularly if interim reports have been filed; such interim reports can easily be combined into a final, over-all report.

The effect of a final accounting and settlement is to close the estate and discharge the executor or administrator. In some jurisdictions the laws require than an executor give public notice for a designated length of time as to his intention to make a final settlement. This gives constructive notice to all parties interested, who thus have an opportunity of contesting the accounts. A settlement of an estate made after the prescribed notice is generally conclusive on all interested parties.

The court will examine the executor's final report and determine whether or not the various expenditures listed therein are proper charges to the estate for which the executor may be reimbursed or credited. It will also hear and rule on any objections which may be raised by creditors or beneficiaries. If everything is in order, the court will then issue a decree of distribution and discharge the executor and cancel his bond.

Form of Report

There is no uniformity whatsoever as to the proper form for an executor's interim or final reports. Most statutes have very little to say about just what kind of report shall be filed, frequently describing it in very general terms, such as "a statement of the estate's receipts and disbursements," but without specifying whether a detailed listing is required or whether a summary will suffice.

Each court is likely to have its own ideas about what a report should consist of. Some may insist on one certain form, others may accept any form which will present the information they need in making their review. It is advisable, therefore, for the estate's accountant to ask the probate judge about his requirements before spending time preparing a report which will not be acceptable to that court. (This will often be a frustrating experience for an accountant because many courts will insist on reports in a much less informative form than the accountant would otherwise be able to prepare.)

Generally, however, a summary cash statement must be prepared, accompanied by detailed schedules of cash receipts and cash disbursements. Cancelled checks supporting the disbursements must also be presented to the court. If the volume of transactions was very large, the detailed schedules might not be required, though the court might later ask for them if more detailed information is needed.

A desirable feature of any executor's report (though not always required by the court) is for it to show, in some way, the disposition of all estate property which came into the executor's hands. The beginning inventory plus gains and income and less losses, expenses, and distributions should be shown to equal the closing inventory of assets being held for final distribution.

Another desirable feature is for the report to show separately the estate's operating income and expenses rather than have them intermingled with receipts and disbursements having to do with the principal of the estate (receipts from sales of assets, disbursements for administrative expenses, debts, and the like). A careful segregation of principal and income is important not only in the report but also in the accounting system, because the income beneficiaries are often not the same people who will receive the estate principal. This is explained more fully in the chapter on estate accounting.

The preparation of a "Charge and Discharge Statement" is generally considered to be the best way for an executor to report to the court. This form will serve for either interim reports or a final report, and it is acceptable to most courts.

A charge and discharge statement shows the executor as being charged with all assets and funds which come under his control—the inventoried assets, those later discovered, gains on sales, estate income, and so forth. There is deducted from this total the disbursements for which the executor claims credit—the decedent's debts, losses on sales, funeral and administration expenses, operating expenses, legacies paid, and other expenditures. The balance is the amount with which the executor is still charged,and it must be represented by cash and other assets still in his possession and distributable to the beneficiaries.

It is preferable to divide a charge and discharge statement into two parts. One should be a statement covering only items relating to the principal of the estate, the other a statement covering only the estate's income and the expenses against that income. Each will show a closing balance and the total of the two balances will agree with the amount of the closing inventory.

To summarize, executors' reports might take any one of many different forms, depending on the legal requirements, the wishes of the governing court, and the size and nature of the estate. The most simple kind of cash statement might suffice for a very small estate. For larger estates, more formal and more complete reports are desirable. In any case, the charge and discharge statement recommended by most accounting writers is the most satisfactory type of report. But, unfortunately, its use is still far from universal, due largely to many courts being unfamiliar with any accounting statement other than a cash receipts and disbursements statement and insisting on some less informative type of report.

Reports Illustrated

A simple cash receipts and disbursements statement, which might serve as an interim or a final report for a small estate, is shown in the following form.

Estate of Allan Griswold
Martin Gross, Executor

STATEMENT OF CASH RECEIPTS AND DISBURSEMENTS

For the Period November 15, 1975 to June 20, 1976

Cash on Hand and in Bank, November 15, 1975		$ 2,086.62
Receipts:		
Nov. 30—Collection of Accrued Salary	$ 300.00	
Dec. 1—Rent on House	65.00	
Dec. 8—Sale of Auto	1,400.00	
Jan. 1—Rent on House	65.00	
Feb. 1—Rent on House	65.00	
Feb. 27—Proceeds from Sale of House	7,900.00	
Total Receipts		9,795.00
Total Cash Accountable		$11,881.62
Disbursements:		
Nov. 22—County Court Clerk, Probate Fees	$ 6.00	
Nov. 24—County Judge, Probate Fee	7.50	
Nov. 28—Bell Telephone Co., Debt	4.26	
Dec. 2—Plaza Pharmacy, Debt	18.50	
Dec. 3—Western Gas Company, Debt	9.97	
Dec. 3—Electric Plant Board, Debt	2.65	
Dec. 3—Troy Laundry, Debt	2.80	
Dec. 3—City Hospital, Debt	180.80	
Dec. 3—Dr. Ralph Harvey, Debt	100.00	
Dec. 29—Geo. Wayne, Appraiser Fee	20.00	
Dec. 29—Alan Mayer, Appraiser Fee	20.00	
Dec. 29—Scott Vance, Appraiser Fee	20.00	
Dec. 29—County Court Clerk, Filing Inventory	7.00	
Jan. 4—White Funeral Home, Funeral Expenses	1,046.50	
Jan. 18—Davis Roofing Co., Repairs to House	18.50	
Jan. 20—First Presbyterian Church, Bequest	500.00	
Feb. 9—Insurance Center, Insurance on House	17.88	
Feb. 27—County Court Clerk, Stamps on Deed	8.80	
Mar. 3—Frances Griswold, Bequest	2,000.00	
Mar. 3—John A. Griswold, Bequest	2,000.00	

Estate of Allan Griswold
Martin Gross, Executor

STATEMENT OF CASH RECEIPTS AND DISBURSEMENTS

(cont.)

Disbursements:

Apr. 15—Internal Revenue Service, Debt	$ 96.27	
Apr. 27—Geo. Barner, Atty., Deed and Title	42.50	
May 1—Dept. of Revenue, Inheritance Tax	426.61	
June 15—Geo. Barner, Attorney Fee	200.00	
June 15—Martin Gross, Executor Fee	800.00	
June 19—County Court Clerk, Settlement Fee	5.25	
June 19—County Judge, Settlement Fee	26.85	
Total Disbursements		7,588.64
Balance, Cash in Bank, June 20, 1976		$ 4,292.98

Although the above report might be accepted by some courts, it has a serious deficiency in that it makes no mention of the estate inventory and furnishes no accounting for the inventoried assets. A much more informative report could be made as follows, with the foregoing statement of receipts and disbursements being attached to it as a supporting schedule.

Estate of Allan Griswold
Martin Gross, Executor

STATEMENT OF FINAL SETTLEMENT

For the Period November 15, 1975 to June 20, 1976

Assets per Inventory, November 15, 1975:		
Cash on Hand and in Bank	$ 2,086.62	
Residence, 1426 Lincoln Avenue	14,250.00	
Rental House, 416 Elm Street	7,800.00	
Salary Receivable	300.00	
Automobile	1,400.00	
Household Furnishings	800.00	
Total Assets		$26,636.62
Less: Inventory Value of Assets Sold:		
Rental House	$7,800.00	
Automobile	1,400.00	
Salary Receivable	300.00	9,500.00
Total Assets Not Sold		$17,136.62
Add: Cash Receipts, per Schedule		9,795.00

Estate of Allan Griswold
Martin Gross, Executor

STATEMENT OF FINAL SETTLEMENT

(cont.)

Total		$26,931.62
Deduct: Disbursements, per Schedule		7,588.64
Estate Balance, June 20, 1976		$19,342.98
Balance Consisting of:		
Cash in Bank	$4,292.98	
Residence	14,250.00	
Household Furnishings	800.00	
Total		$19,342.98

It should be noted that in order to combine a cash statement with what might be considered a fund balance statement it is necessary to eliminate from the inventory the value of any assets sold or realized, because these values are duplicated in the cash receipts.

If the beginning or closing inventories are very lengthy, they should be listed in separate schedules and only the totals shown on the statement.

The above statement with its supporting cash schedules adequately reports on the estate's administration and is in a form which could be easily understood by most people. It still fails to show one important bit of information, however. It makes no distinction between transactions applying to the principal of the estate and those applicable to the estate's income.

This can be corrected by making a segregation of the receipts and the disbursements as follows:

Add: Cash Receipts, per Schedule:		
Principal Receipts	$9,600.00	
Receipts of Income	195.00	$9,795.00
Deduct: Disbursements, per Schedule:		
Principal Disbursements	$7,552.26	
Disbursements of Income	36.38	$7,588.64

Although the above type of statement might be preferred by many courts, it is still a very poor substitute for the recommended charge and discharge statement. A charge and discharge statement does not lend itself only to reporting on a large estate but is adaptable to an estate of any size. As an illustration, the following is a typical charge and discharge statement, using the same small estate that was used in the preceding examples.

Estate of Allan Griswold
Martin Gross, Executor

CHARGE AND DISCHARGE STATEMENT

For the Period November 15, 1975 to June 20, 1976

First as to Principal:

The Executor charges himself with:		
Assets per Inventory (Schedule A)	$26,636.62	
Assets Subsequently Discovered (Schedule B)		
Gains on Realization of Assets (Schedule C)	48.70	$26,685.32
The Executor credits himself with;		
Funeral and Administration Expenses (Sch. D)	$2,159.10	
Debts of Decedent Paid (Schedule E)	415.25	
Losses on Realization of Assets (Schedule F)		
Bequests Paid (Schedule G)	4,500.00	
State Inheritance Tax Paid	426.61	7,500.96
Leaving a Balance of Principal of		$19,184.36
Consisting of:		
Cash in Bank	$4,134.36	
Residence	14,250.00	
Household Furnishings	800.00	
Total	$19.184.36	

Second as to Income:

The Executor charges himself with:		
Rents Received		$195.00
The Executor credits himself with:		
Repairs to Property	$ 18.50	
Insurance on Rental Property	17.88	36.38
Leaving a Balance of Income of		158.62
Consisting of:		
Cash in Bank	$ 158.62	

Schedule A—Assets per Inventory

Cash on Hand and in Bank	$ 2,086.62
Residence, 1426 Lincoln Avenue	14,250.00
Rental House, 416 Elm Street	7,800.00
Automobile	1,400.00
Salary Receivable	300.00
Household Furnishings	800.00
Total	$26,636.62

Estate of Allan Griswold
Martin Gross, Executor

CHARGE AND DISCHARGE STATEMENT
(cont.)

Schedule C—Gains on Realization of Assets

Proceeds, Sale of Rental House	$7,900.00
Less: Deed, Title, Stamps	51.30
Net Proceeds	$7,848.70
Inventory Value of House	7,800.00
Net Gain	$ 48.70

Schedule D—Funeral and Administration Expenses

Funeral Expenses:		
White Funeral Home		$1,046.50
Administration Expenses:		
County Court Clerk, Probate Fees	$ 6.00	
County Judge, Probate Fees	7.50	
Appraisers' Fees	60.00	
County Court Clerk, Filing Fee	7.00	
Geo. Barner, Attorney Fee	200.00	
Martin Gross, Executor Fee	800.00	
County Court Clerk, Settlement Fee	5.25	
County Judge, Settlement Fee	26.85	1,112.60
Total		$2,159.10

Schedule E—Debts of Decedent Paid

Bell Telephone Company	$ 4.26
Plaza Pharmacy	18.50
Western Gas Company	9.97
Electric Plant Board	2.65
Troy Laundry	2.80
City Hospital	180.80
Dr. Ralph Harvey	100.00
Internal Revenue Service	96.27
Total	$ 415.25

Schedule G—Bequests Paid

First Presbyterian Church	$ 500.00
Frances Griswold	2,000.00
John A. Griswold	2,000.00
Total	$4,500.00

Petitions to the Court for Instructions

There is much variance in the statutes regarding the conditions under which an executor must obtain permission from the court before performing certain acts. *For example*, in some states claims must be approved by the court before payment is made. In some, permission must be secured before selling property, before making investments, or performing other duties.

As a general rule, the executor has the authority to pay proper claims and to sell personal property to the extent necessary and desirable, but permission must be obtained before real estate can be sold.

The executor should, therefore, determine just which of his acts require court approval in his state, and he should also keep in mind that he has the privilege of asking the court for advice and instructions at any time, even though court approval may not be required.

It is frequently necessary for the executor to ask the probate court for the construction of a will or for instructions with respect to various matters relating to the administration of the estate. Where there is room for doubt as to the executor's duties or as to the policy that should be pursued, the judge of the probate court should be consulted before any steps are taken that might seriously affect the funds of the estate.

An informal conference with the judge may often be all that is necessary. In other cases, a formal, written petition should be made to the court, and in these cases the court's reply will be in the form of a court order containing the information requested. A court order protects the executor, and although he does not generally need such an order in the ordinary discharge of his duties, he should not hesitate to obtain this protection to cover any acts which are not clearly within his authority as granted by the statutes and the will.

The probate court does not exist just for the purpose of protecting the creditors and the beneficiaries from improper acts of the executor. It is also a very valuable source of help and protection for the executor.

7

Distribution of Assets
and Final Settlement

After the payment of the decedent's debts and the estate expenses and taxes, it is the duty of the executor to distribute the remaining assets to those entitled to them. The procedure is for the executor to file his final accounting with the court, and, after the expiration of the time granted for inspection and objections by interested parties, the court approves the accounting, allows the fees and expenses claimed therein, and issues a decree of distribution which disposes of the balance of the estate.

Time for Making Final Settlement

The time for distributing an estate is controlled by either the terms of the local statutes or the terms of the testator's will, but most statutes are flexible enough to permit the court to grant extensions of time which may be necessary due to unusual circumstances.

Assuming that the executor is able to obtain reasonable extensions of the time within which the estate must be settled, there are a number of important factors which should be considered before deciding on a closing date.

An estate should never be distributed until after the time allowed for the presentation of claims. As pointed out before, an executor must always be sure that the debts and expenses are paid or provided for before making any distributions to the beneficiaries. If the estate is relatively small and has no tax or other complications, the executor has the duty as well as the right to proceed with the settlement promptly after taking care of the claims. He has no right to postpone the settlement, and the beneficiaries are usually anxious for the estate to be distributed as early as possible so that they may receive their shares of the property.

The executor will also be anxious to settle the estate and be discharged from his responsibility as quickly as possible. His compensation is usually based on the amount of the estate rather than on the length of time he spends administering it. His fee might be exactly the same for a six-months term as for a three-year administration, so he seldom has anything to gain by prolonging it.

Settlement of the average small estate is therefore, usually desirable and possible within a month or so after the six-month period ordinarily prescribed for the presentation of claims.

In many estates, however, such an early settlement is neither possible nor desirable. The executor must not only wait until all claims are presented by the decedent's creditors, but he must wait until the estate and inheritance taxes have been determined and settled and until he has been able to accumulate enough cash in the estate to pay the administration expenses, cash bequests, and other expenses. He has no right to force quick sales of estate property at sacrifice prices just in order to obtain the necessary cash to enable him to make an early distribution.

The estate tax return is not due until nine months after the decedent's death, and it will probably be another year at best before it is examined and settled. If the estate is at all sizable, and particularly if it is subject to the Federal estate tax, it is very unlikely that settlement can be made in less than two years, and three years would be a much more probable period of administration.

The administration might even have to extend far beyond this period. *For example*, the estate's fiduciary income tax returns might be questioned by the Internal Revenue Service; the questions might even have to be taken to court, with the resultant additional delay, and it would seldom be wise for an executor to attempt to settle an estate as long as any questions of income tax or estate tax remain unresolved.

There are also cases where still another factor might cause a lengthy extension of the administration period. If there are a number of different beneficiaries, it might be impossible to make a distribution of the remaining estate assets which would be satisfactory to them. They might insist that the executor continue in charge of the estate until he is able to liquidate these assets, finally distributing cash rather than burdening the heirs with various kinds of property which they have no desire to manage.

In these cases, the executor must be guided by his conscience. He has no real duty to devote additional time to the estate just to satisfy the desires of the heirs. But he may realize that his management of the assets would be more productive and efficient than theirs would be, and he should certainly consider their wishes in the matter. These and other complications in effecting a distribution can necessitate a much longer administration than the normal two or three year period. It is not too unusual for an estate to remain in administration for six, eight, or even ten years or more.

The executor should not overlook the fact that a lengthy administration can sometimes be very advantageous for tax purposes. This applies principally to the larger estates where a sizable amount of annual income is involved. If the decedent's will provides that a portion of the estate income each year shall go to one or more beneficiaries with the remainder of the income remaining in the estate, this has the effect of splitting such income among the fiduciary tax return and those of the beneficiaries. The total income, therefore, is taken out of a higher income tax bracket and taxed in two or more lower brackets. (Also, the fiduciary's $600 tax exemption will be used.) The more years this kind of tax splitting can continue, the more income taxes can be saved and the greater will be the total proceeds from the estate to the beneficiaries. However, the Internal Revenue Service will not permit this kind of tax saving device to continue indefinitely. They will insist on a distribution of the estate when there ceases to be any other valid reason for keeping it open.

The proper way to handle an estate's income for tax purposes is not always an easy thing to determine. The decedent's will and state law govern, but the question of who has the right to the income must be settled early in the administration. If the executor finds that the income should be split, he might have a moral (though not a legal) obligation to try to discover valid reasons for holding the estate open longer than would otherwise be necessary.

The same principles would hold true if all the income is taxable to the estate and if the estate income is in a lower tax bracket than it would be if added to the other income of the heir or heirs. (Ordinarily, the income of a decedent's estate during administration is taxable to the fiduciary, unless the will provides otherwise, but some states make this optional with the executor.)

All of the above factors make it difficult to set a target date for closing an estate. This decision must be delayed until all the facts are known. Most executors find that the time they originally estimate for administration must be extended several times before settlement is both possible and desirable. When this time finally comes, regardless of whether it is the end of a tax year or calendar year or even the end of any month, settlement and distribution can be made.

Payment of Fees

All fees and other expenses of administration must be paid—or at least provided for—before settlement of the estate is possible. If some have not actually been paid when the final report to the court is being prepared, they should nevertheless be included in the report so that it will be complete and present all of the expenses which the court needs to approve.

The principal fees are those paid to the estate's accountant and its attorney and the compensation of the personal representative. Of lesser importance are the fees charged by the court clerk and perhaps by the judge of the probate court for the filing of the will, the inventory, and other estate documents. Most of these filing fees will have been taken care of long before settlement of the estate begins, but enough cash should be reserved to cover the fees of the judge and the court clerk in connection with the final settlement itself.

The fees payable to the attorney and the accountant should have been agreed upon at the time these men were retained. Portions of these fees may have been payable periodically throughout the administration period, but a final payment, at least, would certainly have been deferred until the time of settlement. Any such remaining unpaid portion should now be paid. If the fees had not been agreed upon, the attorney and the accountant should be asked to submit statements. If the amounts are reasonable, payment is in order. If there is any question as to whether the amounts are excessive, the court's approval should be sought before paying them.

The executor's fee is usually the largest single administrative expense. It is the one with which the executor is most concerned, but it is also the one which is most difficult to determine; and its determination is often the cause of ill feelings between the executor and the residuary beneficiaries of the estate.

The commission allowed the representative is usually fixed by statute as a percentage, or a series of percentages, applied to the value of the assets received and distributed or disbursed during the administration of the estate. Depending on the wording of the particular statute, these percentages might be applied to the gross appraised estate (including or excluding real property), to the value or amount of the personal property, to the property coming into the executor's hands, and other factors. The laws are seldom very specific, however, leaving the determination of the exact amount to the probate court. In these cases, and in states where the law is silent regarding the executor's fee, the court will attempt to fix a "reasonable" compensation for the services rendered.

The executor can be expected, of course, to try to obtain the maximum compensation permitted by law, and there are a few very general rules which may be helpful to him in this connection (whether he is trying to convince the court or the heirs).

The term "gross estate" usually refers to the total appraised value of the estate inventory, except that real property passing directly to the heirs would have to be eliminated if included in the inventory. Theoretically, the real estate does not have to be administered by the executor so no fee would be allowed on its value. On the other hand, real estate which is sold during administration becomes personal property for this purpose and would be included in the basis for computing the fee. But an executor cannot sell real estate, when such a sale is not required in order to pay debts, just to increase his fee basis.

If the decedent's will indicates a desire for the real property to be included in the administration, or if it gives the executor the power to sell real estate, there would seem to be little question that the total inventory value should be the basis for computing the fee. But it would be logical in any case to adjust the gross inventory value for any gains or losses on realization of the assets during administration.

What if certain inventory valuations are raised or lowered in determining the gross estate for tax purposes? Which base should be used, the inventory valuation or the estate tax valuation? There is no established answer to this question, but the estate tax valuations would tend to be more accurate. This is true because estate tax examining agents usually make a very thorough review of the values, and they also have the advantage of "hindsight" which the appraisers did not have.

The executor's percentage is often also applicable to "funds coming into the executor's hands during administration." Does a statutory provision of this kind refer to cash receipts, to the estate's gross income, or to its net income? Again, there is no definite answer, but the gross income is generally considered to be the "funds" referred to.

Allowance of extra compensation to executors who have carried on the business of the deceased has frequently been made upon the authority of some provision authorizing an extra allowance for "extraordinary" or "unusual" services. To be extraordinary the services must be of a character not ordinarily required and not within the routine of administration. An executor who actively manages estate businesses or who must devote more than the nominal time usually required to the administration of the estate and management of the properties should not overlook claiming this extra compensation. The additional amount will be extremely variable, depending on the exact set of circumstances.

As a rule, if the executor is a lawyer or an accountant he may not claim extra compensation for the professional services he renders the estate, even if he performs duties which he might properly have hired an attorney or an accountant to perform. Some statutes, however, do permit extra fees in these cases.

The above difficult questions become merely academic in cases where the decedent's will specifies the amount of the executor's fee or provides the executor with a bequest in lieu of any fee. In most jurisdictions, if a will provides for a sum less than the legal compensation, the executor has the choice of refusing the appointment or accepting it on the terms fixed by the testator.

The amount of the executor's compensation is almost always a matter of great concern to the decedent's heirs. This often causes trouble between them and the executor. The heirs do have the right to object to the amount claimed by the executor, and the court will try to consider the arguments of both parties. This controversy might arise early in the administration (*for example*, when the amount must be estimated for inclusion in the estate tax return) or not until the time for settlement. Whenever it comes up, the executor should present and explain his position to these heirs, show them the way in which he believes his compensation should be computed, and try to secure their cooperation and support. His attorney and his accountant can be of great help to him at this point. It should be pointed out to the heirs that any compensation allowed the executor will be used as an estate tax or an income tax deduction and will not cost the heirs the full amount claimed. The executor should also be receptive to any arguments advanced by the other parties, and should make every effort to work out a satisfactory compromise and maintain a friendly relationship with the heirs. In some cases, it would be wise to suggest that one or more disinterested outsiders be asked to help in arbitrating the dispute.

If an agreement can be reached, the amount agreed upon will almost invariably be allowed by the court. If no agreement is reached, the only remaining course is to submit all the facts and arguments to the court for a decision—with the resulting rupture of the (much to be desired) friendly relationship between the executor and the heirs.

At what time is the executor's fee payable? Generally, it should be paid in full just prior to final settlement. In some cases, however, the executor may be permitted to draw on it periodically throughout his term. If he is devoting most of his time to the estate and needs the income periodically, and if estate funds are clearly available, the court will usually grant his request for advances on the fee. (Spreading the fee over several tax years rather than receiving it all in one year might also save the executor some personal income taxes.)

Another point should be considered by an executor who is also the residuary legatee of the estate. He may find it advantageous to waive any fee, which would be taxable to him, thereby increasing his nontaxable legacy.

Payment of Legacies

The payment of legacies was discussed in Chapter 5, but it is mentioned again here as a reminder to the executor that the final settlement cannot be effected until the legacies are paid.

Any amounts still payable on bequests or legacies should be taken care of prior to the final settlement so that this report will show them as having been paid. If funds are not available for the full payment of all legacies, an order of the court should be secured directing the proper method of abating the legacies.

The indebtedness of a legatee to the estate may be offset against his legacy.

Decree of Distribution

Upon the filing of the executor's final accounting, the practice in many jurisdictions is for the personal representative to make application for an order of distribution to the court having jurisdiction of the administration. Sometimes an order of distribution follows as a matter of course upon the settlement of the executor's accounts, or a decree adjusting such accounts may operate as an order of distribution.

Exhibit 15

Final Settlement

WASHINGTON COUNTY COURT

IN RE: THE MATTER OF THE ESTATE OF
CARL DAVIS, DECEASED

FINAL SETTLEMENT

The affiant, George Foster, states that Carl Davis died on the 9th day of August, 1975, a resident of this county and state; that his will was probated by the Washington County Court on the 12th of August, 1975, and the affiant was appointed executor of the estate of the said deceased and has continued to act as such executor.

The affiant states that there came into his hands as such executor the following property:

(List the property and its value)

The affiant states that he has made the following disbursements and filed herewith either a receipt or cancelled check supporting each:

(List disbursements and amount of each)

The affiant states that the balance of $_____ has been distributed as follows:

(Set out the distribution made)

The affiant states that he has paid all the debts of the estate including all taxes due the State and estate taxes due the Federal Government.

Wherefore, having performed all of the duties pertaining to his office, the affiant submits this report as his final settlement of his accounts as executor of said estate and prays that this be taken as his final report and that he be discharged, together with his bondsmen, from all further liability in connection therewith.

_____

Subscribed and sworn to before me, a notary public, by George Foster, this the_____
_____ day of_____19__.

_____

NOTARY PUBLIC

In some jurisdictions a specified form is used for a decree of distribution. In others, the estate's attorney will write up a court order directing the distribution of the assets and secure the signature of the probate judge on the order. The order for distribution should be drawn in accordance with the local probate practice.

When the distribution of the property has been directed by will, the decree will merely indicate the amounts going to legatees who have not yet received their prescribed legacies, and to the residuary legatee. When there is no will the distribution follows the statutes covering descent and distribution.

A decree of distribution does not create the title in the distributees or legatees. It is a determination of those who acquire the title of the deceased and becomes final and conclusive on that question if not attacked.

Upon receipt of a decree or order of distribution, the executor may immediately proceed with the actual distribution of the remaining estate assets.

Distribution of Estate Assets

If all of the estate assets have been converted to cash, distribution is easy. Each beneficiary is simply given a check for his proper share of these funds.

More often, however, a distribution in kind must be made. In these cases, a difficult problem often arises when there is more than one person to whom distribution must be made. It is the problem of valuation—should the assets be divided among the beneficiaries at the values at which they were originally inventoried as of the date of death, at the values established for estate tax purposes, or at the current values at the date of distribution? The answer to this question must be firmly established before any distribution is begun.

The laws of a few states specify the proper method of valuation to use in distributing the property. Where the law is silent, local practice governs.

If current values are to be used, a reappraisal of the remaining property must be made and the property distributed on that basis. The theory behind this treatment is that the executor could have sold all the assets on the date of distribution, at the values shown by the reappraisal, and distributed cash only.

The values established for estate tax purposes are frequently used, on the theory that the income tax basis so established for each item of property is the value at which the heir should receive the property. Also, because the testator, in directing the proportions in which the division is to be made, certainly had in mind the values at the date of his death rather than at some indefinite future date, and the tax values are determined as of the date of death.

Inventory values are seldom used for distribution purposes, except where there is no change for estate taxes or where the estate is not subject to such taxes.

A second problem in distributing the property arises if there is dissension among the heirs as to just which items of property each shall receive. *For example*, one piece of property might be more desirable than another of exactly the same value, due to convenience of location, ease of management, and so on. Or, each of two heirs might prefer to receive one large diamond ring rather than two smaller rings of the same value, and so forth.

The executor should try to work out this problem with the heirs and avoid dissension among them, if possible. If the property is in the form of securities, *for example*, he might give each heir his prorata share of each investment. If no satisfactory distribution can be agreed upon, the executor should apply to the court for instructions. The executor might be instructed, as a last resort, to convert any disputed property into cash and distribute cash to the heirs.

Advances may be made to the distributees by the executor prior to final dissolution. Obviously, where such advances have been made, they should be deducted from the respective shares of the distributees upon final distribution of the estate.

Actual distribution of personal property is accomplished by giving the proper heirs physical possession of the property. As for real estate, if it was not administered but passed directly to the heirs, no deed or other formal action is necessary. If title to the real estate did pass to the executor, he must usually deed it to the heir or heirs.

The executor may, and usually does, require a receipt from an heir or legatee upon the payment to him of his share in the estate.

Transfer of Assets to a Trust

The testator may have provided in his will that all, or some portion, of the estate shall be placed in the hands of a trustee. The executor in this case will simply transfer the proper assets to the trustee rather than to individual beneficiaries.

The same person may have been named to act as executor and as trustee. This person may distribute the estate without actually transferring it from himself as executor to himself as trustee, but in such cases his executorship records should be kept entirely distinct from his trusteeship records. The estate and the trust are two entirely separate entities, and the trustee does not take over the duties of the trusteeship until the trust property is turned over to him.

The Executor's Discharge and Cancellation of Bond

When the estate of a decedent has been duly administered and closed, and when all the assets have been distributed to those entitled to them, the heirs and distributees have full ownership of the decedent's property and the executor is discharged from further liability.

The executor must usually apply to the court for this discharge, and this should be done as soon as he has completed the distribution of the estate assets. A formal order of discharge is generally considered as necessary. (*See* Exhibit 16.)

Exhibit 16

Executor's Discharge

WASHINGTON COUNTY COURT

IN RE: THE MATTER OF THE ESTATE OF
CARL DAVIS, DECEASED

ORDER

The foregoing settlement of the account of George Foster as Executor of the estate of Carl Davis, deceased, which was filed last court and ordered to lay over for exceptions, and no exceptions having been filed thereto, is this day confirmed and ordered to be recorded as the final settlement of the said George

Exhibit 16 (cont.)

Foster, executor of the decedent's estate, and he together with his bondsmen are hereby released from any further liability in connection with the settlement of the said decedent's estate.

This the _____ day of _____ 19__.

_____
Judge, Washington County Court

The need for the executor's bond no longer exists when the executor has been discharged from liability in connection with the administration. The rule in some jurisdictions is that final distribution of the property, which will relieve the sureties on the bond, may occur by operation of law. A decree directing the transfer of funds by an executor to himself as trustee may also relieve the sureties on the administration bond from further liability, though the representative will have to execute a new bond in his capacity as trustee. In any case, the surety on the bond should be notified and the bond cancelled.

The administration of the estate is now complete.

8

Estate Accounting Simplified

Many treatises on *estate accounting* seem to emphasize the differences between this kind of accounting and ordinary commercial accounting, and they leave the reader with the impression that estate accounting requires the knowledge of an entirely new, very difficult set of rules which it may require a great deal of study and experience to master.

This simply is not true. It would seem much more sensible to emphasize the fact that estate accounting is basically just the same as any other accounting and that the only cause of difficulty is its relative unfamiliarity to most accountants. There are really only two or three points of difference which the accountant needs to know and understand to be able to design and maintain just as good a bookkeeping system for an estate as he could for any other business entity.

Illustrations of forms and journals for use in estates are generally rather frightening. The reader too often gets the impression that these are standard forms which must be used by all estates, that he must master them and must make his estate's transaction fit into them.

This also is untrue. There are no standard or required bookkeeping forms which any estate must use. Rather, the system for each estate should be designed with that particular estate in mind. As a result, there could be, and probably should be, as much variation in the accounting systems for different estates as there is in those for the corner grocery store and the large manufacturing company.

This discussion of estate accounting, therefore, dwells less on specific forms to be used than on the theory and principles of estate accounting, in the belief that the accountant on the job is the best man to design the actual accounting system—provided he knows and understands just what the system must accomplish.

Principal and Income

The main point of difference between estate accounting and ordinary accounting is caused by the necessity for keeping the books in such a way as to distinguish clearly between the principal (or corpus) of the estate and its income.

The distinction between principal and income is necessary because in many cases the decedent's will designates one person to receive the income (a life tenant, perhaps), and another to receive the principal (a remainderman). It is very common for a will to create a trust of this kind, and although the trust cannot go into operation until the estate is settled, the segregation of income must begin immediately at the date of the testator's death rather than when the property is later transferred to the trust.

Even though it may not be necessary under the will to make such distinctions, the requirements of estate, inheritance, and income tax laws usually make it desirable, if not mandatory, to do so.

A simple example might help to clarify the differences between transactions affecting principal and those affecting income. Suppose an estate consists solely of non-income producing property—the decedent's residence, its furnishings, a vacant lot, and cash in the bank. If the vacant lot is sold for the amount at which it was appraised, one asset (the lot) is simply exchanged for another (cash or a receivable), and neither principal nor income is affected. If the lot is sold for more than the appraisal figure, the amount of the estate principal is increased but this has not produced income; it is just a correction of the appraisal figure. If cash is spent in paying the decedent's debts, the estate administration expenses, and so on, principal is decreased but income is not affected—such expenditures are properly considered as deductions from the estate principal rather than from income. (Obviously, in this case there is no income from which they may be deducted.)

But suppose that the residence is rented to a tenant; the rent received is income. Suppose the proceeds from the sale of the vacant lot are invested in bonds; the interest on the bonds is income though the bonds themselves remain a part of the principal.

Suppose, further, that the net income accumulates in an amount which warrants its investment, and it is invested in bonds. These bonds do not become principal, they are still a part of the assets belonging to income.

The legal theory seems to be that the principal of an estate is not a certain amount of monetary value, but is a certain group of assets which must be capable of isolation from the assets which compose the undistributed net income. These assets of the principal may change in form, or even in amount, but they always constitute the principal of the estate.

Actual separation of cash and other assets between those belonging to principal and to income is difficult, however. It will ordinarily be sufficient to keep one account for cash and one for each type of investment, and to indicate the claims of the principal and the income in the total. This can be accomplished by a carefully planned chart of ledger accounts. Those representing receipts of income minus those representing deductions from income gives the amount of the net income, which will be the amount of the assets making up this undistributed income. It is relatively unimportant just which specific assets comprise this amount, but the more liquid assets will generally be so designated—cash and any securities purchased with net income.

A device, recommended by most estate accountants as an aid in the proper segregation of principal and income, is the use of two separate ledger accounts for cash (although there is only one bank account and one checkbook). Each journal will have a pair of columns for these accounts, "Principal Cash" and "Income Cash." This forces the accountant to make a decision regarding the proper segregation of principal and income each time any receipt or disbursement is entered in the journals. It also results in the ledger accounts showing how much of the asset, cash, belongs to principal and how much belongs to income.

To summarize, the amount of the estate's net income must be carefully built up in the accounts, transactions affecting the estate principal rather than income must be recognized and excluded from income, and some way must be found of identifying the assets into which this net income has found its way.

This represents no radical change from ordinary commercial accounting; it is, rather, just a shift in emphasis. An accountant keeping this in mind should have no great trouble with estate accounting.

Items Applicable to Principal

Accountants generally think of all disbursements for expenses as being deductions from income. In estates, however, there is a certain group of expenditures which do not decrease income but which represent reductions in the principal of the estate.

This group might, as a rule, be classified as those expenditures which would be necessary even if the estate had no income whatsoever against which they might be charged. These non-income deductions are as follows:

1. The decedent's debts, expenses of his last illness, and funeral expenses.

2. The executor's fee, fees paid the estate's attorney and accountant, and all other administrative fees and expenses.

3. Federal estate tax and state inheritance tax.

4. Payments of legacies and other distributions of the principal of the estate.

All of the above expenditures, as well as any gains or losses on the sale of estate assets, are applicable to principal. It might be mentioned that there can be no such thing as any income being applicable to principal.

Items Applicable to Income

Earnings from all estate assets are applicable to income, regardless of whether the assets belong to principal or to income. Such earnings are those ordinarily thought of as being income—interest, dividends, rents, business profits, and others.

The expenses applicable to income are all those generally classed as ordinary operating expenses—office expense, repairs and maintenance, utilities, wages, property taxes, and so on.

The various accounts representing income and deductions from income would, if summarized into statement form, look very much like an ordinary profit and loss statement.

A slight difficulty might be encountered if a certain cash receipt includes both principal and income. *For example*, interest accrued to the date of death is inventoried and is a part of the estate principal. The cash receipt in payment of this interest will usually include, also, interest from the date of death to the date of payment. In this case, debit Principal Cash for the accrued portion, debit Income Cash for the portion earned after death, credit the accrual for its amount, and credit Interest Income for the balance.

Likewise, a single disbursement could include both elements. An example might be a check written in payment of a repairman's wages. The portion covering work performed prior to the decedent's death is a debit to Debts of Decedent, the remainder is a debit to Repairs Expense, Principal Cash is credited with the amount of the debt, and Income Cash is credited with the balance.

Chart of Accounts

At this point it would be well to study an illustrative chart of the accounts which might be found in an estate ledger.

A glance at the example given in Exhibit 17 will show that an estate's chart of accounts is very similar to one which any other business entity might use. The only real difference is that there are two net worth sections, one for Principal and one for Income.

Some of the individual account titles might seem unfamiliar, but these will be explained later. For the present, consider only the functions and interrelationships of the various groups of accounts shown by the chart.

The 100 series, Assets, will cause no difficulty. As with any asset section, accounts are set up for whatever property the estate owns plus any accounts expected to be needed (such as Allowance for Depreciation). The accounts may, of course, be listed in great detail or they may be condensed. *For example,* if the estate owns ten pieces of real estate, there could either be separate ledger accounts for each of the ten or one account including all of them. The only peculiarity in the asset section is the division of the usual cash account into two accounts, Principal Cash and Income Cash, as suggested earlier.

The liabilities section, 200 series, might never be used, as an estate starts out with no liabilities. In handling the business of the estate, however, some liabilities may be incurred, but these are usually current in character. Any entries to this section will be made in accordance with ordinary accounting principles.

Account number 300, Estate Principal, is the equity account, the equivalent of an investment account or a capital stock account. The concept of proprietorship is almost entirely absent in estates, and its place is taken by responsibility or accountability, the amount being determined by the adjusted balance in the Estate Principal account. It is this account which is credited with the total original amount of the estate inventory, for which the executor is accountable. Changes in the amount for which the executor is responsible are recorded through entries to the various accounts in the 400 series. These accounts include the expenses which are applicable to Principal, corrections and adjustments to the original balance, and distributions of principal. They will all finally be closed into the Estate Principal account, but this is not usually done periodically. These accounts are left open until the final closing of the books, at which time (after final distribution of the assets) they are closed into Estate Principal and should entirely eliminate the balance in the Estate Principal account. At any time prior to the final closing, the amount for which the executor is responsible to the principal beneficiaries can be determined by combining the balance in all of the 300 and 400 series accounts. The net credit balance must be supported by net assets belonging to principal.

Exhibit 17

Illustrative Chart of Accounts

Estate of Carl Davis
General Ledger Accounts

Assets:
100—Petty cash
101—Principal cash
102—Income cash
103—Notes receivable
104—Bonds
105—Interest receivable
106—Stocks
107—Real estate
108—Allowance for depreciation
109—Rent receivable
110—Partnership interest
111—Miscellaneous assets
112—
113—

Liabilities:
200—Notes payable
201—Mortgage payable
202—Payroll taxes deducted
203—
204—

Net Worth (Principal):
300—Estate principal
301—Assets not inventoried

401—Debts of decedent
402—Funeral expenses
403—Administration expenses
404—Estate and inheritance taxes
405—Gains on realization

Exhibit 17 (cont.)

Net Worth (Principal):
406—Losses on realization
407—Legacies paid
408—Distributions of principal

Net Worth (Income).
500—Estate income

600—Distributions of income

Income:
700—Interest income
701—Dividends received
702—Rental income
703—Partnership income
704—Other income
705—
706—
707—

Expenses:
800—Salaries
801—Office rent

Expenses:
802—Office expenses
803—Telephone
804—Repairs
805—Insurance
806—Utilities
807—Real estate taxes
808—Payroll taxes
809—Interest expense
810—Travel expense
811—Commissions on collections
812—Depreciation expense
813—Miscellaneous expense
814—Income taxes paid
815—
816—
817—
818—
819—
820—

The other equity, or accountability, account is Estate Income. A credit balance in this account represents the executor's responsibility to the income beneficiaries. This Estate Income account will never have an opening balance. Nothing can appear in it until income is earned. Income and the expenses applicable to income are accumulated in the accounts listed in the 700 and 800 series during each accounting period, and these accounts are closed into Estate Income at the end of each period—just as the nominal accounts of any other business are closed into Investment or Surplus periodically. If distributions are made to income beneficiaries, account number 600, Distributions of Income, is debited.

This account remains open until the final closing, but, at any time, its balance, deducted from the balance in Estate Income, represents the undistributed income for which the executor is accountable. This amount must be supported by the physical assets (frequently cash only) belonging to Income.

Just as an ordinary investment account must always match the net assets of a business, so must the two estate equity accounts always equal the estate's net assets.

Reference should be made to the Charge and Discharge Statement illustrated in Chapter 6, and it will be seen how easily the set of accounts described above will lend themselves to the preparation of such a statement, whether it be an interim statement or a final accounting.

The Bookkeeping System

A very small estate might require no formal bookkeeping system at all. If only a few cash receipts are expected during the period of administration and if only a handful of checks will be written, a simple listing of receipts and disbursements will take the place of a set of books.

Larger and more complex estates will, however, need formal accounting systems, and the style and complexity of these systems will depend on the volume and variety of transactions anticipated during administration.

The basic requirement for such a set of books is a general ledger. The accounts to be set up in this ledger should be very carefully planned with a view to the probable future transactions to be embraced by these accounts. Reference should be made to Exhibit 17 so that the account titles which are peculiar to estates will not be overlooked.

As with any accounting system, common sense and the accountant's good judgment will dictate the details of the chart of accounts finally decided on.

It might be found that subsidiary ledgers are desirable. *For example*, if the decedent owned numerous notes, mortgages, and accounts receivable, a receivables ledger would be necessary; if only two or three receivables existed, it might be more desirable simply to have a separate general ledger account for each. The same principles would apply in the case of securities, real estate, and miscellaneous assets.

As for the journals, great latitude is permitted in their design. A general journal is always desirable, however, for the entering of opening and closing entries, adjustments, corrections, and any other entries which do not readily lend themselves to columnar journals. The average medium-sized estate will usually need only one other book, a combination cash receipts and disbursements journal. The column headings for a journal of this kind might be as follows:

(Column)	(Account Number per Exhibit 17)
Date	
Payee or Explanation	
Check Number or Receipt Number	
Principal Cash—Debit	101
Principal Cash—Credit	101
Income Cash—Debit	102
Income Cash—Credit	102
Notes Receivable—Credit	103
Interest Income—Credit	700
Dividends Received—Credit	701
Rent Income—Credit	702
Other Income—Credit	704

	(Account Number per Exhibit 17)
(Column)	
Debts of Decedent—Debit	401
Administration Expenses—Debit	403
Salaries—Debit	800
Office Expenses—Debit	801
Telephone—Debit	803
Repairs—Debit	804
Insurance—Debit	805
Utilities—Debit	806
Real Estate Taxes—Debit	807
Payroll Taxes—Debit	808
Interest Expense—Debit	809
Travel Expense—Debit	810
Miscellaneous Expense—Debit	813

Other Accounts—Account Number
Other Accounts—Debit
Other Accounts—Credit

Column headings are set up for those accounts expected to be affected most frequently, of course. Entries to any other accounts will be made in the last three columns.

When the volume of transactions is very large, or when so many journal columns are needed that a combination journal would become unwieldy, this journal should be replaced by two others—a cash receipts journal and a cash disbursements journal.

The bookkeeping system described above, together with any necessary subsidiary ledgers and memorandum records, should serve for any estate, and it will be obvious that this system is basically the same as that which is used in any commercial business. The only real difference is the use of the two pairs of cash columns for the separation of principal cash and income cash instead of the usual one pair of columns.

One important fact should be kept in mind in designing the accounting system for an estate—estate books are almost invariably kept on the cash basis rather than the accrual basis, so no accounts need be set up for the many accruals usually necessary for an accrual basis commercial business.

The Accounting Period

The accounting period for an estate is a twelve-month period. The executor may elect a calendar year or a fiscal year ending on the last day of any month. Two factors might enter into the decision regarding the best fiscal year to select—the time of the year at which it will be most convenient to close the books and prepare income tax returns (natural business year) and the possible desirability of having a "short" accounting period from the date of death to the end of the first fiscal year in order to have some of the estate's income taxed in a lower bracket than if a full year's income were reported at one time.

The journals are posted to the ledger each month, of course, and the ledger is closed at the end of each accounting period, at which time all income and expense accounts are closed into Estate Income. No other accounts are closed into the two net worth accounts, however, until the final closing of the books at the termination of the estate.

In short, the rules governing an estate's accounting period are exactly the same as for a corporation.

The Opening Entry

The estate inventory is always the basis for the opening entry in the estate's books, and this entry cannot be made until the inventory is completed. This might cause a delay of several months, but in order to keep from getting far behind in the daily bookkeeping routine the journals may be started at once, delaying only their postings to the ledger until after the opening entry has been entered and posted.

The opening entry will contain a number of debits—debits for each asset shown on the inventory, after combining various items to fit into the asset accounts established in the general ledger. There will be only one credit entry, a credit to Estate Principal for the total amount of the estate as shown by the inventory. No liabilities are included in an estate inventory, so none are entered on the estate books.

(The inventory values are used in the books even though values at the later optional valuation date may be used for estate tax purposes.)

Assets Not Inventoried

Assets erroneously omitted from the estate inventory, but later discovered by the executor, must be entered in the estate books as soon as they are valued.

The credit side of this entry could be made to the Estate Principal account, as the amount of the executor's accountability has been increased, but it is considered better to credit, instead, the account Assets Not Inventoried. By handling the addition this way, the Estate Principal account will continue always to agree with the amount of the inventory originally filed with the court, and the amount of total accountability is the combined total of Estate Principal and Assets Not Inventoried.

Assets Not Inventoried will remain as an open account on the books during the entire life of the estate, and it will be closed into Estate Principal at the time of final closing of the books when the estate is terminated.

Debts of Decedent

Seldom does anyone die without owing debts of some kind, but these debts are never treated as liabilities on the estate books. They are, instead, handled on a strict cash basis, and when they are approved and paid they are charged to the account Debts of Decedent.

Care should be taken to prevent any of these debts existing at the time of death from being charged to expense accounts. They are of a different nature from expenses incurred in the operation of the estate after the decedent's death, as they are payable out of the estate's principal rather than from income.

The Debts of Decedent account is one of the several accounts, therefore, which reduce the amount of the principal for which the executor is accountable, and this account remains open on the books until it is finally closed into Estate Principal upon termination of the estate.

Funeral and Administration Expenses

An estate ledger might contain one account entitled Funeral and Administration Expenses, or, if the estate is very large, there might be one account for Funeral Expenses and others for the various administrative costs, such as Executor's Fee, Attorney and Accountant Fees, Court Costs, and others.

There is no difficulty in determining the payments to be charged to this account, but it must be remembered that, like Debts of Decedent, these charges are not expenses to be offset against the estate's income but are payable out of the estate's principal, and they reduce the amount of the executor's liability. The account itself remains open until it is closed into Estate Principal upon final closing of the estate books.

Estate and Inheritance Taxes

The Federal estate tax and state inheritance taxes paid by an estate are also considered as being payable out of the principal of the estate, and they are charged to a separate account in the group of accounts representing deductions from Estate Principal.

This account is also one of those which remain open on the books until it is finally closed into Estate Principal.

Although the Federal estate tax is always payable by the executor out of the estate assets, the applicable statutes and the decedent's will should be consulted to determine whether the executor or the beneficiaries are liable for the payment of state inheritance taxes.

If these taxes are payable by the beneficiaries out of their shares of the estate, the executor should notify the various individuals of the amount of their liability. The most practical way of handling inheritance taxes, however, is for the executor to pay these taxes and later withhold the payments from the distributions to the beneficiaries. This enables the executor to take advantage of the discount sometimes given for early filing, rather than having to wait for each beneficiary to advance his share of the tax out of his legacy.

Legacies and Distributions of Principal

Specific legacies provided for in the decedent's will are debited to the Legacies account when they are paid. Bequests of personal property other than cash are also charged to this account, and the asset account is credited, when the article is given to the named beneficiary.

Distributions of cash or other property out of the principal of the estate, whether made only at the time of final settlement or at various times during the life of the estate, are charged to the Distributions of Principal account.

The Legacies and Distributions accounts represent the portion of the executor's accountability which has been discharged. These accounts will finally total the same amount as shown in the Estate Principal account (reduced by the contraprincipal accounts for debts, administrative expenses, and the like) which will mean that the executor has completely discharged his liability. Legacies and Distributions will then be closed into Estate Principal.

Gains and Losses on Realization

The values at which the estate assets are appraised and entered on the books are merely intelligent estimates, and it is very unlikely that the actual proceeds from the sale of any asset will be exactly the same as its book value.

An account is needed, therefore, for the recording of any gains or losses on the disposition of estate assets. An account called Gains and Losses on Realization (or two accounts, one for gains and the other for losses) should be included in the estate ledger. The nature of this account is that it represents a correction to the Estate Principal account, into which it will finally be closed. A credit balance in this account means that the executor has that much greater accountability than originally shown by Estate Principal; a debit balance means that he was charged with more value than was actually in the property. The Gains and Losses on Realization account will remain open during the life of the estate for the entering of corrections in inventory valuations disclosed by any sales up to the date of final settlement.

The term "gains and losses" as used here is unfortunate because it might be misleading. From a strict estate accounting standpoint, these gains and losses have nothing to do with income or expense. As suggested above, they simply represent corrections in original valuations and do not enter into the computation of the estate's operating net income. If these entries were made directly to the Estate Principal account, their true nature would be clearer, but the books would not be so informative.

From a tax standpoint, it is only partially true that these items do not represent income or loss. Erroneous valuations disclosed by sales made up to the time of filing the estate tax return are reflected on that return by correcting the inventory valuations to show the amounts realized. There is still no taxable income or deduction caused by these "gains and losses." But property still unsold at the time of filing the *estate* tax return takes as its *income* tax basis the valuation shown thereon, with the result that later sales will usually result in gains or losses in the usual sense of the term, for income tax purposes.

But it must be remembered that, regardless of the tax treatment, only the Estate Principal, rather than Estate Income, is affected. For this reason, the Gains and Losses on Realization account will continue to be used even after the time of filing the estate tax return, and any later taxable gains or losses can be picked up out of this account in preparing the estate's income tax returns.

Income Taxes

Income taxes paid by the fiduciary on the estate's net earnings during administration are applicable to income rather than to principal—they represent a reduction in the amount for which the executor is accountable to the income beneficiaries.

It would not be improper to charge these income taxes to the Estate Income account, but income taxes are usually considered as a more direct reduction of the income to be later distributed to the income beneficiaries—more in the nature of an operating expense—and are charged to an account in the expense section of the ledger. As a result, the estate's net income, which is closed into Estate Income at the end of each accounting period, is the net income after income taxes.

A question arises as to the proper treatment of any portion of the income tax which might have been applicable to the taxable gains on realization described in the preceding section. Should this part of the tax be a charge against principal rather than income? Technically, principal should be charged, but, as a matter of practice, this question is usually ignored unless the decedent's will or state law require otherwise.

Income taxes paid by an executor in filing the decedent's final income tax return, as well as any taxes, penalties, and interest due on prior years, are not subject to the above rules. Such taxes were liabilities of the decedent at the time of death and are simply charged to Debts of Decedent on the estate books.

Business Income

If the fiduciary is authorized to continue a proprietorship business which the decedent had been operating, the net income from the business becomes income to the estate.

The accountant has the choice of incorporating the bookkeeping system of the business into the estate bookkeeping system or of continuing separate books for the business and using only a "control" account in the estate books.

Combining the two sets of books can cause numerous complications, so it is generally considered much more satisfactory to keep them separate.

The business interest will have been given an appraised valuation, along with the other estate assets, and it is this figure which will be debited to an asset account, "Business Interest," in the opening entry. At the end of each accounting period of the business, the estate will debit this asset account for the amount of the business net profit and will credit an income account for the same amount. As the estate makes periodic withdrawals of cash from the business, the Business Interest account will be credited when income cash is debited on the estate books.

The accountant should be careful to determine if the business profits credited to estate income include any capital gains. If so, this income should be segregated into its two elements, ordinary income and capital gains, for proper income tax treatment.

As for the books of the business, they should be continued just the same as before the decedent's death, with one exception. It is highly unlikely that the net worth balance at date of death, as shown by the business books, will be the same as the appraisal figure in the inventory and the estate books, but these two figures must be made to agree. To accomplish this, the book values of the businesses assets will be adjusted to the appraisal figure. This is mandatory because these new valuations become the new tax and depreciation bases for the assets.

One other point to remember is that the annual accounting period of the business must be changed to agree with that adopted by the estate, if the two are not already the same.

The above comments regarding a proprietorship interest are equally applicable to an interest in a partnership which is being continued with the estate taking the place of the deceased partner. The appraised valuation of this partnership interest is set up as an asset on the estate books; the estate's share of net profits, determined at the end of the partnership's fiscal year, is a debit to this asset account and a credit to an income account, and cash withdrawals by the estate are debited to income cash and credited to the Partnership Interest asset account.

Prior Estates

Accounting for an interest in a prior estate which is still in the process of administration can be very complex, but if this interest has been set up on the present estate's books in the proper manner, the problems will be minimized.

It was pointed out in Chapter 4 that it would be incorrect to show this interest as a lump sum figure. Rather, the various items making up this interest should be listed and valued separately, and each should occupy a separate account sheet in the estate's ledger (or be clearly identified by memoranda within one account).

Cash distributions received from the prior estate during the year must be recorded in a temporary manner, by debiting cash and crediting a suspense account, such as "Distributions from X Estate." At the end of the prior estate's fiscal year, a detailed analysis of the source of these distributions must be made.

A portion may have come from the sale of an asset; if so, that asset will be credited on the present estate's books. If capital gain or loss was involved on the sale, entry should be made to an income or expense account set up for this particular purpose, and this account should agree with the taxable gain or loss shown on the prior estate's income tax return.

If the source of some of the cash was from payments on installment obligations, there will be a credit to the asset account for both the principal and income portion of the payment, since both had to be included in the inventory figure. (*See* Chapter 13 regarding further treatment of the income portion, which is "income in respect of a decedent.")

Some of the cash was probably derived from the prior estate's net income; the present estate's share of taxable income shown by the prior estate's tax return will be credited to an income account, "Income from X Estate."

All of the above credits will be offset by a debit to the suspense account originally credited with the distributions received. It is not likely that the suspense account will be exactly balanced out by this entry, unless the prior estate happened to distribute the exact amount of its taxable income and proceeds from sales of assets, but this should cause no concern from year to year. Eventually, the final closing of the prior estate should result in the balancing out of the suspense account and the asset accounts representing the interest in that estate. If not, this will simply mean that the appraisal figures were incorrect and any balances will be closed into the Gains and Losses on Realization account.

If the two estates have different fiscal years, the principles regarding a partnership year ending within a partner's tax year will be followed; the analysis of the prior estate's distributions will be made as of the end of that estate's fiscal year and recorded as of that date on the present estate's books.

Depreciation

Depreciable assets of estate are subject to depreciation, and this must be provided for in the accounts.

The depreciation basis for each asset is its newly acquired inventory valuation, regardless of its original cost or its book value at the date of death. An exception to this rule is that if the alternate valuation date is used for estate tax purposes, the values so reported as of that date will be the proper values for depreciation purposes.

The usual depreciation rules regarding asset life, salvage value, first year depreciation, and so on will be followed.

Depreciation expense is generally a charge against the estate's income, even though the depreciable assets belong to the estate principal.

The decedent's will and local law should be studied carefully for any instructions regarding depreciation. It is not uncommon for these to govern, to some extent, the proper treatment of depreciation in the accounts and particularly its proper income tax treatment. As a general rule, the income tax deduction for depreciation must be apportioned between the fiduciary and the income beneficiaries on the basis of income allocable to each.

Accounting for Liabilities

It was pointed out earlier that liablitites existing at the time of the decedent's death are not recorded on the estate books—they are handled strictly on a cash basis and are recorded only when paid, by a debit to Debts of Decedent.

Since estate accounting is usually on a cash basis, there is seldom any need for liability accounts on the estate books, except possibly for those of a very current nature, such as payroll tax deductions.

This raises the question of how to account for any mortgages, installment notes, or other long-term liabilities existing at the decedent's death. These can be accounted for only by memorandum records. There should certainly be a record of each liability, and memo entries should be made to this record for each periodic payment (excluding interest). A convenient form for these records is to have an ordinary account sheet for each such liability and to place it in a separate section of the estate ledger—flagged in some way to prevent it from being included in a trial balance of the ledger.

The executor is, in a few cases, authorized to mortgage the estate property or to otherwise borrow money in the name of the estate. In the event of any such liabilities arising after the decedent's death, these liabilities must be recorded on the estate books, and their treatment will follow general accounting rules.

Closing the Estate Books

The annual closing of the estate books is very simple. No adjustments for accruals are necessary; generally the only entry is one to close all the income and expense accounts into the Estate Income account.

The final closing, upon termination of the estate, will consist of only three basic entries—an entry closing all income and expense accounts into Estate Income, an entry closing Distributions of Income into Estate Income, and one closing all of the accounts representing adjustments to and deductions from principal into the Estate Principal account.

Theoretically, if all of the estate assets and earnings have been distributed to the beneficiaries, these three entries will result in the balancing of every account in the estate ledger.

The estate assets may or may not have been reduced to cash for final distribution. If property other than cash is included in this distribution, such property is usually credited for its book value and the distribution account is debited. A slight difficulty may arise when local law permits or requires the executor to distribute the assets at their market value at date of distribution. If this is done, another account should be set up, "Gains and Losses on Distribution." Each asset will be adjusted to its market value through this new account, which will then be closed into Estate Principal.

It frequently happens that the estate assets are transferred to a trust at the end of the administrative period. Each asset so transferred will be credited, and a new account, in the name of the trustee, will be charged with the transfer. All accounts will then be closed except this new account with the trustee and the Estate Principal account. The final entry will be to close these two accounts together, and the amount of this entry will represent the total responsibility and accountability which the trustee is taking over from the executor.

The books for the successor trust, or any trust for that matter, can be set up and operated in very much the same way as described for an estate; the concept of responsibility and accountability applies to a trustee in the same way as to an executor, and the segregation of principal and income is as important in a trust as in an estate.

9

Estate and Inheritance
Tax Returns

The preparation of correct estate and inheritance tax returns is one of the most formidable hurdles facing the estate executor, his accountant, and his attorney, and the payment of the taxes shown by these returns usually requires by far the largest cash expenditures to be provided for during the administrative period.

The great importance of these taxes in the total estate administration picture makes a thorough knowledge of the theory and details of estate taxation necessary for anyone concerned with the administration of an estate.

This knowledge is also important to the person engaged in planning an estate, because practically all planning technics must be evaluated in the light of their tax consequences. Estate planning is outside the scope of this book, but it will be found that many of the decisions regarding the operation of an estate during administration will also be based on whether or not they will save estate taxes. This is known as postmortem estate planning.

The Theory of Estate Taxation

The Federal estate tax is an excise tax, levied upon the transfer of the decedent's taxable estate at his death.

The estate tax is neither a property tax nor an inheritance tax. It is not imposed on any particular property, legacy, devise, or distributive share. It is not imposed on any recipient of the property. It is a tax on a person's right to transmit property at death and is measured by the value of the taxable estate that came into being by reason of death. To prevent undue avoidance, the tax also reaches back to certain transfers made by the decedent during his lifetime—transfers which are deemed to be in lieu of disposition by will, such as a gift made in contemplation of death.

The constitutionality of the tax was long ago upheld when the claim was made that it constituted an interference with the rights of the state to regulate descent and distribution, and was an intrusion of the processes of the states.

How the Tax Works

Since the tax is levied on no specific property and on no individual, it is payable out of the gross assets of the estate, and it is the responsibility of the fiduciary to see that it is paid.

The estate tax accrues at the instant of the decedent's death, but the executor is allowed a grace period of nine months within which to file the required return and pay the tax.

In computing the tax, the provisions of the taxing statute in effect at the time of death will be applied, not those in effect at the time of payment. The tax liability generates from death, so the date of death determines the applicable law.

Estates Subject to the Tax

The estate tax law provides for a specific exemption of $60,000, so no estate valued at less than that amount will be taxable, and no return is required.

The law also provides for certain deductions from the gross estate; therefore, if these deductions plus the specific exemption equal or exceed the gross estate, there is no taxable estate and no tax.

The above exemption applies only to the estate of a citizen or resident of the United States. A citizen is a person who was born in the United States, who was naturalized in the United States, or who was given citizenship by treaty or Act of Congress. A resident is one who was residing in the United States at the time of his death, provided this was the place he indicated as his permanent home.

The specific exemption for a nonresident alien is only $30,000. If this decedent's gross estate situated in the United States exceeds $30,000, the estate may be subject to tax. There are a number of special rules applicable to the taxation of estates of nonresident aliens; these will not be covered in this book, but the applicable sections of the law should be studied in these cases.

There is a special exemption for estates of members of the armed forces of the United States dying during an induction period or as a result of wounds or disease suffered in a combat zone, but this exemption is in the form of a special reduction in the estate tax rather than a change in the specific exemption mentioned above. (See Reg. 20.2201-1.)

The Estate Tax Return

A return on Form 706 must be filed for the estate of every citizen or resident of the United States whose *gross* estate exceeded $60,000 in value at the date of death. The value of the gross estate at the date of death governs the filing of the return, even though the executor may elect the alternate valuation date for the reporting of asset valuations. (Form 706 NA must be used for a nonresident alien.)

Form 706 is a sixteen-page return which provides schedules for the listing of all taxable property of the estate, all deductions allowed by statute, the computation of the tax, credits against the tax, and so forth.

This return must be signed by the executor and by the attorney or agent who prepared it, and it must be filed, within nine months after death (fifteen months for estates of decedents dying before January 1, 1971), with the Internal Revenue Service Center for the district in which the decedent had his domicile at the time of his death. (Or it may be hand carried to the office of the District Director.)

If the decedent died testate, a certified copy of the will must be filed with the return.

Computation of the Estate Tax

The estate tax is imposed at the graduated rates shown in Exhibit 18, upon the net value of the taxable estate transferred.

The steps in arriving at the amount of the tax are as follows:

1. Determine the total value of the gross estate at date of death (or the alternate valuation date). The various types of property included in gross estate and their valuations were discussed in the chapters on estate inventory.

2. Deduct from the value of the gross estate the statutory deductions for debts, expenses, losses, and other items discussed in Chapter 10, and the marital deduction explained in Chapter 11.

3. Figure the amount of tax on the net taxable estate, after deductions, by applying the rates given in the estate tax rate table.

4. Deduct from the tax so determined the tax credits permitted by law, which are discussed in Chapter 12.

The result is the amount of the federal estate tax due.

Liability for Payment of the Estate Tax

The Internal Revenue Code provides that the executor shall pay the estate tax. This duty applies to the entire tax, even though the gross taxable estate may consist in part of property which does not come into his possession.

Exhibit 18

Computation of Gross Estate Tax			
Taxable estate equal to or more than—	Taxable estate less than—	Tax on amount in column (1)	Rate of tax on excess over amount in column (1)
(1)	(2)	(3)	(4)
			(*Percent*)
0	$5,000	0	3
$5,000	10,000	$150	7
10,000	20,000	500	11
20,000	30,000	1,600	14
30,000	40,000	3,000	18
40,000	50,000	4,800	22
50,000	60,000	7,000	25
60,000	100,000	9,500	28
100,000	250,000	20,700	30
250,000	500,000	65,700	32
500,000	750,000	145,700	35
750,000	1,000,000	233,200	37
1,000,000	1,250,000	325,700	39
1,250,000	1,500,000	423,200	42
1,500,000	2,000,000	528,200	45
2,000,000	2,500,000	753,200	49
2,500,000	3,000,000	998,200	53
3,000,000	3,500,000	1,263,200	56
3,500,000	4,000,000	1,543,200	59
4,000,000	5,000,000	1,838,200	63
5,000,000	6,000,000	2,468,200	67
6,000,000	7,000,000	3,138,200	70
7,000,000	8,000,000	3,838,200	73
8,000,000	10,000,000	4,568,200	76
10,000,000	----------	6,088,200	77

If there is no duly qualified executor or administrator, anyone in actual or constructive possession of the property is liable for the payment of the tax to the extent of the value of such property in his possession.

The Code further provides that an executor who pays any of the estate's debts, or who distributes any portion of the estate, before paying the Federal estate tax shall be personally liable for the tax to the extent of the assets which came into his possession.

In the absence of any provision of the local law, the estate tax is usually payable out of the residuary estate, but a number of the states have laws providing for the allocation of death taxes among the beneficiaries, unless otherwise directed by the decedent's will. State law should be studied for the proper answer to this question.

Upon payment of the estate tax and its examination and acceptance by the Internal Revenue Service, the executor should request the District Director to send him a written discharge from personal liability in connection with this tax.

It should be remembered that certain U.S. Treasury Bonds may be redeemed at par in the payment of estate taxes, even though their cost or present market value is much lower. This can result in a substantial saving, in spite of the fact that bonds so used must be included in gross estate at the higher of par or market value.

The executor may also make written application to the District Director at the time of filing the return, requesting a determination of the tax and discharge from personal liability for it. Within one year after receipt of the application, the executor will be notified of the amount of the tax and will be discharged upon payment of it. In estates of decedents dying after December 31, 1973, the one-year waiting period for a personal discharge is shortened to nine months.

Refunds of Tax from Beneficiaries

Although the estate tax must be paid by the executor out of the estate assets in his possession, there are two instances in which he is given the right to recover, for the estate, from others, a portion of the tax he paid.

First, any beneficiary of a life insurance policy on the decedent's life (other than the estate itself) may be required to pay a proportionate part of the estate tax unless there is a testamentary direction to the contrary. The executor can recover from the beneficiary such portion of the tax paid as the proceeds of the policy bear to the sum of the taxable estate and the amount of the exemption allowed.

Second, unless the will directs otherwise, if any part of the gross estate on which the tax has been paid consists of the value of property over which the decedent had a power of appointment, the executor may recover from the person receiving such property the proportionate part of the estate tax attributable to the inclusion of this property in the gross estate.

Theory of the Inheritance Tax

An inheritance tax is a tax levied against the property passing from a decedent to a beneficiary, and it is payable by the beneficiary out of his distributive share rather than out of the general estate assets.

The various State inheritance tax laws differ, but they generally tax the decedent's real property only in the state where it is situated, the personal property of a resident wherever it is situated.

As with the Federal estate tax, the first step is a listing of all assets of the gross estate subject to the particular state's inheritance tax. From this total certain deductions are permitted, similar to those allowed under the Federal law. A listing is then made of the various beneficiaries and of the various shares of this net estate that each will receive.

The laws then usually provide for an exemption for each beneficiary against his share, the amount of the exemption often depending on his relationship to the decedent, with the closer relatives being favored.

Each person's distributive share after exemption is then subjected to the inheritance tax, at the rates fixed by law—usually progressive in nature.

Differences in Estate and Inheritance Taxes

The estate tax is a Federal tax; inheritance taxes are levied only by the various states.

They are different in nature in that the estate tax is levied on the *transfer* of the property, the inheritance tax on the *property* itself.

The greatest difference, therefore, is that each beneficiary must give up a part of his distributive share in payment of the inheritance tax, but only the residuary beneficiary suffers from the imposition of the estate tax. However, many states have enacted special legislation providing for the allocation of both State and Federal death taxes among the beneficiaries. (But the decedent's will may provide that both taxes shall be paid by the estate rather than by individual beneficiaries.).

In spite of the difference in the theory of the two death taxes, the actual reporting of the two has many similarities, and it is well to prepare both returns at the same time and to cross-check one against the other, reconciling the net taxable estate as shown by each.

A particular state's laws will have to be studied to determine the details wherein its definitions of gross estate, deductions, and of other items differ from Federal law, but there are several fairly general differences which should not be overlooked, such as:

1. The proceeds of insurance policies on the decedent's life, payable to named beneficiaries other than the estate, are generally excluded from inheritance tax gross estate.

2. Curtesy and dower rights are usually not taxed by the states.

3. The state in which the decedent's property is located governs its inheritance taxability. (Inheritance tax returns might have to be filed in several different states if the decedent owned property in more than one state.)

4. Lifetime transfers and powers of appointment are not always taxed by the state laws.

5. State laws sometimes limit the amount deductible for funeral expenses and various other expenditures.

6. The Federal law allows a *credit* for state death taxes; state laws generally allow a *deduction* for a proportionate part of the Federal tax, based on the portion of the gross estate located in the taxing state.

7. The Federal estate tax return is due to be filed within nine months after death; the due dates for state returns vary, with a cash discount sometimes being offered for early filing. (If the tax is not determinable by the discount date, the payment of an estimated amount is permissible.)

These or any other differences must be searched for in the state law. The time spent will be well spent, because state laws are generally a little more lenient than the Federal law.

Liability for Payment of Inheritance Taxes

Inheritance taxes attach to the property transferred and usually constitute a lien on the property until paid. The recipient of the property is, therefore, primarily liable for the tax, but this liability is most often shifted to the executor by statute—to the extent of the property passing through his administration.

The executor must file the proper tax return with the state and pay the assessed tax. He may then recover the tax from the various devisees and legatees. The tax paid on real estate will be collected from those who took possession of it. The tax paid on a legacy should simply be deducted from the amount due to the legatee, except that the tax on a legacy paid in property other than cash must be collected from the legatee.

Relationship of Gift Tax to Estate Tax

The Federal gift tax is not often a vital concern of the person engaged in estate administration, but because of its close relationship to the estate tax a brief discussion of the gift tax might be well at this point.

The purpose of the gift tax law is to impose a tax on gifts of property made by a living person, in order to compensate for the estate tax which would have been payable on the property if it had not been given away and had remained a part of the estate at death.

An estate can be completely depleted by gifts before death, but the gift tax is a deterrent to this action, being primarily a partial substitute for the estate tax in such cases.

On the other hand, gifts are an effective device in estate planning because the resulting tax is generally substantially less than the estate tax would be. This is true because, first, the rates are only 75 per cent as high as estate tax rates and, second, because of the exemption and exclusions permitted. (*See* Exhibit 19.)

The specific exemption is $30,000, which everyone is allowed to give away during his lifetime without becoming liable for the tax. Besides this, everyone can make, each year, gifts of $3,000 or less to as many different donees as he desires without being taxed. If no one individual is given more than $3,000 in any one calendar year, there is no tax. This is the annual exclusion.

A husband and wife can elect to treat all gifts made by either during any quarter as though they were made one-half by each. One-half of the gift will be taxed to the donor, one-half to the husband or wife, and this has the effect of doubling the annual exclusion and the specific exemption.

The quarterly gift tax return, Form 709, is due to be filed within one and one-half months after the end of the calendar quarter in which the gifts were made. (Gifts made before 1971 were reported on an annual basis.)

Because of the lifetime exemption, the computation of the gift tax for any period must be made on a cumulative basis, taking into consideration the gifts made in all

Exhibit 19

Table for Computation of Gift Tax

(A) Amount of taxable gifts equaling—	(B) Amount of taxable gifts not exceeding—	Tax on amount in column (A)	Rate of tax on excess over amount in column (A)
			Percent
----------	$5,000	----------	2 ¼
$5,000	10,000	$112.50	5 ¼
10,000	20,000	375.00	8 ¼
20,000	30,000	1,200.00	10 ½
30,000	40,000	2,250.00	13 ½
40,000	50,000	3,600.00	16 ½
50,000	60,000	5,250.00	18 ¾
60,000	100,000	7,125.00	21
100,000	250,000	15,525.00	22 ½
250,000	500,000	49,275.00	24
500,000	750,000	109,275.00	26 ¼
750,000	1,000,000	174,900.00	27 ¾
1,000,000	1,250,000	244,275.00	29 ¼
1,250,000	1,500,000	317,400.00	31 ½
1,500,000	2,000,000	396,150.00	33 ¾
2,000,000	2,500,000	564,900.00	36 ¾
2,500,000	3,000,000	748,650.00	39 ¾
3,000,000	3,500,000	947,400.00	42
3,500,000	4,000,000	1,157,400.00	44 ¼
4,000,000	5,000,000	1,378,650.00	47 ¼
5,000,000	6,000,000	1,851,150.00	50 ¼
6,000,000	7,000,000	2,353,650.00	52 ½
7,000,000	8,000,000	2,878,650.00	54 ¾
8,000,000	10,000,000	3,426,150.00	57
10,000,000	----------	4,566,150.00	57 ¾

prior quarters. The rate of tax on gifts in any particular quarter is determined by the aggregate sum of the taxable gifts for preceding years, or quarters.

This, very briefly, is the operation of the gift tax. Of concern to the estate administrator is the fact that even though legitimate gifts were made by the decedent before his death and the proper gift tax paid, the gift property is not necessarily excluded from the gross estate for estate tax purposes. This was explained earlier, when it was pointed out that certain lifetime gifts, such as gifts in contemplation of death, must still be considered a part of the taxable estate.

Will such transfers, then, be subject to both the gift tax paid before death and the estate tax later payable? The answer is that both taxes must be paid, but a credit is allowed against the estate tax for the amount of the gift tax paid on any gift property later held to be includible in gross estate.

The executor should make a review of the decedent's gifts for as many years back as possible. If taxable gifts are found and if gift tax returns were not filed, he should file these delinquent returns and pay the tax, a debt of the decedent.

The Gross Estate

With the foregoing general information about the estate tax in mind, the executor and his accountant should now proceed to prepare the estate tax return itself.

The first step is to refer to the estate inventory and to fill in, from the inventory, each of the schedules on the return wherein the various items of gross estate are to be listed.

The assets to be included and their proper valuations at the date of death were covered in detail in Chapters 3 and 4, to which the reader should refer and follow as a check list in completing the gross estate schedules in the Form 706.

It was suggested in Chapter 3 that all assets owned by the decedent at the time of his death should be included in the inventory and appraisal, because all of them are a part of the *taxable* estate, even though certain assets, such as real estate, life insurance proceeds, and others, might not be a part of the *administrable* estate. Since different assets constitute the estate for different purposes, it seems best to inventory and evaluate *every* asset so that the inventory will contain the complete information needed for *any* purpose.

If this suggestion was followed, all of the asset schedules on the estate tax return can be completed from the information in the inventory, with one exception—the property *not* owned by the decedent at death which might still be a part of the taxable estate, such as certain lifetime transfers, gifts in contemplation of death, and so on.

The Alternate Valuation

The executor's option to use an alternate valuation date instead of the date of death for estate tax purposes was explained in Chapter 2.

If this option is exercised, the schedules on the tax return must not only show the values at date of death but must include, for each item, a brief explanation of the status or disposition governing the subsequent valuation date, such as, "Not disposed of within six months following death," "Distributed," or "Sold," together with the proper valuation date for each and the proper valuation as of that date.

This election need not be made until the return is filed, and is made on the return itself.

The method of entering the required information on the tax return, using either the date of death valuation or the alternate valuation, is illustrated in Exhibit 20.

Exhibit 20

Examples showing use of Schedule A

Example where the alternate valuation is not adopted; date of death, January 1, 1972

Item number	Description	Alternate valuation date	Alternate value	Value at date of death
1	House and lot, 1921 William Street NW., Washington, D.C. (lot 6, square 481). Rent of $900 due at end of each quarter, February 1, May 1, August 1, and November 1. Value based on appraisal, copy of which is attached			36,000
	Rent due on item 1 for quarter ending November 1, 1971, but not collected at date of death			900
	Rent accrued on item 1 for November and December 1971			600
2	House and lot, 304 Jefferson Street, Alexandria, Va. (lot 18, square 40). Rent of $100 payable monthly. Value based on appraisal, copy of which is attached			12,000
	Rent due on item 2 for December 1971, but not collected at date of death			100

Example where the alternate valuation is adopted; date of death, January 1, 1972

Item number	Description	Alternate valuation date	Alternate value	value at date of death
1	House and lot, 1921 William Street NW., Washington, D.C. (lot 6, square 481). Rent of $900 due at end of each quarter, February 1, May 1, August 1, and November 1. Value based on appraisal, copy of which is attached. Not disposed of within six months following death	7/1/72	30,000	36,000
	Rent due on item 1 for quarter ending November 1, 1971, but not collected until February 1, 1972	2/1/72	900	900
	Rent accrued on item 1 for November and December 1971, collected on February 1, 1972	2/1/72	600	600
2	House and lot, 304 Jefferson Street, Alexandria, Va. (lot 18, square 40). Rent of $100 payable monthly. Value based on appraisal, copy of which is attached. Property exchanged for farm on May 1, 1972	5/1/72	10,000	12,000
	Rent due on item 2 for December 1971, but not collected until February 1, 1972	2/1/72	100	100

10

Estate Tax
Deductions— General

The Federal estate tax law permits a number of deductions from the gross estate to arrive at the amount of the taxable estate.

Schedules are provided on the Estate Tax Return, Form 706, for itemizing the various deductions permitted by law, and these schedules should be carefully completed after the items constituting the decedent's gross estate have been entered on the return.

This chapter and Chapter 11 contain a discussion of the deductions which may be claimed and should serve as a check list to prevent the overlooking of any deduction which would reduce the taxable estate and the estate tax.

Types of Deductions Permitted

The taxable estate of a decedent is the excess of his gross estate over the sum of the following items:

1. The statutory specific exemption of $60,000 ($30,000 for a nonresident alien).
2. Funeral expenses and administration expenses.
3. The decedent's debts and other claims against the estate.
4. Losses from casualty or theft sustained by the estate during its administration.
5. Transfers to charitable and similar organizations.
6. The marital deduction.

These are the only items deductible in computing the taxable estate. This listing should be considered only as a general classification, however, because the law includes many conditions and limitations, which will be explained in the following discussions of specific items.

Property Subject to Claims

As a general rule, the debts and expenses included in the above listing are deductible only to the extent that they are payable out of the "property subject to claims," meaning the property coming into the executor's hands as a part of the administrable estate, and they are deductible only to the extent that their payment is authorized by the laws of the jurisdiction under which the estate is being administered.

A special provision, however, permits the deduction of expenses incurred in administering property which is *not* subject to claims but which is included in the gross estate for tax purposes, such as real estate passing directly to the heirs, life insurance proceeds payable to named beneficiaries, and others. But these expenses are deductible only if they *would be* allowed as deductions if the property *were* subject to claims and only if they are actually paid within three years after the due date for filing the estate tax return.

Whether property included in the gross estate should be considered as property subject to claims depends entirely on the applicable state law. Since expenses in connection with both types of property are generally deductible under present law, however, the distinction is not often of great importance except for the fact that the estate tax return does include a separate schedule for the listing of expenses incurred in administering property not subject to claims.

Time Limits for Payment of Expenses

The time limit within which expenses must be paid to be allowable as deductions falls into three categories.

First, as a general rule, the right to deduct a debt or expense does not depend on its actual payment; there is no time limitation. *For example*, a valid and allowable debt of the decedent may not become due until years after his death, but it may still be used as a deduction in computing the taxable estate.

Second, an exception to the above rule provides that if the decedent's debts, expenses, and so forth add up to more than the amount of the "property subject to claims," the excess (paid out of property not subject to claims) must be paid by the due date for filing the estate tax return—nine months after death plus any extension granted.

Third, expenses incurred in administering property not subject to claims must be paid within three years after the due date for filing the return, as explained in the preceding section.

Funeral Expenses

Expenses of the decedent's funeral are allowable as deductions to the extent that they were actually paid, within the proper time limit, but they must be reduced by any reimbursement such as death benefits payable by the Social Security Administration.

In addition to the actual expense of the funeral, there may be deducted in this category a reasonable expenditure for a tombstone, monument, or mausoleum, or for a burial lot, either for the decedent or his family, provided that such expenses are allowable under local law. There may also be deducted the cost of transportation of a person bringing the body to the place of burial.

A reasonable expenditure paid for the perpetual care of a cemetery lot or mausoleum is also deductible, if allowable under local law.

Administration Expenses

The amounts deductible as administration expenses are limited to such expenses as are actually and necessarily incurred in the administration of the estate, that is, in the collection of assets, payment of debts, and distribution of the property to the beneficiaries.

Expenditures which are not essential to the proper administration of the estate but are incurred for the individual benefit of the heirs, legatees, or devisees, may not be taken as deductions.

The administration expenses include the executor's fee, the attorney's fee, and a number of miscellaneous expenses of administration.

It is not necessary that these expenses be paid before filing the tax return (unless subject to the time limits mentioned earlier) or that they be formally allowed by the court. If, at the time of filing the return, they may reasonably be expected to be paid, they should be entered as deductions. The tax return requires that the amounts listed be described either as "paid," "estimated," or "agreed upon."

The Executor's Fee

The principal administrative expense is usually the executor's fee, or commission, and it may be claimed as a deduction from gross estate to the extent that it is within the amount allowable by the local law. If it exceeds the state's fee schedule, the return should be accompanied by proof that it has been allowed by the court having jurisdiction over the estate.

It often happens that the amount of the executor's commission is not known at the time of filing the estate tax return; the probable duration and the exact nature of his services may not be foreseeable. In these cases, a deduction should still be claimed for the amount reasonably expected to be paid. By the time of final audit of the return, the amount may have been established. If not, the Commissioner will still allow the deduction if it is reasonably certain that it will be paid and if it does not exceed the legal amount. But this allowance continues to be tentative, and if the amount is later found to be incorrect the executor must notify the District Director and pay the tax difference with interest.

If the executor waives his commission, there is no deduction. If the decedent's will specified that the executor should serve without compensation, there is no deduction. If the executor is given a bequest in lieu of commission, there is no deduction.

An executor's commission is taxable income to the recipient, but a bequest or legacy is not; the comparative tax advantages for estate and income tax purposes should be considered by an executor who is also the residuary legatee. He may find it advantageous to increase his legacy by waiving his fee.

The Attorney's Fee

A deduction should be claimed for the amount of the attorney's fee actually paid, or an amount which at the time of filing may reasonably be expected to be paid.

If, when the return is finally audited, the fees have not yet been awarded by the court and paid, they will still be allowed if the Commissioner believes that they will be paid and that they are reasonable for the services rendered, taking into account the size and character of the estate and the local law and practice.

The deduction for fees still unpaid at the time of final audit must be supported by an affidavit, or statement signed under the penalties of perjury, of the executor or attorney stating that such amount has been agreed upon and will be paid.

The deductible fees are only those incurred for the benefit of the estate. They do not include fees incurred by beneficiaries incident to litigation as to their respective interests.

Miscellaneous Administration Expenses

In addition to the executor's and attorney's fees, administration expenses may include the fee of the estate's accountant, court costs, surrogates' fees, appraisers' fees, clerk hire, and any other necessary expenses of preserving and distributing the estate, including the cost of storing or maintaining the property of the estate.

A brokerage fee for selling property of the estate is deductible if the sale is necessary in order to pay the debts or other expenses or to effect distribution. Auctioneers' fees and other expenses of such a sale are also deductible.

As in the case of the fees of the executor and attorney, other administrative expenses are deductible only if they relate to the administration and settlement of the estate.

Claims Against the Estate

Deductible claims are those which represent personal obligations of the decedent existing at the time of his death. Only those claims enforceable against the estate are deductible, and only interest accrued at the date of death is allowable, even though the alternate valuation date is used.

Claims against the estate must be itemized in the schedule, "Debts of Decedent and Mortgages and Liens." If the amount of the debt is disputed or the subject of litigation, only such amount may be deducted as the estate concedes to be a valid claim.

The deduction for a claim is limited to the extent that the liability was contracted bona fide and for an adequate and full consideration in money or money's worth (except a charitable pledge).

Typical claims to be deducted as debts might include unsecured notes, property taxes accrued prior to death, income taxes on income received during the decedent's lifetime, gift taxes due on lifetime gifts, claims for services rendered or materials furnished, the balance due on a contract for the purchase of property, alimony decreed by a court but past due, amounts due on judgments against the decedent, checks written by the decedent but not paid by the bank before his death, and any other such obligation of the decedent which existed at the time of his death.

The executor has an option in reporting medical expenses of the decedent paid by the estate within one year after death—they may be deducted as debts of the decedent on the estate tax return *or* as medical expenses on the decedent's final income tax return, whichever produces the greater tax saving.

Charitable Pledges

A pledge made by the decedent for charitable or similar purposes is also deductible as a debt of the decedent, whether evidenced by a promissory note or otherwise, provided it is enforceable against the estate.

In such instances, the consideration requirements are waived, and the deduction will be allowed to the extent that the debt would have been deductible if it constituted a charitable bequest.

Mortgages and Liens

If property included in the gross estate is subject to a mortgage or other indebtedness, a deduction may be claimed for the unpaid amount, as well as for interest accrued on the mortgage up to the date of death.

If the decedent's estate, as a whole, is liable for the payment of the mortgage, the gross appraised value of the mortgaged property is listed as an asset of the estate and the amount of the mortgage is shown as a deduction in the schedule, "Debts of Decedent and Mortgages and Liens."

If, however, the obligation is collectible only against specific property, it should not be shown as a separate deduction but should be deducted from the value of the mortgaged property, and only the net value of the property will be listed as an asset. The tax effect is the same under either treatment, but the official instructions require the difference in handling.

In no case may the deduction exceed the amount which was contracted bona fide and for an adequate and full consideration.

Real estate situated outside the United States does not form a part of gross estate, unless the decedent died after July 1, 1964, so no deduction may be taken for any indebtedness on such property.

Deduction for Taxes

Some of the taxes paid by an estate are allowed as deductions from gross estate, others are not. The several kinds of taxes must, therefore, be considered individually.

Property taxes are deductible if they accrued before the decedent's death. The term "accrued" is not to be used in the accounting sense. Rather, the taxes must have been an enforceable obligation of the decedent at the time of his death, in which case the entire amount is deductible; no apportionment is required. If the tax did not become a lien on the property before death, no part of it may be deducted.

Death taxes, including the Federal estate tax, foreign death taxes, and state inheritance taxes, are not deductible (with one exception), but, as distinguished from their *nondeductibility,* state and foreign death taxes are to some extent allowed as a *credit* against the Federal estate tax. (*See* Chapter 12.)

The exception is that a deduction is allowed for the amount of any *state* death tax imposed on a charitable transfer, provided the resulting decrease in the Federal estate tax inures solely to the benefit of the charitable transferee (*for example*, when the charity is the residuary legatee). This deduction is optional with the executor, because it is possible that the taking of the deduction, which affects the credit for state death taxes, might actually produce a larger estate tax. The option must be exercised by filing a written notice with the District Director.The regulations, which give five examples, should be studied if this election is being considered.

Gift taxes which are due and payable on gifts made by the decedent during his lifetime are deductible, and a tax credit is also allowable if these gift taxes are due as a result of gifts which are also included in the gross estate for estate tax purposes.

Excise taxes incurred in selling property of an estate are deductible as an expense of administration if the sale is necessary in order to pay the decedent's debts, administration expenses, or taxes, to preserve the estate, or to effect distribution.

Income taxes are deductible only if they are on income properly includible in an income tax return of the decedent for a period before his death. Taxes on income received after death are not deductible. Interest on income taxes is limited to the amount accrued up to the date of death.

If income received by a decedent before his death is included in a joint income tax return (filed by the decedent and his spouse or by the estate and the surviving spouse), only the decedent's portion of the joint tax is deductible. This portion is computed on the basis of what the husband and wife would have been liable for if they had filed separate returns. The deductible amount equals,

$$\frac{\text{decedent's separate tax}}{\text{both separate taxes}} \times \text{joint tax}$$

This amount must, however, be reduced by any payments which the decedent had already made on the joint liability, and it cannot exceed any amount agreed upon (between the spouses or between the surviving spouse and the estate) as being the amount to be contributed by the estate toward the joint liability.

Deduction for Losses

A deduction may be taken for losses from fires, storm, shipwrecks, other casualties, or theft incurred during the settlement of the estate. If the loss was fully covered by insurance, however, there is no deduction; if it was only partially compensated for, the excess of the loss over the compensation is deductible.

Losses occurring in connection with assets after their distribution may not be claimed as a deduction.

Charitable Transfers

A deduction from the gross estate is allowed for the value of property transferred by the decedent's will for public, charitable, religious, educational, or other certain uses. Such transfers are also deductible if made during the decedent's lifetime but considered a part of his gross estate, such as a charitable transfer in contemplation of death.

The deduction may never exceed the value at which the transferred property is included in the gross estate.

The Code specifies that the deduction will be allowed only for transfers to or for the use of:

1. The United States, any State, Territory, any political subdivision thereof, or the District of Columbia, for exclusively public purposes;

2. Any corporation or association organized and operated exclusively for religious, charitable, scientific, literary, or educational purposes (including the encouragement of art and the prevention of cruelty to children or animals), if no part of the net earnings of the corporation or association inures to the benefit of any private stockholder or individual (other than as a legitimate object of such purposes), and no substantial part of

its activities is carrying on propaganda, or otherwise attempting to influence legislation;

3. A trustee or trustees, or a fraternal society, order, or association operating under the lodge system, if the transferred property is to be used exclusively for religious, charitable, scientific, literary, or educational purposes (or for the prevention of cruelty to children or animals), and if no substantial part of the activities of such transferee is carrying on propaganda, or otherwise attempting to influence legislation; or

4. Any veterans' organization incorporated by Act of Congress, or of any of its departments, local chapters, or posts, no part of the net earnings of which inures to the benefit of any private shareholder or individual.   .

The deduction is not limited by any percentage limitations such as are applicable under the income tax law.

When a portion of the estate falls into a charitable bequest because of a disclaimer (an absolute and unqualified refusal) by any person entitled to the property under the will, this property becomes a charitable transfer just as if it had been left to the charity by will. The disclaimer should be filed in the probate court before the time of filing the estate tax return.

Property includible in the estate under a power of appointment and which passes to a charitable beneficiary is considered to be a charitable transfer of the decedent. Also, a deduction may be allowed for property transferred in trust with income for life to a spouse who is over eighty and who has a power of appointment over the principal of the trust, provided the spouse makes an affidavit of intent to exercise the power in favor of a charity; this affidavit must be made within six months of the decedent's death and filed with the estate tax return.

When the charitable bequest is an outright transfer of specific property or of a sum certain in money, out of which no death taxes are required to be paid, the determination of the charitable deduction is a simple matter; it is the amount of money or the value at which the property was included in the gross estate.

Very often, however, a bequest will be reduced by Federal or state death taxes, or both, before it reaches the charitable beneficiary. This is particularly true in the case of residuary legacies, which are certain to bear the brunt of at least a part of these death taxes. Since the law makes it clear that only the net transfer received by the charity (after deducting such taxes) will be allowed as a deduction, the correct amount of the deduction may be difficult to determine.

In these cases, the amount the charity will receive depends on the amount of the tax, but the amount of the tax will also depend on the amount of the deduction for the net transfer. The computation of these two unknowns must be made either by use of an algebraic formula or by a series of trial-and-error computations. If, in addition, interdependent Federal and state taxes are involved, the computation becomes highly complicated. Examples of methods of computation in these cases are contained in the supplemental instructions to the estate tax return.

Another situation which causes difficulty in determining the amount of the charitable deduction is caused by property being left in trust for the benefit of certain persons for life, with remainders to charity.

No deduction is allowed for the bequest of a charitable remainder unless the remainder interest is in a farm or personal residence or is a trust interest in an annuity trust, unitrust, or a pooled income fund.

A charitable remainder annuity trust is one that pays only a specific sum to at least one noncharitable income beneficiary for his life or a term of not more than twenty years and transfers the remainder interest to a charity. The income payout must be made at least once a year and cannot be less than five per cent of the value of the property when it was placed in trust.

A charitable remainder unitrust is a trust that pays only a fixed percentage (not less than 5%) of the value of the trust property determined every year. Like an annuity trust, the payment must be made at least annually to at least one noncharitable income beneficiary and the remainder is transferred to a charity. However, the will or trust instrument may provide that the unitrust pay its income to the noncharitable beneficiary even if it is less than the required percentage, but only if the will or trust instrument also provides that the deficit is to be made up from any excess of trust income over the required percentage in subsequent years.

A pooled income fund is a trust that is made up solely of irrevocable remainder interests contributed to the charity that maintains the fund. At the time of death, the decedent also transfers a life income interest in the property for the life of one or more named living beneficiaries. The income is payable by the fund to each beneficiary and is determined by the rate of return of the fund. Income must be distributed currently or within 65 days following the close of the tax year in which the income is earned. The estate is entitled to a charitable contribution deduction for the present value of the charitable remainder interest. This value is the present fair market value of the assets transferred less the present value of the life income interest of the noncharitable beneficiaries. The present value of a contributed remainder interest is computed on the basis of tables found in Reg. Sec. 1.642 (c)-6(d) (3) for the life of one individual and at the highest rate of return in the three years preceding the year of the transfer.

The only charitable income interests that can be deducted are guaranteed annuities or bequests of a fixed percentage distributed yearly of property's fair market value determined annually.

The charitable remainder and income interest rules apply to estates of decedents dying after 1969. However, they do not apply to transfers under wills executed before October 10, 1969 or transfers to trust before October 10, 1969 if, (1) the decedent dies before October 9, 1972 without republishing the will or amending the trust after October 9, 1969; (2) the decedent did not have the right to change the will or trust instrument after October 9, 1969, or (3) the will is not republished or trust instrument not amended before October 9,1972 and the decedent did not have the mental capacity to do so after October 8, 1972. If a transition rule applies, the deduction is allowed if the remainder interest can be ascertained. A power of invasion for the benefit of the life tenant may be allowed if the remainder interest is ascertainable. However, a conditional remainder interest is not deductible when the possibility that the charity will take is negligible.

The estates of decedents dying after 1969 cannot deduct transfers to a private foundation that is subject to tax on loss of exemption or that is not required in the governing instrument to avoid practices that would subject it to penalty taxes. Transfers to foreign private foundations are similarly disallowed.

When Exact Amount Is Not Known

The nine-month period for filing the estate tax return may be too short for the exact determination of every possible deduction, but if a deductible item is ascertainable with reasonable certainty at the time of filing, it should be entered on the return.

Upon final audit of the return, these items will be reexamined. Some amounts may have become definite by then. Others, which are still uncertain, may either be allowed or disallowed.

The important thing to remember is that if any deduction is disallowed by reason of uncertainty of amount, the executor should file a protective claim for refund within three years from the due date of the return. Then, when the amount is determined, a refund may be in order.

Choice Between Deduction for Estate Tax and Income Tax

There is one extremely important option which must be kept in mind when claiming some of the estate tax deductions described in this chapter.

The executor has the choice of using any item of estate administration expenses either as an estate tax deduction *or* as a deductible expense on the fiduciary income tax return. Not only may any item be used in either place, but the executor may split any item between the two in any proportion he wishes.

The executor's decision is governed by the comparative tax advantages. Future estate income must be estimated, and the probable income tax rates compared with the estate tax rates. Sometimes a clear advantage can be foreseen in using one course rather than the other. More often, however, future uncertainties make the choice very difficult up to the time when the estate tax return must be filed.

But there is a way out of this dilemma. The election may be delayed until the time of final estate tax allowance, because the only specific waiver required is the waiver of the deduction for estate tax purposes in order to secure the income tax deduction; this waiver may be filed at any time before final allowance of the item as an estate tax deduction.

The wisest course to follow is to claim *every* deduction on the estate tax return and then, as the picture becomes more complete, to waive any portion of the estate tax deduction needed as an income tax deduction. The greatest possible use should be made of the opportunity to adapt the final decision to the facts as they gradually develop.

A point to remember is that these deductions can be claimed on the income tax return only in the tax year in which they are actually paid, but the executor does not always have the choice of timing the payments for the best income tax advantage. Frequently, however, some one large expense, such as the executor's fee, can be split into a number of different payments which can be timed for the best possible tax saving.

Another point to remember is that if any such deduction is used on the income tax return rather than on the estate tax return, it will have the effect of increasing the "adjusted gross estate" (see Chapter 11) and, therefore, of increasing the allowable amount of the all-important marital deduction.

Deductions in Respect of a Decedent

Certain expense items, classed as "deductions in respect of a decedent," are allowable *both* as estate tax deductions *and* as income tax deductions.

These will be explained more fully in Chapters 13 and 14, but they are mentioned here as a reminder that there is certainly no question of the desirability of including them among the deductions from gross estate for estate tax purposes.

11

Estate Tax
Deductions—
The Marital Deduction

There is one additional deduction from gross estate to be considered along with those described in Chapter 10. This is the "marital deduction."

The *marital deduction* is, in many cases, the largest and most important deduction allowable in determining the taxable estate; it may be as much as one-half of the adjusted gross estate. This deduction is subject to many intricate rules, and finding the allowable amount often requires complex mathematical computations.

Due to its general importance, an entire chapter has been devoted to an explanation of the marital deduction, a discussion of the rules to which it is subject, and the mathematics often required for its determination.

Theory of the Marital Deduction

The marital deduction is intended to equalize estate taxes between residents of community property states and those of other states.

The community property states have a concept of divided ownership of property—that all property acquired during marriage belongs equally to the husband and wife. On the death of one spouse, only the decedent's share of the community property is subject to the estate tax. Residents of such states enjoyed a distinct estate tax advantage because although one spouse might have acquired all the property, only one-half is considered to have been legally his, and only that one-half can be transferred at his death and be subject to estate tax.

The noncommunity property states wanted the same advantage, so, in 1948, Congress changed the estate tax rules by granting a "marital deduction" for noncommunity property left to a surviving spouse, up to a maximum of roughly one-half of a decedent's estate.

(At the same time, Congress added the "split income" provisions to the income tax law, so that all married taxpayers would enjoy the advantage of having one spouse's income "split" and taxed at lower rates, formerly possible only in the community property states.)

Although the concept of divided ownership is still not a part of the Federal estate tax law, the marital deduction gives substantially the same effect taxwise, resulting in the equalization of estate tax treatment for residents of all the states.

What the Marital Deduction Is

The marital deduction is a deduction that is allowed from gross estate for the value of property that passes at death from one spouse to the other. If the estate is entitled to the marital deduction, it must be taken; it cannot be waived.

The amount of the deduction is the net value of the property interests which pass to the spouse, either by will or by law, but it cannot exceed fifty per cent of the decedent's adjusted gross estate.

Thus, *for example,* if the surviving spouse receives only one-third of the decedent's estate, only that amount is a deduction; if she receives two-thirds, the deduction is limited to fifty per cent; or if she receives the entire estate, the fifty per cent limitation still applies.

The term "adjusted gross estate," which is used only in connection with the marital deduction, requires some explanation. It is not the same as the taxable estate. Instead, it is arrived at by subtracting from the estate tax gross estate the sum of all debts, administration expenses, taxes, and losses which are *allowed* for estate tax purposes—not all deductions authorized by law but only those which are actually allowed in the particular case. The $60,000 exemption is not subtracted for this purpose; deductions for charitable bequests are not subtracted.

To summarize, the net value of the property passing to the surviving spouse is determined; one-half of the adjusted gross estate is computed; the lower of these two figures is the amount of the marital deduction, which will be used along with all other allowable deductions in reducing the decedent's gross estate to taxable estate.

Interests Passing to Surviving Spouse

The marital deduction is allowed only for property or interests in property that "pass" to the surviving spouse. It may pass by the decedent's will or by inheritance in the absence of a will; it may have been given as a gift in contemplation of death; it may pass by survivorship in joint tenancy; by the exercise or nonexercise of a power of appointment, and so on.

To be a part of the marital deduction, the interest also must have been included in the decedent's gross estate, even though it may have passed to the survivor before the decedent died.

The interest must have passed to the surviving spouse as beneficial owner, not merely as trustee or subject to a binding agreement by the survivor to dispose of it in favor of third persons.

Dower, Curtesy, and Other Interests

Dower and curtesy interests, or the statutory substitutes for dower and curtesy are also classed as property "passing" to the survivor. Such interests do, as a rule, qualify for the marital deduction, but this depends on the kind of interest which was conveyed.

The local law governs this. A mere life estate, with remainder passing to others, would not qualify; a vested absolute interest would.

If a surviving spouse elects to take a property interest under the applicable state law in preference to the interest given to her by will, the interest taken is considered as having passed to her from her spouse.

Property exempt from execution under local law and set off absolutely for the decedent's widow qualifies as inherited property.

A settlement payment made to a surviving spouse in a will compromise also qualifies as inherited property.

A property interest passing in satisfaction of or in lieu of the survivor's rights under an antenuptial agreement may qualify for the marital deduction.

Effect of Disclaimers

If the surviving spouse makes a complete and unqualified refusal to take the property or interest which would otherwise pass to her, this property is considered as having passed from the decedent to the person receiving it as a result of the disclaimer. It will not qualify for the marital deduction.

However, when the surviving spouse becomes entitled to receive property as a result of a disclaimer made by some other person, such interest is still considered as having passed to the person making the disclaimer, not to the surviving spouse, as if the disclaimer had not been made.

Effect of Death Taxes on the Marital Deduction

The first step in arriving at the marital deduction is to list all the above (and any other) property interests which passed to the surviving spouse, excluding certain "terminable interests," discussed later, which do not qualify as interests passing to the survivor.

Next, the *net* value of this interest must be determined. *Net value* means only the property or interest in property actually received by the surviving spouse. Accordingly, in determining this net value, there must be taken into account the effect that any estate, inheritance, succession, or legacy tax has upon it.

This means that when the spouse's share of the estate must pay part or all of the death taxes imposed by either Federal or state law, such taxes reduce the amount she will actually receive and must, therefore, be deducted to arrive at the marital deduction. There is no marital deduction for money passing to the tax collector.

In these cases, the amount of the estate tax depends on the amount allowed as a marital deduction, but the amount of the marital deduction also depends on the amount of the tax, so this is another case where two unknowns must be determined. Interdependent Federal and state death taxes might further complicate the problem. The use of an algebraic formula or the trial-and-error method, described later in this chapter, is necessary.

Such computations are not necessary, however, if the bequest to the surviving spouse is obviously large enough, after death taxes, to amount to at least fifty per cent of the adjusted gross estate.

Valuation of Interest Passing to Surviving Spouse

There is one other deduction in arriving at the value of the net interest passing to the survivor—a deduction for mortgages or other encumbrances on the property.

If the property is encumbered in any way, or if the surviving spouse incurs any obligation imposed by the decedent with respect to the passing of an interest in it, the amount of the obligation is a deduction.

The value of the net interest passing to the surviving spouse, which will be the amount allowed as a marital deduction (subject to the fifty per cent limitation), is the gross estate value of all property "passing" to the survivor less any encumbrances on this property and less any death taxes which must be paid out of it.

If the alternate valuation date is elected by the executor for estate tax purposes, the starting point in arriving at the marital deduction will be the values as of that date.

The Terminable Interest Rule

Not every transfer to a surviving spouse will qualify for the marital deduction.

No deduction will be allowed for property or an interest in property if that interest can terminate or fail *and* if the interest passes from the decedent to a third person after the termination or failure of the surviving spouse's interest. This is known as the terminable interest rule.

The rule's most common application is when the survivor is bequeathed a life interest in property, with the property passing to someone else upon the survivor's death. Since the survivor's interest is certain to terminate, the terminable interest rule precludes it from being considered for the marital deduction.

An interest can terminate or fail on the lapse of time or on the occurrence or the failure to occur of some contingency. *For example*, no deduction is allowed where the survivor gets a life estate but has no power to dispose of the remainder. The interest is terminable because it ends at her death and somebody named by the decedent then takes the property. The same result would follow where the decedent made a gift to his wife that was to end and go to someone else if she remarried.

But the interest is not "terminable" if nothing passes from the decedent to a third party. *For example,* a deduction can be taken on account of this gift, "I give my wife the right to use the family residence during her life, at her death it shall become part of her estate." Since nothing ever passes *from the decedent* to someone other than the widow, her interest is not "terminable" and the marital deduction will be allowed.

Rev. Proc. 64-19, 1964-1 CB 682, is said to be the most important single ruling on the marital deduction since the provision was enacted in 1948. The ruling says the Internal Revenue Service will not allow the marital deduction when the will contains a "pecuniary bequest" to the surviving spouse which the executor could satisfy by a distribution in kind at estate tax values. Since this permits the executor to satisfy the pecuniary bequest amount with depreciated or wholly worthless assets at the date of distribution, it allows the executor to vary the amount of the bequest from zero to any amount less than the actual bequest. This power to divert some portion of the assets away from the surviving spouse causes the latter to receive only a terminable interest. However, a pecuniary bequest will not be disallowed if the survivor is to receive property with a date of distribution value equal to the marital deduction or where she must share, pro rata, in any appreciation or depreciation in the value of all property. "Fractional Share Bequests," leaving the survivor a *percentage of the residue,* but avoiding a set dollar amount, are not affected by the ruling.

The briefness of this explanation of the terminable interest rule is not intended to minimize its great importance. The rule can have many varied applications because of the many and varied provisions which might be found in a decedent's will governing the disposition of his property. A more thorough study of the applicable law is recommended if this question arises in any particular case.

The problem of identifying specific assets passing to the survivor and four general exceptions to the terminable interest rule are discussed in the following sections.

Interest in Unidentified Assets

At times the decedent fails to identify the property which is to go to the surviving spouse. This occurs when the property passes because of the intestate death of the decedent or when the testator leaves a general legacy or a gift of the residuary estate to the survivor.

When such an interest in unidentified assets passes to the surviving spouse, the terminable interest rule must still be followed. Consequently, if the assets out of which the survivor's interest *may* be satisfied include assets for which no marital deduction would be allowed if they had passed specifically to her, then the survivor's interest must be reduced by the total value of these particular assets, for the purpose of the marital deduction.

Spouse's Survivorship

One exception to the terminable interest rule is designed to take care of cases where the surviving spouse's interest depends on her surviving the decedent for a stated length of time.

The survivorship condition does not affect the marital deduction for the property passing if the required period of survival is not more than six months and the spouse does in fact survive for the specified period.

Another instance involving a question of survivorship is the so-called common disaster clause of a will. If a will provides that the spouse's interest will terminate or fail if there is a common disaster involving the spouses, the marital deduction will not be lost if in fact such failure or termination does not occur.

Life Estate with Power of Appointment

Another exception to the terminable interest rule permits the marital deduction of the full value of a life estate passing to the surviving spouse if the spouse is entitled for life to *all* the income from the entire interest, payable at least annually, *and* if she has a general power of appointment over the property which she may exercise during life or by will.

Also, when the spouse is to receive only a part of the income with a power of appointment over a corresponding part of the principal, the deduction is allowed for that part.

The spouse must have the power to appoint the entire interest (or a corresponding part of the interest when she receives only part of the income) either to herself or to her estate. She may also have one or more lesser powers, such as one to appoint any part of the principal to someone else, but this is not necessary.

Estate Trusts

Property is not subject to the terminable interest rule if it passes to the surviving spouse's estate—if the trust income is payable to the wife for life and on her death the corpus is payable to her estate, or if the income is to be accumulated for a term of years or for her life and the corpus plus accumulated income is to be paid to her estate.

The interest passing to the surviving spouse is not a terminable interest because no one other than the surviving spouse or her estate has any interest in the property.

If the income from property is made payable to another individual for life or for a term of years, with remainder absolutely to the surviving spouse or her estate, the marital deduction is based on the present value (at the time of the decedent's death) of the remainder.

Insurance Proceeds

A marital deduction can be taken for insurance proceeds that are included in the decedent's gross estate for tax. There is no difficulty when the proceeds pass to the surviving spouse outright and in a lump sum. But there is a special rule when the insurance, annuity, or endowment contract provides that the proceeds shall be held by the insurer and paid out in installments or when interest only is to be paid.

The deduction may still be taken under an exception to the terminable interest rule if (1) all payments of installments or interest are to be made to the surviving spouse and no one else; (2) these payments begin not later than 13 months after the decedent's death; (3) such amounts are payable annually or more often; and (4) the surviving spouse has a full power to appoint all (or a specific portion) of the proceeds still held by the insurer at her death or they are payable to her estate.

Community Property Marital Deduction Rules

There is no Federal estate tax on the half of the community property the surviving spouse takes on her spouse's death, so there is no marital deduction to be computed.

The marital deduction applies only when the decedent also leaves separate property. It is allowed—up to one-half of the adjusted gross estate—for interests which pass to the surviving spouse and which are included in the decedent's estate for tax.

In these cases, a special rule applies to the determination of the adjusted gross estate. There is first deducted from the gross estate (including the separate property and the decedent's one-half of the community property) the value of the decedent's one-half of the community property. Next, there is deducted a *proportionate* part of the debts and expenses—the proportion which the separate property bears to the gross estate.

The balance is the adjusted gross estate, one-half of which is the maximum marital deduction.

In some states, a wife has only an "expectant" interest in community property—she really does not have ownership until the husband dies. In such a case the "community" property is treated as separate property for Federal estate tax purposes.

Execution of Schedules on Return

The estate tax return includes a schedule for the listing and description of property interests passing to the surviving spouse.

Everything to be listed in this schedule will already have been listed in the various schedules provided for showing the assets constituting the gross estate, so each item listed on the marital deduction schedule should refer to the schedule and item number where the property interest was first listed. The value at which it is shown on the marital deduction schedule must agree with the value at which it was included in the gross estate.

These values will be the gross values before taking into account the effect of any death taxes to be paid out of them. After totaling these gross values, a deduction is made for Federal estate tax or any other death taxes payable out of the property interests. The balance is the amount of the marital deduction—subject to the limitation of fifty per cent of adjusted gross estate.

Marital Deduction Mathematics

The computation of the marital deduction can become very complex when death taxes are payable out of the share of the estate left to the surviving spouse. The amount of the estate tax is dependent on the amount of the marital deduction; the marital deduction is, in turn, dependent on the amount of the tax.

In many cases, the two unknowns must be determined to arrive at the correct amount of the marital deduction and of the estate tax.

However, in any case where the interests passing to the surviving spouse will obviously be more, even after the reduction for death taxes, than fifty per cent of the adjusted gross estate, no computations are necessary. This is because the percentage amount to which the marital deduction is limited, rather than the amount of the bequest less taxes, will establish the deductible amount.

When a computation is necessary, this can be done either by algebra or by the "trial-and-error" method.

The use of the trial-and-error method is illustrated in the following example, which assumes the most simple set of circumstances which can exist when two unknowns will have to be determined:

A husband, having a gross estate of $150,000 made a specific bequest of $80,000 to his son, the balance to his wife. Debts and administrative expenses amounted to $30,000. There are no state or foreign death taxes, but the Federal estate tax must, of course, be paid out of the residuary legacy passing to the wife.

Adjusted gross estate amounts to $120,000 ($150,000—$30,000). One-half of this, $60,000, is obviously more than the $40,000 before taxes the wife will receive, so a computation is necessary. The trial-and-error formula for this computation follows:

| Adjusted Gross Estate | | Marital Deduction | | | | Specific Exemption | | Trial Taxable Estate | | Estate Tax Rate | | Tentative Estate Tax |
		Before Tax	Trial Tax									
— $120,000	—	(40,000	—)	—	60,000	=	20,000.00	× rate	=	1,600.00
— $120,000	—	(40,000	— 1600.00)	—	60,000	=	21,600.00	× rate	=	1,824.00
— $120,000	—	(40,000	— 1824.00)	—	60,000	=	21,824.00	× rate	=	1,855.36
— $120,000	—	(40,000	— 1855.36)	—	60,000	=	21,855.36	× rate	=	1,859.75
— $120,000	—	(40,000	— 1859.75)	—	60,000	=	21,859.75	× rate	=	1,860.36
— $120,000	—	(40,000	— 1860.36)	—	60,000	=	21,860.36	× rate	=	1,860.45
— $120,000	—	(40,000	— 1860.45)	—	60,000	=	21,860.45	× rate	=	1,860.46

In each line of the computation, the tentative tax determined in the preceding line is used as a trial tax to be subtracted from the marital deduction figure.

After carrying the computation for six or eight lines, further computations will not change the results. The amount of the marital deduction, the taxable estate, and the estate tax will have been determined.

The problem may be further complicated by the existence of a state death tax, the amount of which is dependent on the amount of the Federal tax. The basic formula illustrated above may still be used, but it will have to be expanded to incorporate the state tax computation.

A number of other situations may exist, each of which will necessitate a modification of the formula—the widow may pay only a part of the estate tax; state death taxes may be apportioned among various beneficiaries; the surviving spouse may receive only a portion of the residue; a portion of the residue after taxes may go to a charitable organization; and so forth. Still, the trial-and-error method of successive approximations may be used to solve any problem involving interrelated death taxes and deductions.

Methods and illustrations of computing the unknowns in these and other cases are given in the supplemental instructions to the estate tax return. These instructions should be carefully studied and applied to the existing circumstances whenever a computation of this kind is necessary.

If any difficulty is experienced, a request for a solution of the problem may be submitted (a reasonable time before the due date of the return) to the Commissioner of Internal Revenue, Washington, D.C. 20225. Such request should be accompanied by a copy of the will, a statement showing the distribution of the estate under the decedent's will or under state law, a computation of the state death tax showing the amount payable by the spouse, and such documents as may be necessary in the analysis of the legal situation.

12

Estate Tax Credits
and Computation
of the Tax

In addition to the *deductions* from gross estate discussed in the preceding chapters, the Code permits several *credits* which may be claimed against the estate tax itself.

These credits are explained in this chapter, and they should be studied with a view to obtaining the greatest possible benefit from them in every case where they are applicable.

The latter part of this chapter is a summary of the rules governing the computation and payment of the estate tax.

Credit for State Death Taxes

A credit is allowed against the Federal estate tax for any inheritance, estate, legacy, or succession tax paid to any state or territory or the District of Columbia with respect to property included in the decedent's gross estate.

The credit is generally limited to such taxes as were actually paid and for which the credit is claimed within four years after filing the estate tax return.

If the state tax has not been paid by the time the Federal return is filed, the amount of the credit may be claimed and will be allowed provided the payment is actually made within the four-year period.

The state tax cannot always be exactly determined by the time the Federal return is due. The proper procedure is either to pay the Federal tax without claiming the credit and file a refund claim or to pay on the basis of an estimated credit and apply for an extension of time for payment of any additional tax due to an incorrect estimate of the state tax credit.

In determining the amount of state death taxes actually paid, penalties and interest are excluded and a discount for payment within a specified period is deducted. A certification from the proper officer of the taxing state, showing these amounts, should be attached to the return.

In any case, the amount of the credit is limited to a maximum amount which is determined from a table provided in the Code. This table is shown in Exhibit 21.

Exhibit 21

Computation of Maximum Credit for State Death Taxes

Taxable estate equal to or more than — (1)	Taxable estate less than — (2)	Credit on amount in column (1) (3)	Rate of Credit on excess over amount in column (1) (4)
			(Percent)
0	$40,000	0	None
$40,000	90,000	0	0.8
90,000	140,000	$400	1.6
140,000	240,000	1,200	2.4
240,000	440,000	3,600	3.2
440,000	640,000	10,000	4.0
640,000	840,000	18,000	4.8
840,000	1,040,000	27,600	5.6
1,040,000	1,540,000	38,800	6.4
1,540,000	2,040,000	70,800	7.2
2,040,000	2,540,000	106,800	8.0
2,540,000	3,040,000	146,800	8.8
3,040,000	3,540,000	190,800	9.6
3,540,000	4,040,000	238,800	10.4
4,040,000	5,040,000	290,800	11.2
5,040,000	6,040,000	402,800	12.0
6,040,000	7,040,000	522,800	12.8
7,040,000	8,040,000	650,800	13.6
8,040,000	9,040,000	786,800	14.4
9,040,000	10,040,000	930,800	15.2
10,040,000	- - - -	1,082,800	16.0

It should be noted that no credit is granted any estate unless the taxable estate exceeds $40,000.

Many states have their inheritance tax rates geared to the amount of the maximum Federal credit, but there are several factors which might cause the state taxes to be greater than the credit for them—the state rate might be higher than necessary to absorb the credit; the estate may be subject to taxation by more than one state, and the total taxes might be greater than the allowable credit; state and Federal tax structures might differ as to inclusions, deductions, or credits against the tax.

The maximum credit determined from the table might be lowered by the application of a special rule relating to the state death taxes paid out of a charitable bequest. It was pointed out in Chapter 10 that the executor could elect to use such taxes as a *deduction* from gross estate. If this is elected, no *credit* will be allowed for any state death tax for which the deduction is taken.

The Gift Tax Credit

To ease the hardship when a gift made by a decedent during his life is later held to be includible in his estate and is taxed under both the estate and gift taxes, the gift tax paid can be claimed as a credit against the estate tax.

The credit is allowable even though the gift tax is paid after the decedent's death and is deductible from the gross estate as a debt of the decedent.

Two problems arise in determining the amount of the gift tax credit.

The first is to determine exactly how much gift tax was actually paid on a piece of property which is a part of the gross estate. This problem arises when the donor had made several gifts within a calendar year or quarter and only a part of these transfers were included in his gross estate.

The gift tax paid on transfers made during the period must be allocated; the credit will be limited to an amount which bears the same ratio to the total gift tax paid as the value of the gift (less any annual exclusions, charitable deductions, or gift tax marital deduction) bears to the total taxable gifts during the year (determined without benefit of the gift tax specific exemption).

The amount of the gift tax paid on the property included in the donor's estate equals:

$$\frac{\text{Included property less annual exclusion less gift tax marital deduction}}{\text{Total gifts less charitable gifts less annual exclusion less gift tax marital deduction}} \times \text{Total gift tax paid}$$

The $30,000 lifetime specific exemption does not enter into the above computation.

After the gift tax attributable to the gift property included in the estate has been determined, the next problem is to determine whether this gift tax may be credited in full against the estate tax or is subject to limitation.

The limitation is that the credit cannot exceed an amount which bears the same ratio to the estate tax (reduced by the credit for state death taxes) as the value of the gift less the exclusion used (for purposes of the estate tax or the gift tax, whichever is lower) bears to the value of the entire gross estate (reduced by the charitable deduction and the marital deduction).

The formula for computing this limitation on the credit is:

$$\frac{\text{Value of the gift}}{\substack{\text{Value of gross estate less marital} \\ \text{deduction and charitable deduction}}} \times \substack{\text{Gross estate tax} \\ \text{less credit for} \\ \text{state death taxes}}$$

The gift tax credit allowable against the estate tax is, therefore, the amount of gift tax actually paid on property included in the estate, subject to the maximum limitation arrived at by use of the above formula.

Credit for Tax on Prior Transfers

To reduce the burden of successive estate taxes when property passes through more than one taxable estate within a ten-year period, a credit is allowed against the second and subsequent estate taxes for some or all of the tax paid by the previous estate.

The credit is permitted for property transferred to the present decedent if he died within two years before the death of the transferor decedent or within ten years after.

There is no requirement that the property be identified in the estate of the transferee or that it even be in existence on the date of his death. It is sufficient for the allowance of the credit that the property was taxed in the prior decedent's estate and that the specified period of time has not elapsed.

The credit is based on the value of the property in the estate of the prior decedent; but when the present decedent was the surviving spouse of the prior decedent, that value must be reduced to the extent of any marital deduction which was allowed in the prior estate.

The credit must be calculated in two different ways, and the lower of the two is the one allowed (subject to the percentage limitation explained later).

First, the credit cannot exceed the amount of the estate tax paid by the prior estate on the property transferred to the present decedent. This first trial credit is determined by using the following formula:

$$\substack{\text{Prior decedent's estate tax} \\ \text{paid (plus gift tax credit and} \\ \text{prior transfer credit allowed} \\ \text{in that estate)}} \times \frac{\text{Value of transferred}}{\substack{\text{property in prior estate} \\ \text{Prior decedent's taxable es-} \\ \text{tate reduced by all death} \\ \text{taxes and increased by} \\ \text{specific exemption}}} = \substack{\text{Maximum} \\ \text{Credit} \\ \text{that} \\ \text{will be} \\ \text{allowed}}$$

The second way of calculating the credit is to determine the amount of estate tax the present decedent's estate would pay on the transferred property included in that estate. To compute this ceiling:

1. Determine the present estate's tax after deducting credits for state death taxes and for gift taxes.

2. Recompute the estate's tax after reducing the gross estate by the value of the transferred property included therein, and after deducting the credits for state death taxes and gift taxes.

3. Subtract (2) from (1). This is the second trial credit.

In computing the two trial credits, the property transferred to the present decedent has the same value as it had in the prior estate for tax purposes, after being reduced to the extent of Federal or state death taxes imposed on it and to the extent of any marital deduction allowed.

The lower of the two trial credits will be allowed in full against the estate tax if the present decedent dies within two years after the death of the prior decedent. If he dies later than that, the credit is reduced by twenty per cent every two years, so that no credit is allowed after the tenth year. The following table shows the percentage of credit allowed:

Period of time exceeding	Not exceeding	Per cent Allowable
—	—	100
2 years	2 years	80
4 years	4 years	60
6 years	6 years	40
8 years	8 years	20
10 years	10 years	None

When property included in the present estate has come from more than one prior decedent, the first trial credit must be computed separately for the property transferred from each. The second trial credit, however, need be computed only once, as above. The percentage limitation must, of course, be applied to the credit determined for each prior decedent's transfers. The estate tax instructions contain excellent examples of all necessary computations.

Credit for Foreign Death Taxes

The decedent may have owned property outside the United States which is subject to death taxes levied by the foreign country in which it is located. This property may also be includible in the gross estate and be subject to the Federal estate tax.

To give the estate some relief from this double taxation, there is a credit against the estate tax allowable for the death taxes paid to the foreign country.

Briefly, the foreign death tax credit cannot exceed the lower of:

1. The amount of the foreign death tax attributable to property situated in the country imposing the tax and included in the decedent's gross estate for Federal estate tax purposes.

2. The amount of the Federal estate tax attributable to the property situated in the foreign country, subjected to death tax in that country and included in the decedent's gross estate for Federal estate tax purposes.

The detailed rules governing these computations will not be discussed here, due to the limited application of this credit, but the estate tax regulations should be studied if the problem of the foreign death tax arises.

Recovery of Credited Taxes

When any state or foreign death tax claimed as a credit is later recovered, the executor must notify the Revenue Service within thirty days. The Revenue Service will redetermine the estate tax on the basis of the recovery, and the additional tax due must be paid upon notice and demand.

No interest is charged on the additional tax due for any period before the refund is received.

Computation of the Estate Tax

Up to this point, all elements involved in the determination of the estate tax have been discussed. This section provides an over-all picture of the way these elements are combined to arrive at the amount of the estate tax liability.

The steps are as follows:

First—Determine the total gross estate, by listing and totaling all includible assets from the estate inventory (Chapters 3 and 4) in the following schedules of the estate tax return, where applicable:

Schedule A—Real Estate
        B—Stocks and Bonds
        C—Mortgages, Notes, and Cash
        D—Insurance
        E—Jointly Owned Property
        F—Other Miscellaneous Property
        G—Transfers During Decedent's Life
        H—Powers of Appointment
        I—Annuities

Second—Determine the total allowable deductions, by completing and totaling the following applicable schedules:

Schedule J—Funeral and Administration Expenses (Chapter 10)
        K—Debts of Decedent and Mortgages and Liens (Chapter 10)

L—Losses During Administration (Chapter 10)

L—Expenses Incurred in Administering Property not Subject to Claims (Chapter 10)

M—The Marital Deduction (Chapter 11)

N—Charitable and Similar Bequests (Chapter 10)

Third—Subtract the allowable deductions and the $60,000 specific exemption from the total gross estate. This balance is the taxable estate.

Fourth—Compute the gross estate tax, using the tax rate table provided (Exhibit 18).

Fifth—Deduct the tax credits, discussed in this chapter, for,

State Death Taxes

Federal Gift Taxes

Tax on Prior Transfers

Foreign Death Taxes

The balance is the amount of net Federal estate tax payable.

Payment of the Tax

The estate tax is ordinarily due and payable in full within nine months after the decedent's death and must be paid with the estate tax return by the executor or administrator, or where there is no duly qualified executor or administrator, by the persons in actual or constructive possession of the property.

However, an extension of time for payment of up to twelve months may be granted at the request of the executor if the facts disclose that this request is based on reasonable cause; interest at 4% is added, but this increases to 9% for liabilities outstanding on or arising after July 1, 1975. Then decreases to 7% on February 1, 1976. For undue hardship, the time for paying may be extended up to ten years.

The legal representative is personally liable for the tax to the full extent of the assets coming into his possession. A transferee may also be liable for payment of the tax, up to the value of the property he received.

Installment Payment of the Tax

An executor has a very important option relating to the payment of the estate tax in certain cases.

An estate that consists largely of an interest in a closely held business, or businesses, might have a serious problem in raising enough cash within nine months to pay the estate tax without liquidating the business—possibly at a sacrifice.

If the estate qualifies under the installment payment provisions in Sec. 6166 of the law, the executor may elect to pay the estate tax attributable to the business interest in up to ten annual installments, provided the election is made on or before the due date for filing the return and paying the tax.

It is not necessary to show hardship or inability to pay to be entitled to this extension, and the only cost is four per cent interest payable annually on the unpaid installments, increased to nine per cent on July 1, 1975. Then decreases to 7% on February 1, 1976.

To qualify, the value of the closely held business interest included in the estate must exceed thirty-five per cent of the gross estate *or* fifty per cent of the taxable estate.

To be considered a "closely held business interest" the interest must be either:

1. A proprietorship interest, or

2. A partnership interest in a partnership having no more than ten partners *or* in which the decedent's interest is at least twenty per cent of the total partnership capital, or

3. A stock interest in a corporation having no more than ten shareholders *or* in which the decedent's interest is at least twenty per cent of the voting stock.

Two or more businesses may be treated as one for the 35 per cent—50 per cent rule, if more than fifty per cent of the value of each business is included in the gross estate.

The District Director may require payment of the tax in full if any installment is not paid on time. The tax also must be paid in full when fifty per cent or more of the decedent's interest is withdrawn from the business or disposed of.

Payment of Tax on Remainder Interest

The executor may also elect to postpone payment of the tax on a reversion or remainder interest until six months after the precedent interests in the property terminate. He may get a further extension of up to three years in case of hardship.

This election must also be exercised before the due date for paying the tax, and the executor must provide a surety bond in at least double the amount of the postponed tax and estimated interest.

Stock Redemptions

A way in which the executor might be able to obtain cash for the estate is provided by Sec. 303 of the Code.

If the estate includes corporate stock which, at its estate tax valuation, exceeds either thirty-five per cent of the gross estate or fifty per cent of the taxable estate, a redemption of the stock by the corporation is not deemed to be a dividend; it is a sale, not a distribution of earnings. But such a redemption cannot exceed the sum of the estate's death taxes and funeral and administrative expenses.

Even if there is no urgent need for cash by the estate, a Sec. 303 Redemption might be desirable in substituting income-producing cash for a non-income-producing asset.

This privilege extends to either the estate or any beneficiary who acquires the stock interest in question.

Executor's Discharge from Liability

The executor may make a written application to the District Director for a determination of the tax and a discharge from personal liability.

This makes it necessary for the District Director to complete an examination of the estate tax return within one year after the filing of the return (or one year after the receipt of such application, whichever is later), or to accept the return as filed without audit. In estates of decedents dying after December 31, 1973, this one year waiting period is shortened to nine months.

Upon payment of the tax so determined, the executor will be entitled to a receipt from the District Director showing his discharge from personal liability for any deficiency in the tax thereafter found to be due (*see* Exhibit 22).

Exhibit 22

DISCHARGE FROM ESTATE TAX LIABILITY

U.S. TREASURY DEPARTMENT
INTERNAL REVENUE SERVICE
DISTRICT DIRECTOR

Mr. George Foster, Executor   Date of your application: June 4, 1976
1018 Greystone Street
Brownsville, Ohio

Pursuant to your application a certificate of release from personal liability for any deficiency in estate tax appears below.

UNITED STATES ESTATE TAX
CERTIFICATE OF RELEASE FROM PERSONAL LIABILITY

The Federal estate tax liability of the estate named below having been determined and satisfied, by directionof the Commissioner of Internal Revenue and in accordance with the provisions of Section 2204 of the Internal Revenue Code of 1954, I DO HEREBY CERTIFY that the following are released from personal liability for any deficiency in estate tax that may be hereafter found due from such estate.

Very truly yours,

District Director

Estate of Carl Davis		Date of death August 9, 1975
Name	Title	Address
Mr. George Foster	Executor	1018 Greystone Street Brownsville, Ohio

Effective for estates of decedents dying after December 31, 1970, the executor can also obtain a discharge from the decedent's income tax liability and gift tax liability by filing a written application.

13

Income in Respect of
a Decedent

Income in Respect of a Decedent is an obscure little tax accounting concept which had its origin in Federal tax law in 1942. It is something which is peculiar to estates; it has practically no counterpart in ordinary tax or accounting work.

Importance of Understanding This Concept

Frankly, it is not always of any very great importance. It may not even be encountered in the average small estate, but it can be of great importance in the large estates, and also the estate taxman will find that a thorough understanding of this one little topic can be his key to a complete understanding of the entire complex interrelationships between the Federal estate tax return, the Fiduciary income tax return, and the income tax returns of the beneficiaries of an estate. No one of these returns can stand completely on its own, and in preparing either one of them its relationship with the others must be kept in mind. Income in respect of a decedent is one phase of estate taxation which must be considered when any one of the returns is prepared, so a knowledge of it will help the practitioner to remember that the various returns must be considered as a unit rather than as unrelated, separate parts of the total estate tax picture. Also, income in respect of a decedent gives rise to an important income tax deduction which should never be overlooked.

Meaning of the Term

The term "income in respect of a decedent" refers principally to income of a cash basis taxpayer which was accrued, but not collected, as of the date of his death. It includes (but is not limited to) such items as accrued interest on notes, mortgages, and bonds (except that the executor may elect to report the increment of interest on Series E Bonds on the decedent's final income tax return, in which case it is not income in respect of a decedent though it is still an estate asset); dividends declared but not paid at the date of death; rents receivable up to that date; salaries receivable; the income portion of installment obligations; and any other accrual of income up to the date of death. It would even include the accounts receivable of the average cash basis professional man—anything which would have been taxable income to the decedent if he had collected it the day before his death. The profits of a partnership up to the date of death of a partner are not considered accrued income if the partnership agreement or state law provide for the dissolution of the partnership by the death of the partner. These profits would be reported on the decedent's final income tax return and included in the total valuation of the partnership interest for the estate tax, but if the partnership continues with the estate taking the place of the deceased partner the profits up to the date of death must be considered accrued income, therefore income in respect of the decedent, as of that date.

Inclusion in the Estate Tax Return

Such income is not ordinarily accrued at any time, of course, but at the death of a cash basis taxpayer it is accruable *because* of his death. This accrued income may not be reported on the decedent's final income tax return, because he was on the cash basis and had not collected it prior to his death, but it must be considered in preparing the estate tax return, the fiduciary income tax return, and the income tax returns of any other individuals who might later be recipients of the income.

Therefore, the accountant should insist that all accrued income as of the date of death be determined and included by the appraisers in the inventory of the estate, along with all other assets of the decedent, such as cash, real estate, receivables, stock, bonds, business interests, and the rest, so that this inventory may be complete and may serve both as a basis for the opening entry on the estate books and as a basis for preparation of the estate tax return.

Since income in respect of a decedent is an asset of the decedent and a part of his gross estate, it must be reported on the Federal Estate Tax Return, Form 706, and the estate tax must be paid on it. Now, up to this point, this treatment will make good sense to accountants—accruals of this kind are assets, assets are a part of gross estate, and gross estate must be reported on the estate tax return.

Subject to Income Tax

From this point on, however, the required treatment may not seem so logical. The valuation of these items on the estate tax return may not be treated as a basis to be recovered tax-free. As mentioned above, accrued income is not properly includible on the cash basis decedent's final income tax return; instead, it becomes taxable income for income tax purposes when it is collected, and it must be reported on some income tax return at that time. If the fiduciary collects the income and has the right to it he must report it on the Fiduciary income tax return, Form 1041. If some beneficiary has the right to the income he must report it on his personal income tax return. The recipient is required to report this income in the year in which he receives it, whether or not he uses the cash method of accounting.

A decedent's income which must be reported by the recipient, as stated above, retains the same nature it would have had in the hands of the decedent. *For example*, if the income would have been capital gain to the decedent it is capital gain to the recipient; the recipient of installment payments will report as income the same portion of the payments as that which would have been taxable income to the decedent; interest receivable by the decedent becomes interest income to the recipient; if the amounts received would have been subject to special treatment under Code Sections 1301 to 1305, relating to income attributable to several taxable years, such sections apply to the recipient; exempt income remains exempt income to the recipient (but not exempt from the estate tax). This is based on the "conduit" principle of estates, which means that an estate serves as a pipeline which will eventually channel the decedent's assets into the hands of the proper beneficiaries, but without changing the nature of those assets. So the person who must report the accrued income which he collects will report it as rent income, interest income, capital gain, or whatever it happens to be.

Reason for Double Taxation

There is, then, double taxation on a decedent's income—the estate tax on the amount accrued at the date of death and the income tax to which it is subject when it is received. This may not seem very fair, but there is a logical reason for this treatment being required. The theory is that this will place the final recipient of the income in a similar position, after both taxes, to that which he would have been in if the decedent had collected it before his death. If the decedent had collected this income, he would have had to pay income tax on it, and its remaining value after income tax (in the form of cash, *for example*) would have been a part of his gross estate when he died and would have been subject to the estate tax. So in that case, also, the recipient would have ended up with the net value after both taxes. The net amount would not be exactly the same in both cases, but would be similar in that it would have been subject to both the estate tax and the income tax.

Deduction for Estate Tax Paid

It is important to remember not only that income in respect of a decedent is subject to double taxation but that there is a very worthwhile income tax deduction available in most cases where both taxes have had to be paid on it. Some of the edge is taken off the double tax by this deduction, which is provided for by Code Section 691 (c). This section permits the person reporting the receipt of the income to deduct the amount of *estate* tax paid which was attributable to the inclusion of this income in the decedent's estate.

Computation of the Deduction

The regulations under Code Section 691 (c) prescribe the exact method of computing the amount of this deduction. A two step computation is required, as follows:

1. Determine the *net* amount of the income in respect of the decedent. This is done by totalling the various accruals of income and deducting from this total the amount of any deductions and credit in respect of the decedent. Deductions in respect of a decedent consist of expenses, interest, property taxes, and so forth, described in Sections 162, 163, 164, and 212 which were payable by the decedent at the time of his death but which were not properly allowable as deductions on his final income tax return (since he was on the cash basis and had not paid them). The credit mentioned is the one provided by Section 33 for foreign taxes. Since these payables will be used as deductions from gross estate on the estate tax return it is only fair that they be subtracted from the gross accrued income in determining the *net* income in respect of the decedent. Obviously, if these deductions in respect of the decedent exceed the income in respect of the decedent there can be no net income in respect of the decedent, the computation will stop at this point, and there can be no deduction for estate tax paid.

2. Recompute the estate tax, excluding this *net* value as determined above, and adjusting any estate tax deductions (such as the marital deduction) which may have been based on the gross estate. The resulting estate tax figure, substracted from the estate tax originally computed and paid, gives the amount of that tax which was attributable to the inclusion of income in respect of a decedent, and it is this amount which may be claimed as an income tax deduction by the recipient of the income.

Obviously, this deduction might often be a sizable one, and it should never be overlooked.

Who Is Entitled to the Deduction

If all of the income in respect of the decedent is collected within the same taxable year by one person, either the fiduciary or some beneficiary, it will all be reported as income on his income tax return for that year, and he should claim as a deduction the total amount of estate tax paid on such income, as computed above. There is even a line on the Federal Fiduciary Tax Return, Form 1041, for this deduction. More often, however, more than one recipient is involved, in which case each may deduct a proportionate part of the attributable estate tax paid. In making the computation of this proportionate part, the *net* income in respect of the decedent does not apply and the deduction will be the proportion which the *gross* income received bears to the total *gross* income in respect of the decedent. This may be illustrated by the following example:

Total income in respect of a decedent included in the decedent's gross estate	$10,000.00
Total deductions in respect of the decedent (deductible expenses payable by him at date of death)	2,000.00
Net income in respect of the decedent	$8,000.00
Portion of estate tax paid by the estate which was attributable to the inclusion of the above $8,000.00 in the estate tax return	$ 1,600.00
Amount of the accrued income which was collected during the year	$ 4,000.00
Amount of the allowable deduction for estate tax paid (4,000/10,000 of $1,600.00)	$ 640.00

Time for Claiming the Deduction

Since most accruals of income are usually liquidated within a relatively short time, probably within the fiduciary's first fiscal year, consideration of this subject is likely to be eliminated from later periods. If all of the accrued income is collected during the first year, all of the matching deduction for estate tax paid will have been claimed and there will be nothing to carry forward to following years. There are cases, however, when the collection of the income is delayed and may be spread over a period of several years, as, *for example*, when it consists of the income portion of installment receivables on which periodic payments are being made. Each year a portion of the payments received will be taxable income, and the recipient should claim a deduction for the proportionate part of the estate tax paid which is applicable to the portion being reported in that year. The computation of this proportionate part will be made in the same way as shown by the above example.

Occasionally the amount of income actually collected will be less than the amount at which it was valued in the gross estate for estate tax purposes. In this case, the lower amount must be used in computing the amount of estate tax deductible, rather than the amount at which it was valued on the estate tax return.

The important thing to keep in mind, therefore, is that each time any income in respect of a decedent is reported on a person's income tax return, there is likely to be a matching deduction for the proportionate part of the estate tax paid applicable to that part of the income being reported. Again, this may be a very valuable deduction and should not be overlooked.

Income in Respect of a Prior Decedent

Another interesting possibility is that there might be income in respect of a *prior* decedent. Normally, unless the two deaths occurred fairly close together, the chances are that the second decedent would have had time before his death to collect the accrued income of the prior decedent, to report it on his income tax return, and to claim his deduction for the attributable estate tax paid by the first estate, because accruals of income are usually collected rather quickly, leaving nothing to carry over to another estate.

However, there are cases where the collection of income is delayed for so long that some of the accrued income in the first decedent's estate may remain uncollected and may again be accrued income, and therefore income in respect of a decedent, in the second estate—or possibly in the third or more successive estates. *For example*, the first decedent's estate might have included installment obligations receivable, the income portion of which was income in respect of a decedent in that estate. Income retains the same nature in the hands of a beneficiary (or that beneficiary's estate) that it had in the hands of the decedent, so the remaining value of such obligations would have to be considered as a part of the gross estate of the beneficiary and the income portion would again be income in respect of a decedent in that estate. The result, then, is that estate tax will have to be computed on the same accrued income, or at least the remaining uncollected portion of it, in the second estate as in the prior decedent's estate.

But the final recipient of this income will be allowed a double deduction when he collects it and reports it on his income tax return, one for the applicable estate tax paid by the prior decedent's estate and one for that paid by the second decedent's estate. The amount of each deduction will again be based on the proportionate part of the income being received and becoming subject to income tax in the current year.

Another help in offsetting the double estate taxation is the credit for tax on prior transfers, described in Chapter 12, which may be claimed on the second estate's tax return. The allowance of this credit does not rule out the allowance of the two deductions for estate tax which may be claimed on the income tax return.

Illustration of Tax Treatment

Again, the important thing to remember any time any income in respect of a decedent is reported on any income tax return is to claim a deduction for the estate tax paid on this income by *each* estate through which the income has passed. The following example is an illustration of the correct method of computing the two deductions when two or more successive estates include the same income in respect of a decedent.

Mr. A died on January 1, 1974. Among his assets there were a number of installment receivable, the income portion of which amounted to $40,000.00. He had no other accruedincome. At the same time he had deductions in respect of a decedent, consisting of payables for repairs, insurance, property taxes, and others amounting to $2,000.00. An estate tax return was prepared, the estate was in the 30 per cent estate tax bracket, and estate tax in the amount of $42,700.00 was paid. Computation of the tax applicable to the income in respect of the decedent follows:

Gross income in respect of a decedent	$40,000.00
Less: Deductions in respect of a decedent	2,000.00
Net income in respect of a decedent	$38,000.00
Estate tax originally computed and paid	$42,700.00
Recomputation of the estate tax, omitting the above $38,000.00 and making adjustments required by this change, shows that the estate tax would have been	$31,300.00
Portion of estate tax paid by A's estate attributable to the inclusion of the above $38,000.00	$11,400.00

During the year 1974, Mr. A's heir, Mr. B., collected $15,000.00 of the accrued income, included it in gross income on his income tax return, and claimed a deduction for estate tax paid in the amount of $4,275.00 (15,000/40,000 of $11,400.00).

Mr. B. died on January 1, 1975 and there was included in his estate the remaining uncollected portion of the accrued income, $25,000.00. He had certain payables classified as deductions in respect of a decedent amounting to $1,000.00. His estate was taxed in the 25 per cent bracket and the estate tax paid amounted to $9,000.00. Estate tax attributable to income in respect of a decedent in this estate was computed as follows:

Gross income in respect of a decedent	$25,000.00
Less: Deductions in respect of a decedent	$ 1,000.00
Net income in respect of a decedent	$24,000.00
Estate Tax originally computed and paid	$ 9,000.00
Recomputation of the estate tax, omitting the $24,000.00 net income in respect of a decedent and making adjustments required by this change, shows that the estate tax would have been	$ 5,000.00
Portion of estate tax paid by B's estate attributable to the inclusion of the above $24,000.00	$ 4,000.00

During the year 1975, Mr. B's heir, Mr. C., collected another $15,000.00 of this accrued income, included it in gross income on his income tax return, and claimed two deductions for estate tax paid, as follows:

Portion of attributable estate tax paid by Mr. A's estate (15,000/40,000 of $11,400.00)	$ 4,275.00

Portion of attributable estate tax paid by Mr. B's estate
  (15,000/25,000 of $4,000.00) $ 2,400.00
Total income tax deduction $ 6,675.00

To carry the illustration further one more year, assume that the same recipient, Mr. C., finally collected the remaining $10,000.00 of accrued income in 1976. His deduction for 1976 will be as follows:

Portion of attributable estate tax paid by Mr. A's estate
  (10,000/40,000 of $11,400.00) $2,850.00
Portion of attributable estate tax paid by Mr. B's estate
  (10,000/25,000 of $4,000.00) $1,600.00
Total income tax deduction $4,450.00

State Income and Death Taxes

State laws governing the treatment of a decedent's income differ greatly and should be studied if the state requires death tax returns or income tax returns. Generally, however, if a death tax return is required the accrued income must be considered a part of gross estate just as it is under the Federal law. If income tax returns are required the Federal treatment is usually followed—the income when collected must be reported as taxable income and the deduction for *Federal* estate tax paid will be allowed. However, most states do not provide for a similar deduction for the amount of *state* death tax paid attributable to the inclusion of the accrued income on the state death tax return.

Accounting Treatment

The estate ledger should have a separate asset account for each of these accrued income items, such as "Rents Receivable," "Accrued Interest," "Salary Receivable," and the rest. The proper entry to these accounts upon receipt of this income presents a bookkeeping problem which has no completely satisfactory solution. It would appear that the receivable account should be credited, but if this is done the income will not appear on the income statement, where it must appear for income tax purposes. On the other hand, if an income account is credited when cash is received, the asset account will remain on the books although the asset no longer exists. It appears to be a case where two credits are needed for the same debit, which is impossible; so the best procedure would be to credit the receivable account, thus eliminating it, and to make some kind of memorandum or single entry record of the amount of this income to be picked up and added to the book income figure for preparation of the income tax returns.

Fortunately, since these receivables are usually liquidated soon after the date of death and within the fiduciary's first fiscal year, this eliminates any such problem in subsequent periods.

Other Considerations

There are several other points in connection with the handling of a decedent's income which the accountant should be aware of and for which he should be on the lookout:

1. Income in respect of a decedent, when received, must be reported by the one who has the *right* to this income. If the decedent's estate acquired this right from the decedent, the fiduciary must report the income. If a certain beneficiary acquires the right by reason of the death of the decedent, he shall report it. If the estate has the right, then later distributes it to a beneficiary, the estate shall report the amount it receives and the beneficiary shall report the income thereafter.

2. If the estate or person entitled to income in respect of a decedent transfers this right, by sale or by gift, to someone not otherwise entitled to this income, the transferor must include in gross income the fair market value of the right at the time of the transfer or the consideration received, whichever is greater. This provision does not apply, however, to transfers made by an estate to a specific or residuary legatee (except when transferred in satisfaction of all or part of a specific legacy), or transfers to the estate or other beneficiary of the transferor by reason of his death.

3. Income in respect of a decedent might also be accompanied by deductions in respect of a decedent, explained more fully in Chapter 14, which will be allowable to the fiduciary if liable for their payment or to the person who by reason of the decedent's death acquires an interest in the property, subject to such obligation. *For example*, accrued taxes on real property passing directly to an heir are deductible when paid by the heir; income taxes imposed by a foreign country during the decedent's life, payable out of the income received by the heir, entitle the heir to the credit provided by Section 33 when he pays the tax; the deduction for percentage depletion is allowable to the person receiving the income to which the deduction relates, even though he does not receive the property from which such income is derived.

4. Annuity payments received by a surviving annuitant under a joint and survivor annuity contract are treated as income in respect of a decedent to the extent provided for in Section 691 (d). This section requires the determination of a special value for the surviving annuitant's payments for inclusion in the deceased annuitant's gross estate. The portion of estate tax attributable to this value is allowable as a deduction to the surviving annuitant over his life expectancy period.

14

The Fiduciary
Income Tax Return

A Federal income tax return must be filed for each tax year during which an estate is in the process of administration.

The estate is a new taxable entity which came into being upon the death of the decedent and, as such, must periodically report its gross income, deductions, and taxable income much as any other business entity must do.

The estate's *income tax* return must not be confused with the *estate tax* return. One must be filed periodically throughout the life of the estate, the other is filed only once—as of the date of death. One reports a tax on net income earned over a period of time, the other a tax on the value of property at a specific date.

There are, altogether, three types of Federal tax returns for which the estate executor is responsible—the decedent's individual income tax returns and the estate tax return, both discussed earlier, and the estate's income tax return, which is the subject of this chapter.

The Income Taxation of Estates

Generally, the income earned by an estate during the period of its administration is taxable only once, either to the estate itself or to the beneficiaries, or in part to each. The disposition of the income, as directed by the decedent's will and by state law, governs its taxability.

If the income is to be accumulated by the estate rather than being distributed to beneficiaries, the estate must pay the tax on this income. If the income is required, by will or by law, to be turned over to certain beneficiaries, the estate will not have to pay the tax on it, but the recipients must include such income in their individual tax returns and pay the tax on it. If a portion of the income is retained by the estate and a portion is distributed, the estate is taxable on the retained portion and the distributees on the portions they receive.

Regardless of which of the above possibilities exist, the executor must file an income tax return reporting all of the esate's income and deductions for the period if the estate's gross income for the taxable year is $600 or more or if any beneficiary is a non-resident alien. The return to be used is Form 1041, U.S. Fiduciary Income Tax Return.

This return is, in effect, a cross between an individual income tax return and a partnership income tax return.

If all the income is taxable to the estate, it is taxable very much like an individual's income—a $600 personal exemption is allowed and the tax rate schedule for a married person filing a separate return is used.

The $600 exemption is lost if the estate does not have retained income at least equal to that amount. Thus, there is no exemption for the final year in which distribution of assets is made. No beneficiary may claim that exemption even though the estate has lost the tax benefit of the deduction.

If all the income is distributable to others, the Form 1041 becomes merely an information return showing the names of the various distributees and the amounts of the several kinds of income (ordinary income, capital gains, dividend income, and others) which each received. The distributees pick up these figures from the fiduciary return in preparing their individual returns, just as the members of a partnership obtain their income figures from the partnership tax return.

In those cases where only a part of the income is distributed, the fiduciary must pay tax on the retained portion; the distributed portion is shown as being taxable to the recipients—the return is both an income tax return and an information return at the same time.

The tax return allocation of the estate's income is accomplished by showing any proper distributions to beneficiaries as a *deduction* from the net income for the period, previously detailed on the form. The balance remaining, if any, is taxable to the estate; a distribution schedule, Schedule K-1, is provided for giving the names of recipients and other details of the deduction claimed.

If income in respect of a decedent is reported and includes earned income of more than $26,000, the tax is computed on Form 4726, attached to the return.

An estate must pay the minimum tax on the same tax preference items as individuals, and the tax is computed in the same way. However, the preference items are apportioned between the estate and the beneficiaries on the basis of the estate income allocable to each. The $30,000 exclusion is shared by the estate and the beneficiaries in the same proportion. Form 4626 is used and attached to the return.

Although the income taxable to an estate is subject to similar exemptions and rates as that of an individual, there are several basic differences—there is no such concept as "adjusted gross income"; there is no deduction for dependents; the percentage limitation on charitable contributions does not apply; there is no self-employment tax; no declaration of estimated tax is necessary, and others.

The following sections will consider, first, the gross income which must be reported on the fiduciary tax return; second, the allowable deductions from income; and, finally, the credits against the income tax which are available to an estate.

The Estate's Gross Income

The fiduciary of an estate must report the same categories of gross income as must be reported by an individual, that is, dividends, interest, income from partnerships, gross rental income, gains, and the rest.

There must be included any collections of income accrued to the decedent at the time of his death, as explained in the preceding chapter.

The principal complication in connection with gross income is caused by the fact that under state laws the title to certain property frequently vests directly in the decedent's heirs or devisees. Who must report the income from such property? As a rule, the person *entitled* to the income must report it. The executor must examine the scope of his power and authority in the light of any applicable provisions in the will or in the state law. He may have only the power to collect the income and may be no more than an agent for the beneficiaries, who as principals are accountable for the income. Or he may have broader powers (*for example*, the power to sell property) which indicate that the estate is entitled to the income and must, therefore, include it as gross income— even though those who possess the property may have collected the income.

The fiduciary includes in gross income only those income items actually belonging to the estate, not items belonging to the decedent's heirs, devisees, or beneficiaries. Once he has distributed an asset, the income from that asset must be reported by the distributee, even though otherwise the estate continues to be in the process of administration.

Total dividends received are included in gross income. The $100 exclusion is later claimed as a *deduction* rather than as an income *exclusion*.

Other exclusions from gross income (such as state and municipal bond interest) follow the same rules as for an individual.

Deductions from Income

Estates get basically the same deductions as individuals, except that they may not use the standard deduction.

Allowable deductions might include taxes, interest, repairs, office expenses, certain administrative expenses, depreciation, losses, contributions, and so forth, as well as the $600 deduction for personal exemption. But the $600 personal exemption deduction is not allowed if final distribution of the estate's assets was made during the year. It is lost in this final year because no deduction for the exemption is allowable in computing distributable net income or the excess deductions on termination.

A number of deductions are subject to certain exceptions and different rules from those for an individual, and these will be pointed out in the following sections covering specific deductions.

Deduction for Distributions to Beneficiaries

From the viewpoint of the fiduciary, the most important potential deduction is the one allowed for income "distributed or distributable" to beneficiaries. It is possible for this deduction to eliminate entirely the estate's taxable income and leave the fiduciary with no tax to pay.

This may or may not be desirable. Income not taxable to the fiduciary is taxable to the beneficiaries, who might be in higher tax brackets than the estate would be in. It is usually best if a portion of the income is taxable to the estate and a portion to the beneficiaries, thereby splitting the income into lower bracket amounts; if the executor has any choice whatsoever as to distributing the estate's income, he should try to do it in such a way as to save income taxes by having it taxed in the lowest possible brackets.

The executor, however, usually has little or no choice regarding the distributions. This is governed by the decedent's will or, in the absence of instructions in the will, by state law.

The executor must definitely determine the legal requirements applicable in his case. It is up to the testator to decide what part of the income the fiduciary should be required to distribute periodically, but if the will does not authorize any distributions of estate income during administration, the income is taxable to the estate, because in most states income earned during administration is not considered as being distributable. In some jurisdictions, however, the executor does have the option of distributing or not distributing income when the will is silent, and this gives him an excellent opportunity for saving taxes by sprinkling income among several different taxable entities. Spreading income over different years, when possible, also effects a tax saving.

And, if a testamentary trust has been provided for, property might well be turned over to it as soon as possible, thereby creating another taxable entity for spreading income.

After establishing the legal status of the estate's distributions, the next problem is the determination of the proper amount of these distributions to be claimed as a deduction on the fiduciary income tax return.

This determination is subject to an extremely complicated set of rules, but these must be understood not only to arrive at the correct deduction but also because the treatment of some of the other tax deductions depends on the way the distributions are handled.

Basically, the deduction is the lower of
1. Income required to be distributed currently, or
2. The estate's distributable net income.
Each of these concepts, "currently distributable income" and "distributable net income," requires some explanation, given in the following sections.

Currently Distributable Income

Currently distributable income is any portion of the estate's income which is required (by will or by local law) to be distributed currently to the beneficiaries, *and* any other amounts paid, credited, or required to be distributed for the tax year.

As for income required to be distributed, neither the fact that the income is of such a nature as to make its distribution difficult, nor that it cannot be exactly ascertained until after the close of the year affects its nature as currently distributable income. It does not have to have been actually distributed within the tax year to qualify as currently distributable income; it qualifies even though it is not distributed until after the end of the year.

But as for the "other amounts paid or credited," these are included as currently distributable income only if they were actually distributed during the year, or at least made available upon demand. There are cases where the executor is not authorized to distribute all of the current income but may make distributions out of corpus; such distributions, if properly paid or credited, will qualify as currently distributable income to the extent that they are actually paid out of income—that is, to the extent of current income less any portion required to be distributed.

Currently distributable income means, generally, *net* accounting income. The charges to income are usually the ordinary expense deductions familiar to accountants, but it is possible for the will or state law to redefine some of these, so the accountant must be sure to know the correct definition of "charges" applicable to his particular case.

Currently distributable income can never include amounts which did not enter into taxable gross income in the first place—tax-exempt interest, *for example*. And the expenses attributable to tax-exempt income must also be excluded in determining the currently distributable income.

To summarize, currently distributable income consists of the portion of the estate's taxable net income required to be distributed plus any amounts properly paid or credited during the year, out of either the income itself or out of corpus.

One distinction should be kept in mind. Amounts paid under the terms of the will as a gift or bequest of specific property or of a specific sum of money, being tax exempt to the beneficiary, are not deductible by the fiduciary as currently distributable income, provided they are paid all at once or in not more than three installments.

Distributable Net Income

The deduction for currently distributable income is subject to a ceiling known as "distributable net income." This ceiling not only limits the fiduciary's deduction but also the amounts the beneficiaries must include in their gross income.

The estate's *taxable* net income is the starting point in computing distributable net income. To this figure there must be added back:

1. The $600 personal exemption.
2. The $100 dividend exclusion.
3. The deduction for distributions.
4. The 50 per cent long-term capital gain deduction
5. Tax-exempt interest (unless allocable to charitable contributions) less expenses applicable to such income.
6. Net capital losses.

Next, capital gains allocable to corpus are deducted, and so are capital gains which are not paid, credited, or required to be distributed to any beneficiary during the taxable year.

The result is the distributable net income of the estate for the year. (The "throwback" rules do not apply to estates, only to trusts.)

Character of the Amounts Distributed

If the distributable net income includes various kinds of income subject to special tax treatment, such as tax-exempt interest, dividends, and others, it is necessary to determine how much of each type of income was distributed to each beneficiary.

An estate is considered as a "conduit" through which income is channeled to the beneficiaries, but without changing the nature of the income; that is, the income retains the same income tax status in the hands of the beneficiaries that it had in the hands of the fiduciary. The recipients of the distributions need to know the character of these amounts in order to properly report them on their income tax returns; the fiduciary needs the same information about any portion of the income retained by the estate.

To make this determination, each item of *gross* income being distributed is first reduced to *net*. Any deduction directly allocable to a particular class of gross income should be deducted from that class; unallocable deductions may be applied against any other income which was included in figuring distributable net income.

Each item of the *net* income is then apportioned among the beneficiaries on a simple proportion basis.

The executor should, of course, inform each beneficiary of the income tax status of the various distributions and give a Schedule K-1 to each.

Deduction for Operating Expenses

In addition to the all-important deduction for distributions, the fiduciary may claim a number of other deductions.

These are the familiar "ordinary and necessary expenses" paid or incurred by the estate if they are trade or business expenses; expenses for the production or collection of income or for the management, conservation, or maintenance of property held for the production of income; expenses in connection with the determination, collection, or refund of any tax; or reasonable administration expenses (subject to the option explained in the following section). Also deductible are non-business casualty losses in excess of $100, but funeral, medical, and dental expenses are never deductible. Nor is there any deduction for interest or other expenses allocable to tax-exempt income.

The operating expenses are itemized on the tax return and subtracted from gross taxable income. But although all such deductions must be listed by the fiduciary, his right to them is limited to the portion remaining after allocation to the beneficiaries of their proper share of these deductions. Obviously, this is of little practical importance because it is *net* income which may be distributable and the deductions will either go along with the distributions or stay with the undistributed income.

Optional Treatment of Deductions

It was explained in Chapter 10, in connection with estate tax deductions, that the executor has the option of using certain administrative expenses as *either* estate tax deductions *or* as income tax deductions, or that he may split them in any proportion he may wish.

The first fiduciary income tax return might be filed before the time for filing the estate tax return. If so, it is at this time that a tentative decision must be reached as to the comparative tax savings to be achieved through using these deductions in one place rather than the other.

To deduct any administration expenses on the fiduciary income tax return, a statement that they have not been deducted on the estate tax return must be filed in duplicate. This statement is required even though the gross estate is not large enough to require an estate tax return. The statement must constitute a waiver to deduct these particular expenses at any time for estate tax purposes.

However, this does not mean that the estate forfeits its right to deduct, as estate tax deductions, administrative expenses paid *in another year.* The option may be exercised differently *each* year for the amounts paid during that year. The only requirement is that deductions used on the income tax return must be used on the return for the year in which they were actually paid—on the cash basis.

Deductions in Respect of a Decedent

Deductions for business and nonbusiness expenses, interest, and taxes incurred by the decedent before his death but not actually paid until after his death, by his estate, are known as deductions in respect of the decedent.

This class of expenses may be claimed as deductions on *both* the estate tax return and the fiduciary income tax return, provided the estate pays them or is liable for them. (If they are paid by an heir or other beneficiary who got property subject to them, he gets the deduction.)

When paid by the executor, these expenses are charged to the account, "Debts of Decedent," and are automatically included in that category of estate tax deductions. But since this account is not an expense account, it is easy to overlook using them as income tax deductions also, so the executor should be reminded to pick up any such items from the debts account when preparing the estate's first income tax return—and for later periods too in the unlikely event that any of this class of expenses is paid later than in the estate's first fiscal year.

Deductions of the decedent other than those mentioned above are not available to the estate or beneficiaries. *For example,* a decedent's net capital loss carry-over may not be used by his estate.

Depreciation and Depletion

The rules governing the computation of depreciation and depletion—basis, life, rates, first year allowance, and so forth—are the same as for an individual, but there is a special rule governing their deduction on the fiduciary income tax return.

A depreciation schedule must first be filled out showing the total allowable depreciation, and a separate schedule must give the details of any allowable depletion. These allowable deductions are then apportioned between the estate and the income beneficiaries on the basis of the income of the estate (before depreciation) that is allocable to each.

Only the fiduciary's portion of the deductions enters into the computation of the estate's net income. The portions allocable to the beneficiaries are shown in the distribution schedule, Schedule K-1, from which these beneficiaries obtain the amounts of their deduction, along with other items of income or credits allocable to them.

Charitable and Similar Deductions

An estate may take an income tax deduction for amounts which, under the terms of the will, are paid or permanently set aside for charitable, religious, educational, or similar purposes. Unlike the charitable deduction allowed individuals, there is no percentage limitation on the amount that can be deducted.

To be deductible, the contributions must be made from the *gross* income of the estate. No deduction is allowed for a contribution out of the estate principal. However, a contribution from income that is allocable to corpus, such as capital gains, will qualify for the deduction, since such income is included in the gross income of the estate.

When an estate has both taxable and tax-exempt income, the contribution deduction is allowed only for the portion considered as coming from the gross taxable income. This is computed on a simple proportion basis—the proportion which the gross taxable income bears to the total income.

An adjustment must also be made when a part or all of the contribution is made out of long-term capital gains. The proportionate part of the contribution coming from long-term capital gains is computed and this figure is reduced by fifty per cent; this, plus the portion of contributions coming from ordinary income, is the amount of the allowable contribution deduction.

A contribution is deductible even though it is made out of income accumulated in prior years.

Net Operating Loss Deduction

An estate is entitled to the net operating loss deduction, and the rules for carry back and carry forward of a net operating loss are the same as for an individual. (A net operating loss sustained by the decedent during his last tax year is deductible only on his final return, not on the estate's return.)

In computing the net operating loss, an estate cannot consider deductions for charitable contributions or for distributions to beneficiaries.

A loss sustained by the fiduciary cannot be carried back to the decedent's individual tax return, only to a prior year of the estate. When carried back, the loss may reduce the distributable net income for the prior year, so that the beneficiaries who received distributions for that year may be entitled to a refund of taxes paid by them. The fiduciary may also be entitled to a refund.

Upon termination of the estate, any unused net operating loss carry forward is transferred to the beneficiaries and is the same in the hands of the beneficiaries as in the estate in which it originated. It may be used by a beneficiary as a deduction in arriving at adjusted gross income. However, it is still subject to the five-year limitation, and the last taxable year of the estate and the first taxable year of the beneficiary to which the loss is carried over constitute separate years.

If on termination the estate has "excess deductions," that is, deductions in excess of gross income, these excess deductions may be used by the beneficiary on his tax return for the year in which or with which the estate terminates. This deduction, however, may be used only as an itemized deduction on the individual return.

Deduction for Estate Tax Paid

An estate which collects and reports income in respect of the decedent may claim a deduction for the portion of *estate tax* paid which was attributable to the inclusion of this accrued income in the gross estate.

This is often a valuable deduction, which should not be overlooked. The details of income in respect of a decedent and the related deduction for estate tax paid were discussed fully in Chapter 13, to which reference should be made when preparing the fiduciary income tax return.

Capital Gains and Losses

Gains and losses from sales and exchanges of capital assets and other property are generally taken into account in computing taxable income just as if the estate were an individual. A Schedule D (Form 1041) is used.

Any part of the net gain that is properly paid, credited, or required to be distributed during the year to a beneficiary is deductible by the fiduciary as a distribution and is taxable to the beneficiary to the extent of the distributable net income, even if the gain is allocated to corpus.

A net capital loss, however, is usually deductible only by the estate, not by the beneficiary, and the rules for individuals apply—the loss deduction is limited to $1,000, and so forth.

An important new provision applies to the estates of decedents dying after 1970—although the holding period of property acquired from a decedent starts at the date of death, property acquired from the decedent and sold within six months after his death will be deemed held over six months. Thus, if an executor has to sell an estate's capital assets to get cash, the sale qualifies for long-term capital gain treatment even if made within six months after death.

Undistributed net long-term capital gain, taxable to the fiduciary, is subject to a fifty per cent reduction in arriving at taxable income, and the alternative tax computation is used when taxable income includes net long-term capital gains and exceeds $26,000.

Gains and losses from the sale or exchange of property other than capital assets are reported on a separate line and must be supported by a Form 4797.

Any unused capital loss carry over remaining at the time of termination of the estate may be used by the distributees as a capital loss carry over on their individual returns.

A sale of property within a relatively short time after death is frequently helpful in establishing the property's correct date-of-death valuation. If the sale indicates that the inventory valuation was incorrect, and if the estate tax return has not been filed, the correct valuation as indicated by the sale should be used on the Form 706. If this happens to be the same as the sale price, there will be no taxable gain or loss. But the basis of property still unsold when the estate tax return is filed is fixed at the valuation reported and accepted so that subsequent sales usually produce a taxable gain or loss.

The Dividend Exclusion

The $100 dividend exclusion is treated as a deduction on the fiduciary income tax return rather than as an income exclusion.

The fiduciary is entitled to this deduction on the dividends not allocated to beneficiaries. He must report the total dividends received and then deduct a *proportionate* part of the $100, depending on the proportion of dividends retained by the estate.

This proration does not affect the beneficiary. He reports the dividends received from the estate on his individual return and claims the proper dividend exclusion up to the full $100.

Credits Against the Tax

After computing the amount of the tax, if any, which is due by the estate, this tax should be reduced by any of the several tax credits which may be available.

Foreign tax credit. If a credit is claimed for foreign taxes, Form 1116 must be filed with the return together with a receipt for the foreign tax payment. The fiduciary may deduct any part of this credit which is not allowable to the beneficiaries.

Credit for tax-free covenant bond interest. The credit allowable to the fiduciary is the total credit less the share of the credit allocable to the beneficiaries.

Tax previously paid or withheld. The fiduciary may deduct such items as tax paid on a tentative return or income taxes withheld from the salary of the decedent when the return includes such income as income in respect of a decedent.

Investment tax credit. If the estate acquired any qualifying property during the year, the qualified investment must be allocated among the estate and the beneficiaries in the same proportion the estate income is allocated. Form 3468 must be attached to the return and must show how the investment in new and used property was allocated to each beneficiary, with the life years assigned to the property. The tax credit on the portion allocated to the estate will be claimed on the fiduciary tax return. Recapture of the credit is also possible, as with an individual.

Work incentive (WIN) credit. If an estate is engaged in a trade or business, it is allowed a credit for its share of salaries or wages of employees certified as being under a work incentive program. If this credit is claimed a Form 4874 must be attached to the return.

An estate might also be entitled to a credit for Federal tax on nonhighway gasoline or lubricating oil, attaching Form 4136, but it may not claim the political contribution credit or deduction allowed to individuals.

The executor should inform each beneficiary of the amount of any of the above tax credits available to him from the estate.

Filing the Fiduciary Income Tax Return

The executor may select any fiscal year he wishes for keeping the estate books and filing its income tax return. No application is necessary, and a return for a period of less than twelve months need not be placed on an annual basis unless the short period results from a change in the accounting period.

The fiduciary income tax return must be filed by any estate having a gross income of $600 or more (or by an estate of which any beneficiary is a nonresident alien), and it must be filed on or before the fifteenth day of the fourth month following the close of the taxable year. It is filed with the Internal Revenue Service Center for the state where the executor has his principal place of business.

An estate may elect to pay its income tax in installments rather than in one lump sum. The installments are due on or before the fifteenth day of the 4th, 7th, 10th, and 13th months following the close of the fiscal or calendar year.

An estate files no estimated tax return and therefore pays no tax before the return for the year is due.

The first return for an estate, when gross income is $5,000 or more, must be accompanied by a copy of the will. It must also contain a statement by the fiduciary indicating the provisions that determine the taxability of the income to the estate or beneficiaries.

The return must be signed by the fiduciary, who is responsible for its filing and who may become personally liable for failure to pay the tax, and by the person preparing the return.

One final responsibility of the executor should be mentioned in connection with tax return requirements—a fiduciary who pays, credits, or is required to distribute any amount taxable to a beneficiary who is a nonresident alien must make a return on Form 1040 NR and pay the tax for the nonresident alien, unless the beneficiary has appointed a person in the United States to act as his agent for the purpose of filing income tax returns.

Taxation of the Beneficiary

Although the executor never has any real responsibility in connection with income tax matters of a beneficiary of the estate, he will often assume this responsibility out of courtesy to the beneficiary, particularly when the beneficiary is the surviving spouse, elderly, uninformed about business and tax matters, and other details. Some knowledge of the taxation of beneficiaries is, therefore, desirable.

Basically, the beneficiary's income tax return must reflect the deduction claimed by the fiduciary for any actual or required distributions. It was explained earlier that the income of an estate is taxable either to the fiduciary or the beneficiary, or in part to each; therefore, the portion not taxable to the estate by reason of proper distribution must be reported on the beneficiary's individual tax return.

The correct amount to be reported will be obtained from the distribution schedule of the fiduciary tax return. The character of the income to be reported—whether ordinary income, capital gain, dividends, tax-exempt interest, and so on—must also be obtained from the fiduciary, and each type of income will be entered in the proper place for that type on the beneficiary's individual income tax return.

Most deductions connected with the estate's income are taken by the fiduciary and benefit the beneficiary only indirectly by reducing the amount taxable to him. But the deductions for the beneficiary's share of depreciation and depletion, and the fifty per cent long-term capital gain deduction, are taken directly by the beneficiary. He also deducts his share of any *estate tax* paid which was attributable to income in respect of the decedent.

The beneficiary must also obtain from the fiduciary the amount of all credits against the tax, such as the investment credit, which are available to him.

Carry-overs of a net operating loss or a capital loss, not absorbed by the fiduciary by the time of termination of the estate, may be picked up by the beneficiary and used in determining his taxable income, subject to the usual rules limiting the deductibility of such losses. Also, "excess deductions" on the termination of the estate may be used by the beneficiary, as mentioned earlier.

If the beneficiary has a different taxable year from the estate, he reports for his taxable year the distributions shown by the estate for its tax year ending within the beneficiary's year—the same method used by a partner in reporting his income from a partnership.

15

Handling a Typical
Decedent's Estate
from Start to Finish

Many of the principles and procedures described throughout this book might best be illustrated by a detailed study of a large estate from start to finish.

The decedent in this case was James T. Sinclair, who died on September 1, 1974 at the age of seventy-three. Mr. Sinclair died testate, his will naming Douglas Young as executor.

Mr. Sinclair was the owner of a successful retail business, but had amassed a large part of his fortune over the years from local rental property, from buying and selling such property, and by investing in real estate.

His will was relatively simple. After providing for seven bequests of $10,000.00 each to close friends and associates and the bequest of a valuable diamond ring to a nephew, Mr. Sinclair directed that the entire balance of his estate should go to his wife, Marie R. Sinclair. He directed that all death taxes should be paid by the estate so that the bequests could be made in full, without a tax deduction.

Mr. Sinclair realized that his estate would be difficult to administer because there would be a heavy demand for cash to take care of the taxes, bequests, and expenses, so he gave his executor the power to sell and convey his real estate and to use his judgment in investing and reinvesting the proceeds.

Finally, since Mrs. Sinclair has no income of her own, Mr. Sinclair wisely directed that one-half of the estate's net income during administration should go to his wife.

The Preliminaries to Administration

The day after Mr. Sinclair's burial, Douglas Young had his attorney draw up a petition for probate of the will. The will and the petition were presented to the probate court; the will was authenticated by the witnesses to it and was accepted by the court. Mr. Young qualified as executor, took the oath of office, and made arrangements for an insurance company to provide the bond required by the court. Letters testamentary were then granted to Douglas Young as executor.

Young immediately had Mr. Sinclair's cash in bank transferred to a new account in the name of "Douglas Young, Executor, James T. Sinclair Estate." Next, he engaged an attorney, on a flat fee basis, to handle all matters of a legal nature during the estate's administration; he engaged a Certified Public Accountant to handle all accounting, income tax, estate tax, and inheritance tax matters for the estate, and a flat fee was agreed upon for these services.

Mr. Sinclair's bank lockbox was opened, in the presence of a state inheritance tax agent, and was found to contain only the securities owned by Mr. Sinclair. These were listed in detail by both Young and the tax agent.

An immediate problem was presented by the question of whether Mr. Sinclair's proprietorship business should be sold, liquidated, or continued. The will was silent on this question, but the executor felt that continuing the business would place no undue burden on him, since this business had not required much of Mr. Sinclair's time in recent years, but that an enforced sale would result in an unnecessary loss to the estate. It was necessary to petition the court for an interpretation of the will on this question and for instructions as to how to proceed. The court, recognizing the validity of Mr. Young's arguments and also considering the fact that Young had been given broad discretionary powers in connection with the decedent's real estate, directed him to continue the business indefinitely, or until such time as he felt that its sale would be beneficial to the estate.

Since the business was being continued, Mr. Young decided to use that office as the office for the estate operations. This would also make it unnecessary to employ any office help, as the business office employees were already accustomed to handling Mr. Sinclair's personal collections, disbursements, record keeping, and other duties.

Mr. Young completed the necessary preliminaries to administration by inserting in the local newspaper a notice to creditors of the estate and by having the probate court confirm and approve his selection of three men to serve as appraisers of the estate.

The Estate Inventory

By October 29, 1974 Mr. Young had completed a detailed listing of every item of real and personal property he had been able to locate in Mr. Sinclair's name, so a meeting of the appraisers took place on that date and the valuation of the listed property was begun. Three full days were spent in inspecting the various assets and deciding on the fair market value of each as of September 1, 1974. The summarized results of this appraisal were as follows:

Cash on Hand—$216.08. This consisted of Mr. Sinclair's undeposited cash receipts for August 31, 1974, deposited in the executor's bank account immediately after his qualification.

Cash in Bank—$24,620.86. This was the bank's balance in Sinclair's only bank account on September 1, 1974. Several checks written by Sinclair were presented to the bank by the payees after that date, but the bank refused to pay them and Young paid them from his new account, charging the payments to Debts of Decedent.

Accounts Receivable—$683,302.55. This was the total of the balances due on 127 mortgages, notes, and title bond contracts. All appeared to be well secured and fully collectible.

Interest Receivable—$2,322.60. Accrued interest to the date of death was computed on each of the above receivables, totaling this amount.

Corporate Stocks—$89,776.50. All of the stocks were listed or over-the-counter stocks for which September 1 market values were readily available, except for one block of stock in a close corporation. Valuation of this holding was difficult, but was arrived at by examining the corporation's financial statements, earnings prospects, and other pertinent factors. There were no declared but unpaid dividends on any of the stocks.

Municipal Bonds—$121,434.87. Mr. Sinclair's broker furnished the appraisers with the correct September 1 market values to assign to the portfolio of municipal bonds.

Accrued Interest On Municipal Bonds—$465.27. Computation was made of each bond's accrued interest. This was included as an estate asset even though it would not be income taxable.

Business Interest—$150,000.00. A fair appraisal of Mr. Sinclair's retail business was most difficult. All of the factors mentioned in Chapter 4 had to be considered. Although the book net worth was only $128,416.65, the probable goodwill, past earnings, future earnings prospects, and lack of competition appeared to warrant the above valuation as being the price which a willing buyer would pay to a willing seller. In this case, it did not seem that the loss of the business's owner would have any depressant effect on the price at which it would probably sell as a going business.

Real Estate—$182,500.00. The appraisers inspected each of the fifty-eight small rental houses and apartments included in this total and valued each in accordance with the principles described in Chapter 4.

The Sinclair residence was not included, as it was in Mrs. Sinclair's name, having been deeded to her when purchased by Mr. Sinclair sixteen years earlier. There were no gift tax consequences to this transaction, as the value of the property at the time was considerably less than the donor's gift tax exclusion. No other lifetime gifts were discovered, certainly none within the three years prior to death.

None of the real estate was held jointly with other parties.

Accrued Rents—$780.00. Rents accrued to September 1 were computed for each rental unit, and the total was included as an estate asset.

Diamond Ring—$3,150.00. The diamond ring mentioned as a specific bequest was listed separately and valued at the figure at which two local jewelers, at the request of the estate appraisers, had appraised it.

Other Jewelry—$2,000.00. Other jewelry belonging to Mr. Sinclair was appraised at $2,000.00. Jewelry belonging to Mrs. Sinclair, acquired by her by inheritance, gift, or purchase over the years, was identified and was, of course, excluded.

Household Furnishings—$8,465.00. Mr. Sinclair owned a number of valuable pieces of furniture, rugs, and works of art which could hardly be considered as belonging to Mrs. Sinclair; it was difficult to separate these from the items which Mrs. Sinclair insisted were hers as gifts from her husband. A room by room itemization of all furnishings was made, and those items considered (sometimes arbitrarily) as belonging to Mrs. Sinclair were eliminated, the remaining items being appraised at the above figure.

Several of the rental units had contained a very small quantity of furnishings, but it had practically no sale value and was ignored except for its small effect on the values assigned to the units themselves.

Automobiles—$7,150.00. Two automobiles owned by the decedent were appraised, with the help of a local auto dealer, at $7,150.00.

Directors Fee Receivable—$75.00. Mr. Sinclair was a director of a local bank. His fee for meetings in August, paid after his death, had to be inventoried as a receivable as of the date of death.

Social Security Receivable—$116.00. Another receivable at the date of death was Mr. Sinclair's monthly Social Security benefit check, received the day after his death.

Other Interests—When listing the estate assets, Mr Young and his attorney and accountant made a careful search for any other property interests which might have had to be included in the taxable estate. No lifetime transfers or gifts were discovered other than the gift of the residence and a number of personal items to Mrs.Sinclair. Mr Sinclair had no life estate in property and no powers of appointment over property. He had no life insurance.

It was believed, therefore, that the inventory was complete, and a summary of the appraisal filed with the court on November 15, 1974 is presented below:

Inventory and Appraisal

Cash on Hand	$ 216.08
Cash in Bank	24,620.86
Accounts Receivable	683,302.55
Interest Receivable	2,322.60
Corporate Stocks	89,776.50
Municipal Bonds	121,434.87
Accrued Interest on Bonds	465.27
Business Interest	150,000.00
Real Estate	182,500.00

Inventory and Appraisal
(cont.)

Accrued Rents	780.00
Diamond Ring	3,150.00
Other Jewelry	2,000.00
Household Furnishings	8,465.00
Automobiles	7,150.00
Directors Fee Receivable	75.00
Social Security Receivable	116.00
Total	$1,276,374.73

The Accounting System

General Ledger accounts were debited for each of the above balances, Estate Principal being credited for the total. Two subsidiary ledgers were opened, one for the receivables and the other for the real estate. A cash receipts journal and a cash disbursements journal were opened a week after Mr. Sinclair's death, although the opening entry to the ledger could not be made until November 15, 1974. A general journal completed the accounting system.

It was decided to operate the estate on a calendar year basis for tax and reporting purposes, having a "short" four-month period for the first reports.

The First Accounting Period

Operations during the period September 1, 1974 to December 31, 1974 were largely routine. No assets were sold, but cash increased due to the normal collections on receivables, rents, dividends, and other items, and a $10,000.00 cash withdrawal from the retail business. The diamond ring was sent to the nephew; operating expenses were paid as incurred; the decedent's debts were paid as presented and approved.

It was discovered in December that Mr. Sinclair had a $10,000.00 savings account in a bank he did not normally do business with. This necessitated an entry debiting Cash in Bank and crediting Assets Not Inventoried.

Early in January 1975 Mr. Young's accountant prepared the following interim charge and discharge statement, which was filed with the court.

Estate of James T. Sinclair
Douglas Young, Executor

CHARGE AND DISCHARGE STATEMENT

For the Period September 1, 1974 to December 31, 1974

First as to Principal:
The Executor charges himself with:

Assets per Inventory (Schedule)	$1,276,374.73	
Assets not Inventoried	10,000.00	$1,286,374.73

Estate of James T. Sinclair
Douglas Young, Executor

CHARGE AND DISCHARGE STATEMENT
(cont.)

The Executor Credits himself with:

Funeral Expenses	$ 2,400.00	
Administration Expenses	76.20	
Debts of Decedent (Schedule)	13,726.18	
Bequests Paid	3,150.00	19,352.38
Leaving a Balance of Principal of		$1,267,022.35

Consisting of:

Cash in Bank	$ 42,514.91
Accounts Receivable	669,574.40
Stocks and Bonds	211,211.37
Business Interest	146,040.00
Real Estate	180,066.67
Jewelry, Furnishings, Autos	17,615.00
	$1,267,022.35

Second as to Income:

The Executor charges himself with:

Income from Retail Business	$ 6,040.00	
Interest, Dividends, Rents (Schedule)	21,398.70	$ 27,438.70

The Executor Credits himself with:

Operating Expenses (Schedule)	$ 8,626.05	
Depreciation	2,433.33	11,059.38
Leaving a Balance of Income of		$ 16,379.32

Consisting of:

Cash in Bank	$16,379.32

Income Tax Returns

Two income tax returns had to be filed by the executor on April 15, 1975.

The first was the 1974 individual income tax return for the decedent. Mr. Sinclair's income and deductions for the period January 1, 1974 to August 31, 1974 were determined, and a joint return was filed by the executor with Mrs. Sinclair, who had no 1974 income of her own except her one-half share of the net income of the estate for the last four months of the year.

The total tax shown by this return was $14,626.21. By making a proration on the basis of net income reported, it was determined that Mrs. Sinclair's share of this tax was $2,437.70, which she paid. Of the balance, Mr. Sinclair had made estimated advance payments of $10,000.00, leaving a balance due of $2,188.51 to be paid by the executor. This payment was charged to Debts of Decedent.

The second return filed by Mr. Young was the Fiduciary Income Tax Return, covering the period September 1, 1974 to December 31, 1974. This return reported all of the estate's income (except municipal bond interest) and expenses. From the net income there was deducted the portion of the income distributable to Mrs. Sinclair, the fiduciary's share of the estate tax attributable to the net accrued income in the decedent's estate, and the $600.00 personal exemption. Applying the tax rates to the balance disclosed a tax liability of $1,642.20. This payment was charged to the income tax expense account.

Estate and Inheritance Tax Returns

During the year 1975 Mr. Young was faced with the very difficult problem of accumulating enough cash to pay the death taxes for the estate.

The first deadline requiring a large cash disbursement was May 31, 1975. This was the date, nine months after death, by which the state inheritance tax could be paid with a five per cent discount.

The second deadline was also May 31, 1975, the due date for paying the Federal estate tax.

Also, Mr. Young determined to make every effort to pay the $70,000.00 in cash bequests within one year, by September 1, 1975.

Source of Cash. Much of the above cash requirement was provided by the normal collections of principal and interest on the receivables. A large portion of the corporate stocks and municipal bonds had to be sold. About one-third of the rental houses were sold during the year, some at small gains over the appraisal figures, other at small losses. Cash withdrawals from the retail business added another $20,000.00 to the estate funds during the year.

State Inheritance Tax. It was estimated that the inheritance tax would amount to approximately $80,000.00. This amount had been accumulated by May 31, 1975, so Mr. Young decided to take advantage of the five per cent discount offered for early payment. He sent the state a check for $76,000.00, reserving the statutory right to wait until eighteen months after death to file the tax return itself and to pay any additional tax shown to be due over the estimated $80,000.00.

Federal Estate Tax. The Federal estate tax return was prepared by the estate's accountant and was filed by Mr. Young on May 31, 1975. It was accompanied by the estate's check for $153,102.12 in full payment of the tax.

The question of whether to use the alternate valuation date in filing the return had been raised, but the valuations at the date of death were used, due largely to the fact that values had risen slightly during the year after death.

A summary of the Form 706, Estate Tax Return, showing the computation of this tax, follows:

Gross Estate:

Real Estate (including accrued rentals and net gains and losses on sales of houses)	$ 183,750.00
Stocks and Bonds (including accrued interest)	211,676.64

Mortgages, Notes, and Cash (including accrued interest)	720,462.09
Other Miscellaneous Property (including the business interest, jewelry, furnishings, autos, and other items)	170,956,00
Total Gross Estate	$1,286,844.73

Deductions:

Funeral and Administrative Expenses (excluding $30,000.00 used as income tax deductions)	$ 53,168.00
Debts of Decedent	15,914.69
Marital Deduction (one-half of gross estate less above deductions)	593,881.02
Specific Exemption	60,000.00
Total Deductions	$ 722,963.71
Taxable Estate	$ 563,881.02
Gross Estate Tax	$ 168,058.36
Credit for State Death Taxes	$ 14,955.24
Estate Tax Payable	$ 153,103.12

As noted in the summary, it was decided to withhold $30,000.00 of the executor's fee from the estate tax deductions and to use it as an income tax deduction—$20,000.00 in 1975 and $10,000.00 in 1976—because the income tax rate would otherwise be higher than the estate tax rate.

Mr. Young requested an immediate examination of the estate tax return. This examination was completed in February 1976. Differences in opinion as to the valuation of several pieces of property resulted in an additional assessment of $1,496.13. Appeal did not seem to be warranted, so the assessment was paid.

The state inheritance tax return was prepared at the time of preparing the Federal return; the total tax shown by this return was $85,355.77. Since $80,000.00 of this had been prepaid in May 1975, the balance, $5,355.77, was remitted with the return filed on December 8, 1975.

Payment of Bequests. Collections and sales were unusually good during the summer of 1975, enabling Mr. Young to pay the last of the seven $10,000.00 bequests within a short time after one year from the date of Mr. Sinclair's death.

Completing the Year 1975

After closing the estate books as of the end of the year, December 31, 1975, the estate's accountant prepared another interim charge and discharge statement for the executor to file with the court.

This statement was in the same form as that shown above for 1974, but it covered the entire elapsed period of administration, September 1, 1974 to December 31, 1975.

Next, the fiduciary income tax return for the year 1976 was prepared and was filed on April 15, 1976. This return again reported the estate's gross income and operating expenses and showed deductions for the one-half of the income distributable to Mrs. Sinclair as well as the $600.00 personal exemption.

Due to the claiming of $20,000.00 of the executor's fee as an operating expense deduction on the income tax return, the taxable income for the year was reduced to the point where the income tax amounted to only $467.82.

Completing the Administration

Soon after the beginning of the year 1976, Mr. Young reviewed his administration, noting what had been done and what remained to be done, and he decided on June 30, 1976 as a target date for closing the estate.

The estate and inheritance taxes had been paid, the decedent's debts and the bequests had been paid, the income taxes had been paid through 1975, and a portion of the administrative fees and expenses had been paid. The only remaining cash requirements were for the balance of the fees, about $45,000.00, and about $20,000.00 of income which Mr. Young felt should be distributed to Mrs. Sinclair before closing the estate.

Mr. Young believed that these amounts could be accumulated during the next six months through normal operations and a few additional property sales. If not, there remained about $50,000.00 in securities which could be cashed, although Mrs. Sinclair preferred to have the securities turned over to her on closing rather than real estate.

The only thing which might prevent closing the estate on June 30, 1976 would be the failure of the estate tax and inheritance tax agents to examine the returns and give Mr. Young his release from liability for these taxes. Fortunately, these examinations were completed and the liability settled in February 1976.

During the first six months of 1976, the collections on receivables, withdrawals from the retail business, sales of real estate, and interest and dividends produced enough cash to take care of the operating expenses, pay the balance of the fees due to the executor, attorney, and accountant, and to distribute $20,000.00 to Mrs. Sinclair.

There was no longer any valid reason for keeping the estate open, though it would have been desirable to do so to continue splitting the taxable income between the estate and the beneficiary.

The Final Reports

Within a few days after June 30, 1976, the estate's accountant prepared the final fiduciary income tax return, covering the period January 1, 1976 to June 30, 1976. No $600 personal exemption deduction was permitted on this final return.

This return showed a tax of only $290.12 payable by the estate, due to using $10,000 of the executor's fee as a deduction on this return, as mentioned above. A check was written for this amount and recorded on the books as of June 30, 1976.

Mr. Young ascertained the amount of the fees which would be due to the probate court for filing his final report and granting his release, and he wrote a check for this amount, recording it also as of June 30, 1976.

The estate books were then closed and the following final report was prepared and filed with the probate court:

Estate of James T. Sinclair
Douglas Young, Executor

CHARGE AND DISCHARGE STATEMENT

For the Period September 1, 1974 to June 30, 1976

First as to Principal.
The Executor charges himself with:

Assets per Inventory (Schedule)	$1,276,374.73	
Assets not Inventoried	10,000.00	$1,286,374.73
The Executor credits himself with:		
Funeral Expenses	$ 2,400.00	
Administrative Expenses (Schedule)	80,844.20	
Debts of Decedent (Schedule)	15,914.69	
Estate and Inheritance Taxes Paid	235,955.02	
Net Losses on Realization (Schedule)	538.60	
Bequests Paid	73,150.00	408,802.51
Leaving a Balance of Principal of		$ 877,572.22
Consisting of:		
Cash in Bank	$ -0-	
Accounts Receivable	595,527.30	
Corporate Stocks	19,369.90	
Municipal Bonds	21,188.19	
Business Interest	138,512.75	
Real Estate	85,359.08	
Jewelry	2,000.00	
Furnishings	8,465.00	
Automobiles	7,150.00	
	$877,572.22	

Second as to Income:
The Executor charges himself with:

Income from Retail Business	$33,512.75	
Interest, Dividends, Rents (Schedule)	74,899.89	$108,412.64
The Executor credits himself with:		
Operating Expenses (Schedule)	$38,454.76	
Depreciation Expense	12,945.92	
Income Taxes Paid	2,400.14	
Distributions of Income	40,000.00	93,800.82
Leaving a Balance of Income of		$ 14,611.82
Consisting of:		
Cash in Bank	$ 4,973.14	
Municipal Bonds	9,638.68	
	$14,611.82	

The above charge and discharge statement was accompanied by the schedules mentioned in the statement and by detailed listing of the remaining receivables, stocks, bonds, and real estate.

The estate's attorney prepared an application for an order of distribution, which was presented to the court along with the charge and discharge statement.

The court approved the settlement, directed the executor to distribute the remaining assets in accordance with the will, discharged Mr. Young from his office, and cancelled his bond.

Mr. Young gave Mrs. Sinclair a deed to the remaining real estate (since the real property had in this case been a part of the administrable estate) and gave her physical possession of the remaining personal property.

The administration of a large estate was successfully completed.

Glossary

Administration. The collection of a decedent's assets, the payment of his debts, and the distribution of any assets remaining.

Administrator. One named by a court to take charge of the assets of an intestate and to dispose of them in accordance with law or ruling of the court.

Administratrix. A woman named by a court to administer an estate.

Ancillary. Subordinate; auxiliary; as "ancillary administration," meaning an auxiliary administration required in other states than the one in which a decedent had his residence.

Appraise. To establish cost or value by systematic procedures that include physical examination, pricing, and often engineering estimates.

Appraiser. One who appraises property, such as the property in a decedent's estate.

Beneficiary. One who is lawfully entitled to the proceeds of an estate or property, the title to which is vested in another, such as an executor or trustee.

Bequest. A gift of property by will; specifically, a gift of personal property rather than real estate; a legacy.

Charge and Discharge Statement. A tabular summary prepared for an executor, administrator, trustee, or other fiduciary, accounting for the principal and income for which he has been responsible and constituting a part of an interim or final report on his activities.

Codicil. A written change in, or addition to, a will.

Decedent. A person who has died.

Devise. The disposition of real estate by will.

Devisee. One who receives real estate by will.

Descent. The disposition of the real property of an intestate.

Distribution. The apportionment and disposition, by authority of a court, of the balance of an intestate's personal property after payment of debts and costs.

Estate. The property of a person, often a decedent's property in the process of administration.

Estate Accounting. The preparation and keeping of accounts for property in the hands of executors, administrators, or trustees acting under the jurisdiction of a probate court or similar authority.

Estate Income. The revenue or income of an estate as determined under the provisions of a will or deed, or of Federal or state laws and regulations.

Executor. A person named in a will as the fiduciary who is to take charge of the deceased's estate and administer or dispose of it as directed in the will.

Executrix. A woman named in a will to serve as the fiduciary in charge of the deceased's property.

Fiduciary. Any person responsible for the custody or administration, or both, of property belonging to another; as, a trustee, executor, or administrator.

Fiduciary Accounting. The preparation and keeping of accounts for property in the hands of a trustee, executor, or administrator, whether under the direct jurisdiction of a court or acting by virtue of a deed of trust, will, or other instrument of appointment.

Gift. The transfer of property from one individual to another without consideration.

Heir. One who on the death of another becomes entitled by operation of law to succeed to the deceased person's estate; any one inheriting from a deceased person.

Inheritance. The property received from a deceased person, by succession or by will; strictly, property received by descent rather than by devise.

Intestate. A person who dies without making a will.

Intervivos Trust. A trust created between living persons, as contrasted with a testamentary trust.

Irrevocable Trust. A trust that cannot be set aside by its creator.

Joint Tenant. Any one of two or more persons who together own an item of real or personal property, whereby upon the death of any one of them his interest passes to the other without becoming a part of his administrable estate.

Legacy. A gift of personal property by will. A general legacy is one to be paid from the general assets of the testator; a specific legacy is one involving a specified sum of money or personal property; and a residuary legacy is the gift of the balance of a testator's estate after payment of debts and costs and other legacies.

Legatee. A person who receives a legacy.

Letters Testamentary. A court order admitting a will to probate and approving and giving authority to the person named as executor.

Letters of Administration. A court order appointing and giving authority to the person selected to be the administrator of an intestate's estate.

Life Tenant. One entitled to the use or income of property during his life.

Personal Property. Property of a temporary and movable character, as contrasted with real property.

Principal. The original amount of an estate or fund together with accretions which may, but usually do not, include income.

Probate. The formal, legal proving of a will and its acceptance by the court having jurisdiction over the administration of estates.

Real Property. Land and land improvements, including buildings and appurtenances.

Remainderman. One entitled to the corpus or principal of an estate upon the expiration of a prior estate, such as a life tenancy.

Residuary Legatee. One entitled to receive the balance of an estate after specific bequests, taxes, and other liabilities have been satisfied.

Revocable Trust. A trust terminable at the pleasure of or under certain conditions by its creator.

Tenant in Common. Any one of two or more persons who together own an item of real or personal property, whereby upon the death of one his share of the property is included in his estate, there being no right of survivorship as in joint tenancy.

Testamentary. Pertaining to a testator or his estate.

Testamentary Trust. A trust created by will.

Testator. One who makes a will.

Testate. Having made a will before decease.

Trust. A right, enforceable in courts of equity, to the beneficial enjoyment of property, the legal title to which is in another. The person creating the trust is the creator, settlor, grantor, or donor; the holder of the legal title is the trustee; and the holder of the beneficial interest is the beneficiary.

Will. A document prepared by a natural person in contemplation of death and containing instructions for the disposition of his property.

Index